Fragments, Genius and Madness
Masks and Mask-Making in the fin-de-siècle Imagination

LEGENDA

LEGENDA is the Modern Humanities Research Association's book imprint for new research in the Humanities. Founded in 1995 by Malcolm Bowie and others within the University of Oxford, Legenda has always been a collaborative publishing enterprise, directly governed by scholars. The Modern Humanities Research Association (MHRA) joined this collaboration in 1998, became half-owner in 2004, in partnership with Maney Publishing and then Routledge, and has since 2016 been sole owner. Titles range from medieval texts to contemporary cinema and form a widely comparative view of the modern humanities, including works on Arabic, Catalan, English, French, German, Greek, Italian, Portuguese, Russian, Spanish, and Yiddish literature. Editorial boards and committees of more than 60 leading academic specialists work in collaboration with bodies such as the Society for French Studies, the British Comparative Literature Association and the Association of Hispanists of Great Britain & Ireland.

The MHRA encourages and promotes advanced study and research in the field of the modern humanities, especially modern European languages and literature, including English, and also cinema. It aims to break down the barriers between scholars working in different disciplines and to maintain the unity of humanistic scholarship. The Association fulfils this purpose through the publication of journals, bibliographies, monographs, critical editions, and the MHRA Style Guide, and by making grants in support of research. Membership is open to all who work in the Humanities, whether independent or in a University post, and the participation of younger colleagues entering the field is especially welcomed.

ALSO PUBLISHED BY THE ASSOCIATION

Critical Texts
Tudor and Stuart Translations • *New Translations* • *European Translations*
MHRA Library of Medieval Welsh Literature

MHRA Bibliographies
Publications of the Modern Humanities Research Association

The Annual Bibliography of English Language & Literature
Austrian Studies
Modern Language Review
Portuguese Studies
The Slavonic and East European Review
Working Papers in the Humanities
The Yearbook of English Studies

www.mhra.org.uk
www.legendabooks.com

STUDIES IN COMPARATIVE LITERATURE

Editorial Committee
Chairs: Dr Emily Finer (University of St Andrews)
and Professor Wen-chin Ouyang (SOAS, London)

Dr Ross Forman (University of Warwick)
Professor Angus Nicholls (Queen Mary, University of London)
Dr Henriette Partzsch (University of Glasgow)
Dr Ranka Primorac (University of Southampton)

Studies in Comparative Literature are produced in close collaboration with the British Comparative Literature Association, and range widely across comparative and theoretical topics in literary and translation studies, accommodating research at the interface between different artistic media and between the humanities and the sciences.

ALSO PUBLISHED IN THIS SERIES

20. *Aestheticism and the Philosophy of Death: Walter Pater and Post-Hegelianism*, by Giles Whiteley
21. *Blake, Lavater and Physiognomy*, by Sibylle Erle
22. *Rethinking the Concept of the Grotesque: Crashaw, Baudelaire, Magritte*, by Shun-Liang Chao
23. *The Art of Comparison: How Novels and Critics Compare*, by Catherine Brown
24. *Borges and Joyce: An Infinite Conversation*, by Patricia Novillo-Corvalán
25. *Prometheus in the Nineteenth Century: From Myth to Symbol*, by Caroline Corbeau-Parsons
26. *Architecture, Travellers and Writers: Constructing Histories of Perception*, by Anne Hultzsch
27. *Comparative Literature in Britain: National Identities, Transnational Dynamics 1800-2000*, by Joep Leerssen
28. *The Realist Author and Sympathetic Imagination*, by Sotirios Paraschas
29. *Iris Murdoch and Elias Canetti: Intellectual Allies*, by Elaine Morley
30. *Likenesses: Translation, Illustration, Interpretation*, by Matthew Reynolds
31. *Exile and Nomadism in French and Hispanic Women's Writing*, by Kate Averis
32. *Samuel Butler against the Professionals: Rethinking Lamarckism 1860–1900*, by David Gillott
33. *Byron, Shelley, and Goethe's Faust: An Epic Connection*, by Ben Hewitt
34. *Leopardi and Shelley: Discovery, Translation and Reception*, by Daniela Cerimonia
35. *Oscar Wilde and the Simulacrum: The Truth of Masks*, by Giles Whiteley
36. *The Modern Culture of Reginald Farrer: Landscape, Literature and Buddhism*, by Michael Charlesworth
37. *Translating Myth*, edited by Ben Pestell, Pietra Palazzolo and Leon Burnett
38. *Encounters with Albion: Britain and the British in Texts by Jewish Refugees from Nazism*, by Anthony Grenville
39. *The Rhetoric of Exile: Duress and the Imagining of Force*, by Vladimir Zorić
40. *From Puppet to Cyborg: Pinocchio's Posthuman Journey*, by Georgia Panteli
41. *Utopian Identities: A Cognitive Approach to Literary Competitions*, by Clementina Osti
43. *Sublime Conclusions: Last Man Narratives from Apocalypse to Death of God*, by Robert K. Weninger
44. *Arthur Symons: Poet, Critic, Vagabond*, edited by Elisa Bizzotto and Stefano Evangelista
45. *Scenographies of Perception: Sensuousness in Hegel, Novalis, Rilke, and Proust*, by Christian Jany
46. *Reflections in the Library: Selected Literary Essays 1926–1944*, by Antal Szerb
47. *Depicting the Divine: Mikhail Bulgakov and Thomas Mann*, by Olga G. Voronina
48. *Samuel Butler and the Science of the Mind: Evolution, Heredity and Unconscious Memory*, by Cristiano Turbil
49. *Death Sentences: Literature and State Killing*, edited by Birte Christ and Ève Morisi
50. *Words Like Fire: Prophecy and Apocalypse in Apollinaire, Marinetti and Pound*, by James P. Leveque

Fragments, Genius and Madness

Masks and Mask-Making in the fin-de-siècle Imagination

Elisa Segnini

Studies in Comparative Literature 56
Modern Humanities Research Association
2021

Published by Legenda
an imprint of the Modern Humanities Research Association
Salisbury House, Station Road, Cambridge CB1 2LA

ISBN 978-1-78188-854-4 (HB)
ISBN 978-1-78188-858-2 (PB)

First published 2021

All rights reserved. No part of this publication may be reproduced or disseminated or transmitted in any form or by any means, electronic, mechanical, photocopying, recording or otherwise, or stored in any retrieval system, or otherwise used in any manner whatsoever without written permission of the copyright owner, except in accordance with the provisions of the Copyright, Designs and Patents Act 1988, or under the terms of a licence permitting restricted copying issued in the UK by the Copyright Licensing Agency Ltd, Saffron House, 6–10 Kirby Street, London EC1N 8TS, England, or in the USA by the Copyright Clearance Center, 222 Rosewood Drive, Danvers MA 01923. Application for the written permission of the copyright owner to reproduce any part of this publication must be made by email to legenda@mhra.org.uk.

Disclaimer: Statements of fact and opinion contained in this book are those of the author and not of the editors or the Modern Humanities Research Association. The publisher makes no representation, express or implied, in respect of the accuracy of the material in this book and cannot accept any legal responsibility or liability for any errors or omissions that may be made.

Trademark notice: Product or corporate names may be trademarks or registered trademarks, and are used only for identification and explanation without intent to infringe.

© *Modern Humanities Research Association 2021*

Copy-Editor: Richard Correll

CONTENTS

	Acknowledgements	ix
	Note on Translations	x
	Introduction	1
1	From Objects to 'Things': Masks and Mask-Making in *fin-de-siècle* Europe	17
2	Mask-Makers: From Ensor to Rodin, via Japan	41
3	Masking *Dorian Gray*: Fetishism and Ego-Mania in Beerbohm and Le Gallienne	73
4	Fragments: Gabriele D'Annunzio and Medusa's Head	95
5	Masks-Phobia: Jean Lorrain	121
6	Masquerades: The Child, the Criminal and the 'Savage' in Hofmannsthal and Bely	143
	Conclusion	167
	Afterword	171
	Bibliography	173
	Index	187

To Icaro and Cosimo,
who love masks

ACKNOWLEDGEMENTS

This book has its origin in a project developed at the University of Toronto, which was supported by the George C. Metcalf Research Grant. I would like to thank my colleagues at the Centre for Comparative Literature at the University of Toronto for early feedback and encouragement. I am also thankful to The University of Western Ontario and The University of British Columbia for providing funding to present the project at a broad range of conferences. Thanks to the School of Modern Languages and Culture at the University of Glasgow for providing a term of study leave, which enabled me to finish the book.

I am deeply indebted to the anonymous peer reviewer for their helpful feedback. I would also like to thank the editorial staff at Legenda for their hard work. Finally, a special thought goes to my husband and my children, for their unconditional love and remarkable patience.

NOTE ON TRANSLATIONS

All primary texts in Italian, French, German and Russian are quoted in the original, followed by an English translation. When available, I referred to published translations as listed in the bibliography. I have occasionally taken the liberty of modifying the translated text to render the text's meaning more closely. When translations were not available, they are my own. The exception is Kido Okamoto's *Shuzen-ji Monogatari* [The Tale of Shuzenji], for which, due to my own limitations, I rely on the English translation.

INTRODUCTION

> [Nordau] is so utterly mad on the subject of degeneration that he finds the symptoms of it in the loftiest geniuses as plainly as in the lowest jailbirds, the exception being himself, Lombroso, Krafft-Ebing, Dr. Maudsley, Goethe, Shakespeare and Beethoven. (Shaw 1911: 89)

In the last decades of the nineteenth century, faith in progress was questioned in medical, anthropological, philosophical and aesthetic fields by the paradigm of regression. In the same years, masks flourished as portraits, props and disguises in sculpture, theatre and literary texts. This book examines tales that revolve around masks and mask-making in relation to the debate that, in *fin-de-siècle* Europe, developed around the notion of degeneration. It is concerned with the role of the mask as a figuration of alterity, its link to faraway spaces and the historically remote, its capacity to enable fluid gender identities. Why were masks, at the turn of the nineteenth century, used in conjunction with an imagery of madness, regression and decline? Under what circumstances does the mask becomes a fetish for the Western artist, and to what extent we can speak of a 'misogyny of the mask'? Why do masks, in *fin-de-siècle* texts, acquire uncanny connotations? How is the configuration of masks as uncanny reconciled with the embracement of gender performances and the understanding of gender as performative? To what extent do references to sexology and psychoanalysis reinforce established discourses, or contribute to the development of an alternative point of view? By examining tales of masks and mask-making against the background of nineteenth-century thought, this study aims to answer these questions.

Each of the chapters revolves around different types of masks, from funerary effigies to theatrical props to carnival costumes, and follows a trajectory across media, with particular attention to the work of writers in which masks and masking become dominant tropes. While the primary focus is on literary and dramatic texts, each narrative is read in conjunction with artistic or performance practices and placed in a cultural and historical context. In all the texts considered, masks feature as object, trope and as a symbolic structure; at the same time, they address a concern with regression, madness and perversion. Scholars of nineteenth-century thought have underlined how the flexible yet encompassing notion of degeneration, in the last decades of that century, transitioned from individual disease to societal phenomenon, and began to be applied to the cultural sphere (Pick 1989: 22; Schaffner 2012: 64). By exploring narratives of masks and mask-making in light of medical, sociological, and anthropological debates, this book initiates a discussion on how late nineteenth- and early twentieth-century authors brought masks into relation with madness and the return of the repressed, genius as a form of atavism, sexual inversion as symptom of arrested development, and barbarism as a response to cultural exhaustion.[1]

Regression as a Nineteenth-Century Paradigm

Inquiries into regression shaped medico-sociological discourses from the second half of the nineteenth century (Richter 2011). Before the advent of evolutionary biology, Bénédict Morel (1809–1873), author of the influential *Traité des dégénérescences physiques, intellectuelles et morales de l'espèce humaine* [*Treatise on Physical, Intellectual, and Moral Degeneration of the Human Species*] (1857), had defined degeneration as a pathological deviation from the norm, a state that could be inherited and that was discernible through physical signs. In *Degeneration, a Chapter in Darwinism* (1880), the biologist Edwin Ray Lankaster (1847–1929) combined Morel's notion of degeneracy with Ernst Haeckel's recapitulation theory. Extending the logic of evolution to the social sphere, he argued that degeneration was the response of adaptation to a less challenging environment: just as a lack of stimulation could lead an organism to an inverted development, the lack of challenge in contemporary European society would cause its atrophy.

The Italian anthropologist Cesare Lombroso (1835–1909) drew on the notion of 'atavism', a term Darwin had used to define the phenomenon through which traits cast off by a species can emerge in individual organisms at later stages of development, and applied it to his own study of criminality. In several influential treatises, among which *Genio e follia* [*Genius and Madness*] (1864) and *L'uomo delinquente* [*Criminal Man*] (1876),[2] he illustrated the relationship between physical signs and mental issues in relation to regression and degeneracy, and concluded that criminality, madness and genius were closely related. The criminal, he reasoned, was an evolutionary throwback, an atavistic being with the same instincts as prehistoric men. The epileptic displayed similar features, while the man of genius could be considered a degenerate who paid for excessive intellectual capability through the atrophying of other organs. In 1893, he expanded his line of inquiry with an investigation into women criminals, *La donna delinquente, la prostituta e la donna normale* [*The Criminal Woman, the Prostitute and the Normal Woman*], written in collaboration with Guglielmo Ferrero. Since women were considered less evolved, and therefore closer to their prehistoric past and comparable to children in their moral development, he concluded that the typical crime for women was prostitution, which, he stressed, was endemic among indigenous people.[3] Darwin saw gender blurring as characterizing early species and argued that evolution led to a progressive differentiation; in line with this insight, Lombroso described the born criminal as effeminate, the woman offender as masculine, and elaborated on the similarities between homosexuality and criminality (Lombroso 1906).

The physician, journalist and cultural critic Max Nordau (1849–1923) built on Lombroso's study of genius to argue that the level of development reached by a society was documented by its artistic output. With *Degeneration*, originally

Fig. I.1. Death masks of criminals originally displayed in Cesare Lombroso's museum, by kind permission of the Museum of Criminal Anthropology, University of Turin

published in German in 1892 and subsequently re-issued in numerous editions and broadly disseminated across Europe through translation, he set out to explore the 'pathological character' of the works of Symbolists, aesthetes and decadents, starting from the premise that 'they have their source in the degeneracy of their authors' (1993: 6). In Nordau's view, the concentration of the population in large cities, the increased industrialization, and the development of new technologies had exhausted the European city dwellers. The overstimulation of the nerves, he argued, led to 'moral insanity, imbecility, and dementia' (1993: 6), as exemplified by *fin-de-siècle* literary and philosophical trends. Building on Lancaster and Lombroso, he noted that decadents and aesthetes, with their cult of masks and personas, increasingly blurred gender categories, and remarked that the effacement of differences between the sexes was typical of primitive civilizations and societies in decline.

Richard von Krafft-Ebing (1840–1902), Paul Moreau de Tours (1844–1905), Jean Martin Charcot (1825–1893) and Valentin Magnan (1835–1916), whose studies contributed to the modern articulation of sexuality, argued that the aim of the 'healthy' sexual drive was reproduction and classified any deviation from heterosexual genital intercourse as perversion. In Magnan and Krafft-Ebing's theories, perversions also enacted a regression on the phylogenetic ladder, a return

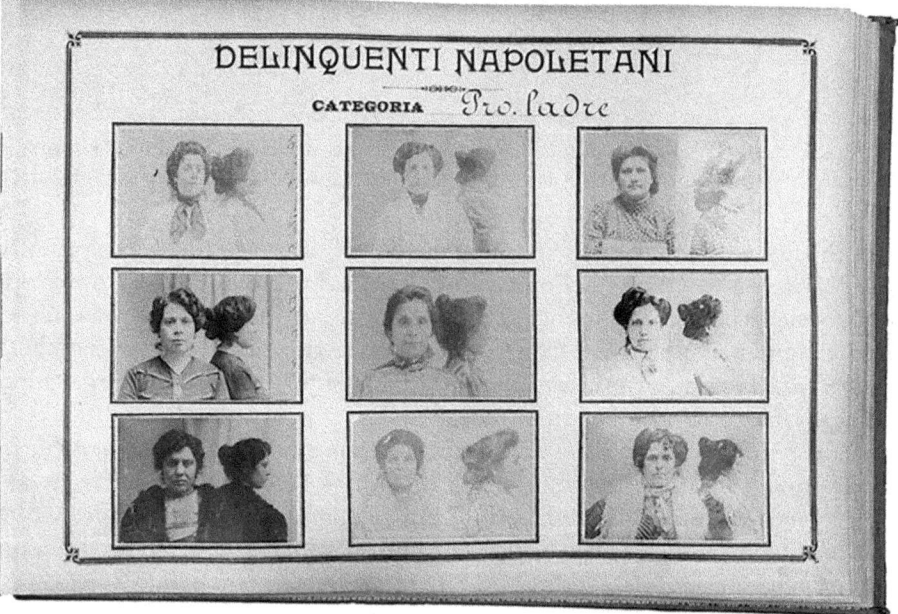

Fig. I.2. 'Neapolitan Delinquents', photograph by De Blasio, by kind permission of the Museum of Criminal Anthropology 'Cesare Lombroso', University of Turin

to a pre-civilized state (Schaffner 2012: 67). These psychologists all underlined the importance that masks and costumes played for subjects suffering from sexual inversion — a label that encompassed phenomena as diverse as homosexuality, bisexuality, androgyny, transvestitism and transsexuality. It is crucial to remember that, at this time, gender-crossing hinged on costumes and make up. For Krafft-Ebing, men who identified with the opposite sex to the point of feeling the urge to dress and behave like women represented one of the gravest cases on the ladder of perversions. This judgement was not based on sexual activity, but motivated by the fact that, by taking on a new identity, these subjects challenged patriarchal authority and the identity received at birth (1965: 188). In an exemplary case study, Krafft-Ebing presented the autobiography of a subject who 'only wears the mask of a man' and 'in everything else fees like a woman' (1965: 206). This person, he stressed, developed from an early age a fascination with masquerades, and felt great excitement at the thought of men dressed in female clothing: 'My only happiness is to see myself dressed as a woman without a feeling of shame; indeed, when my face is veiled or masked, I prefer it so, and thus I think of myself' (1965: 210). Charcot and Magnan similarly stressed how 'inverts' enjoyed dressing up as people of the opposite sex during carnival (Charcot and Magnan 1882: 56). Satisfying deviant sexual urges, in the views of these sexologists, was necessary for the mental health of individuals, but dangerous for the structures of society as it could lead to the disruption of the established order (Oosterhuis 2012: 142).

Although psychoanalysis shifted the focus of the debate on sexual deviances from heredity to childhood experiences, it continued to engage with the paradigm of regression, as deviations from reproductive sexuality featured as 'relics from the past, or insufficiently mastered developmental stages keyed to evolutionary stages' (Brickman 2003: 86). Magnan, Freud stressed, was wrong to consider inverts as degenerate, as many homosexuals 'are indeed distinguished by especially high intellectual development and ethical culture' (Freud 1953: 139). However, by arguing that homosexuality is found in childhood and in primitive stages of society, Freud, just like Magnan, characterized it as an arrested development. In the *Three Essays on Sexuality*, and in the 1914 essay 'On Narcissism: An Introduction', Freud defined homosexuality as a particular kind of narcissism through which the subject identifies with the mother to the point where he chooses the same love object as her (Freud 1978b). Since, according to Freud, the child always experiences a phase of primary narcissism that he then overcomes in adulthood, his understanding of homosexuality involved a regression from the mind of the adult to that of the child (Bredbeck 1994: 54). Furthermore, since primitive men, in Freud's theories, are compared to children in experiencing a lasting narcissistic phase, it also entailed a shift from civilization to the pre-civilized, from consciousness to the unconscious (Brickman 2003: 86–87).

Anachronisms and Icons of Modernity

The extraordinary changes that Nordau perceived as straining the nerves of the artists of his generation were also the trademarks of modernity, which in these years was articulated as a concept involving excitement about a new age and anxieties about disintegration (Felski 1995: 30). In the *fin-de-siècle* imagination, masks reflected this ambivalence by functioning at once as anachronistic objects and as icons of modernity, as exemplified by the so-called *Inconnue de la Seine*, a plaster cast of a young woman drowned in Paris. The death mask, the legend says, was made in the 1880s so as to identify the victim at the morgue, but soon found its way into the homes of artists and collectors. Today we know that the cast could not have been taken from a deceased subject: the features in the *Inconnue* are too well preserved, the skin too smooth to be that of a victim of drowning (Phillips 1982: 321). At the end of the nineteenth century, however, the legend increased its appeal, and the artefact became a highly sought-after object: Richard Le Gallienne, Rainer Maria Rilke, and Albert Camus all owned a copy which they proudly exhibited in their living rooms (Pinet 2002: 175–90).[4] As a death mask, the cast was believed to have touched the face of the deceased, and therefore embodied a sense of authenticity that Walter Benjamin, in his 1935 essay, argued had withered in the age of technical reproducibility (1999: 215). On the other hand, the rate at which this effigy was reproduced and sold for profit involved the substitution of a plurality of copies for a unique object and underlined the role of the mask as a commodity. As the *Inconnue de la Seine* entered the realm of literature — including Le Gallienne's *The Worshipper of the Image* (1900), Jean Lorrain's *Monsieur de Phocas* (1901) and Rainier Maria Rilke's *Die Aufzeichnungen des Malte Laurids Brigge* [*The Notebooks of Malte Laurids Brigge*] (1911) — it embodied the pre-modern and inspired fantasies that revolved around perversions and challenged established social and sexual norms.

Other masks that became icons of modernism — such as Rodin's portraits of the Japanese actress Hanako, the East Asian masks painted by Emil Nolde and James Ensor, or the mask-like faces carved by Picasso — were inspired by or associated with non-Western artefacts, and reflected the belief in renewal through the contact with the 'barbaric' and the 'primeval'. On the one hand, such practices rested on the assumption of the superiority of the Western subject, and on the perception of areas such as Japan and North Africa as as what Anne McClintock calls 'anachronistic spaces', positioned 'forward in geographical space but backward in historical time' (McClintock 1995: 30). On the other, they mirrored the loss of faith in historical progress, the doubt that Western culture, perceived as the latest manifestation of civilization, may be at an impasse, at need of new energy sources (Adamson 2015: 18). Together with an external crisis, these masks reflect an inner one. In capturing the 'primitive', the 'foreign', the 'oriental', they became metaphors for the Western unconscious and for the loss of belief in a cohesive self.

In *fin-de-siècle* artistic circles, it was common to compare and conflate masks originating in a European past (ancient Greece, the Middle Ages) and in the cultures that in this period were considered less evolved (such as North Africa and East Asia). These conflations become evident in the case studies examined

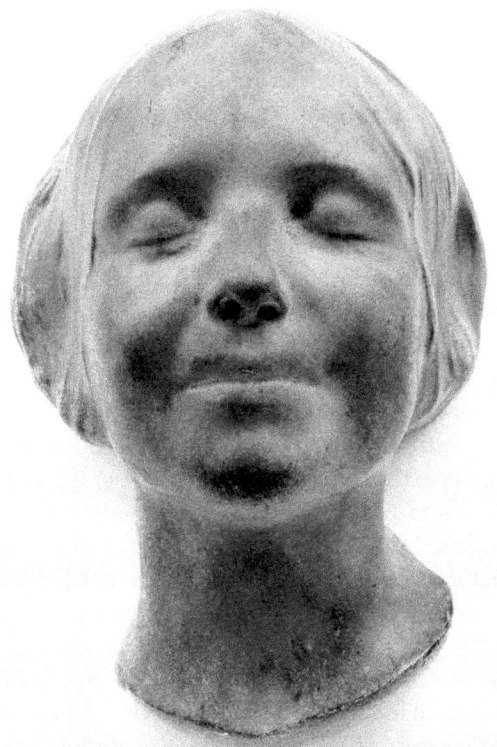

Fig. I.3. Anonymous, *L'Inconnue de la Seine*. *Deutsches Literaturarchiv*, Marbach. Photo by Chris Korner. By kind permission of DLA Marbach.

in this book, and exemplify the 'denial of coevalness' that Johannes Fabian sees as characterizing nineteenth-century anthropology. As Fabian has stressed, the perception of contemporary cultures as existing in other times created a distance between the observer and the observed, and therefore complied with a colonial agenda (1983: 25). In decadent and modernist texts, masks confront the Western subject with alterity in ethnic, gender and social terms, as well as with a fragmented consciousness, childhood experiences and a return to pre-history.

Uncanny and Fetish Objects

In the texts examined in this study, masks evoke unsettling feelings while exercising overpowering attraction. This duality reflects the *fin-de-siècle* connection between disguises and 'sexual deviances', and is enhanced by the frequency with which masks are juxtaposed to images of decapitation.

In his essay on the Uncanny, Freud noted that, in literary texts, descriptions of human fragments such as 'dismembered limbs, a severed head, a hand cut off at the wrist' have 'something particularly uncanny about them' (1955a: 244). In addition, he argued that the experience of the uncanny can be evoked when 'the distinction between imagination and reality is effaced, as when something that we have hitherto regarded as imaginary appears before us in reality, or when a symbol takes over the full functions of the thing it symbolizes' (1955a: 244).[5] The latter is, according to Freud, the operating mechanism in the mind of a child, the 'savage' and the neurotic — all of whom are unable to distinguish the figurative from the real. In Freud's thought, the uncanny, which is associated with the return of the repressed, is therefore from the outset linked to language, and can be triggered by a literal interpretation. At the end of the essay, Freud adds that the uncanny is evoked when surmounted primitive beliefs are confirmed or repressed infantile complexes are revived by impression. Among these, a crucial role is played by castration anxiety, which is also central to Freud's concepts of fetishism and homosexuality.

Freud's early understanding of fetishism, as articulated in *Three Essays on Sexuality*, referred to both anthropological and sexual practices, encompassing the fetish 'in which savages believe that their gods are embodied' and the contemporary Western 'affection for sexual objects' (1953: 153). In the latter case, Freud explained fetishism as a phenomenon that arises when the male child sees the mother's genitals and is unable to overcome the idea that she does not have a penis, which would lead to castration anxiety.[6] In creating a substitute for the 'lost' penis, the fetishist's psyche remains fixed on the last thing he looked at before the discovery of the mother's genitals or an object linked to it by contiguity, and therefore operates by metonymy.[7] In obsessing with an object only partly associated with the original object of desire (the mother), the fetish substitutes the part for the whole and follows the logic of synecdoche. Before Freud, the centrality of metonymy and synecdoche in the formation of the fetish had already been noted by Binet, while Krafft-Ebing had underlined that the fetishist, in translating fantasies into concrete scenarios, literally realizes a metaphor (Schaffner 2012: 57). In the essay on fetishism, Freud built on this intuition by describing the case of a fetish that originates in mistranslation.[8] Elaborating on this note, Jacques Lacan and Wladimir Granoff argued that fetishism is a function of language, that takes place when language 'is simultaneously literalized and its fully symbolic dimensions are denied' (1956: 272).

As manifestations of the uncanny, the masks that appear in the following chapters evoke the return of the repressed, and often merge with the impulses and desires they symbolize, to the point at which they become substitutes for them. Like any fetish object, they simultaneously conceal and reveal, and are situated at the junction of the Symbolic, the realm of language and culture, and the Imaginary, the territory in which 'meaning seems lost' and 'fetishism is connected to the death drive' (Lacan and Granoff 1956: 268). Through the connection to the death drive, they disrupt the Symbolic, and the societal norms it supports, through the emergence of the Real.

Medusa's Head and the Gaze of the Mask

Far from being limited to an individual pathology, Freud's conception of fetishism involved a social dimension, as it relied on the premise that the fetish functioned as a tool to maintain patriarchy. In the 1927 essay, Freud compared the child's feelings in discovering the mother's genitals and the ensuing castration anxiety to the adult's panic in the face of a radical change in socio-political order: 'In later life a grown

Fig. I.4. Caravaggio, *Medusa*, 1595–96, oil on canvas mounted on wood, 55 cm, Uffizi gallery, Florence.

man may perhaps experience a similar panic when the cry goes up that Throne and Altar are in danger, and similar illogical consequences will ensue' (1978a: 152).[9]

The Gorgon's head, for Freud, functioned as an emblem of this anxiety. In an essay dedicated to the Greek myth, Freud addressed how the Gorgon's head is worn as an ornament — a mask — on the dress/shield of the goddess Athena, and argued that, by displaying the mother's genitals, Athena stands for the unapproachable woman who 'repels all sexual desire'. According to Freud, this representation derived from how widespread homosexuality was among the Greeks, a phenomenon that led them to imagine woman as 'a being who frightens and repels because she is castrated' (2003: 85). As a fetish, 'a token of triumph over the threat of castration and a safeguard against it' (Freud 1978a: 154),[10] the head of Medusa fills the viewer with terror while at the same time mitigating his fear.

In most versions of the legend, Medusa is a former priestess of Athena, a beauty punished for having desecrated the goddess's temple through her relationship with Poseidon. Transformed into a monster, she has the power to kill by turning those who meet her gaze into stone. Perseus succeeds in beheading her by wearing a helmet that endows him with invisibility and by looking at the monster's reflection in his shield. After using Medusa's head as a weapon to petrify his enemies, he places it on the shield of Athena, his protector. Feminist critics have challenged Freud's reading of the Greek myth and pointed out the ambiguity of Perseus's use of the shield as a mirror: 'Is it that his deflected gaze permits him to look upon her with impunity? Or does a mirror image shown to Medusa seem to stupefy her with her own appearance? In other words, is it his gaze or hers that costs her her life?' question Marjorie Garber and Nancy Vickers (2003: 6). In Barbara Spackman's view, the emphasis of the myth is 'seeing without been seen, about making sure to remain a subject rather than being turned into an object' (1996: 101).

These reflections build on the concept of the gaze as developed by Lacan in his seminar XI. For Lacan, the gaze is associated with the uncanny feelings that emerge when the object of the look looks back at the observer. Lacan's example of the gaze revolves around a skull hidden in a Renaissance painting, Hans Holbein's *The Ambassadors* (1533). Through a display of symbolic objects, the painting apparently celebrates wealth, science and art. If, however, viewers approach the canvass from the bottom left, they realize that the blurred spot at the centre bottom of the composition is a human skull. Lacan argued that this skull, by looking back at the viewer and confronting them with death, challenges their illusion of control and confronts them with the Real (Lacan 1977: 67–105).

The theatrical mask shares with the skull fixity, symmetry and anonymity, as well as empty orbits (Weihe 2009: 21), features that give it the potential to trigger the Lacanian gaze. For the philosopher Jean-Luc Nancy, every mask is essentially an image of death, as masks signify by juxtaposition to the permanent becoming of the face (2008: 14). In this light, every mask can be compared to the death mask, which involves petrifying, objectifying the features of a living being. Elaborating on Heidegger's discussion of death masks,[11] Nancy stresses that the death mask exemplifies 'the dead look', or 'the death of the look', as well as the mechanism through which the Other presents itself as the same:

> In the ground of the image there is the imagination, and in the ground of the imagination there is the other, the look of the other, that is, the look into the other as look — which also opens, consequently, as an other of the look, a fore-seeing non-look. The other approaches me face-to-face, and thus shows itself as other. The image is first of all other and from the other, altered and altering. It gives the other according to which the same can be shown.
>
> Thus, the other essentially does not show itself as such: what it gives must be seen as the same. The same is altered in its image and it is thus that it makes itself the same as itself — visible, imaginable and presentable. (Nancy 2005: 97)

The gaze, and overall the motif of looking, are central themes in *fin-de-siècle* narratives that revolve around masks and mask-making, where Medusa so often features as an implicit or explicit reference. In many of the tales analysed in the following chapters, the mask is introduced as a female portrait, a fragment that, just like Medusa's head, is characterized by doubleness, at once mesmerizing and terrifying. In some of them, as in D'Annunzio and Lorrain's texts, masks overlap with images of decapitation. Hélène Cixous challenged the misogynistic strain that underpins Freud's theory, and described Medusa as a subversive beauty and as a source of inspiration for *écriture féminine*, a writing that challenges patriarchal

Fig. I.5. Benvenuto Cellini, *Perseus with the Head of Medusa*, c. 1554, bronze, Loggia dei Lanzi, Piazza della Signoria, Florence.

authority by valuing feminine difference (1976: 875–93). The stories considered below, however, are far from such an insight. The work of art that best describes the dynamic at the core of these narratives is Benvenuto Cellini's statue of Perseus (1545–54), which features prominently in D'Annunzio's novel *Il Fuoco* [*The Flame*] and portrays the hero holding Medusa's head immediately after her decapitation. In this statue, Perseus stands holding the Gorgon's head, displaying his muscular body in tension. The Gorgon's headless corpse, which lies supine at the hero's feet, shows full, naked breasts, but also strong, muscular arms and legs, while the heads of avenger and victim are strikingly similar, almost a mirror of one another. Likewise, in many other tales, the mask undergoes a shift from a representation of the Other to a screen for the fantasies of the artist, and the dichotomy between self and other is challenged by the recognition of Otherness as component of the very self.

Masks, Fragments and the *pars-pro-toto* Debate

Fin-de-siècle texts deploy, deflect and repeat the connection between masking and non-normative sexual practices. Kevin Ohi notes that queerness expresses itself at a stylistic, as well as at a thematic level (2011: 17). In *fin-de-siècle* tales of masks and mask-making, manifestations of queerness are accompanied by a focus on belatedness, which involves the deferral of meaning from signifier to signifier, as well as the splitting of the signifier and the signified. On a thematic level, they are linked to the idea of 'the End' — which, as Marja Härmänmaa and Christopher Nissen underline, has both a singular and collective dimension, concerning individuals and larger social units (2014: 19).

In the preface to the 1869 edition of Baudelaire's *Les Fleurs du mal* [*The Flowers of Evil*], Théophile Gautier made these points by stressing how Decadent style was continuously stretching the boundaries of language in the attempt to express 'all the subtle confidence in neurosis, the dying confessions of passion grown depraved, and the strange hallucination of the obsession which is turning to madness'. In defining decadent style as 'nothing else than art which has reached the point of extreme maturity that characterizes aging civilizations as their suns begin to set', 'a language necessary and fatal for people and civilizations where artificial life has replaced natural life and man has developed unknown needs', he identified a link between this stylistic attitude and cultural deterioration (Gautier 1869: 17). In another essay on Baudelaire, originally published in 1881, Paul Bourget compared decadent style to a social organism that begins to degenerate because of excessive individualism, and identified the trademark of decadent style in the dominance of the part over the whole: 'The social organism enters into decadence as soon as the individual life becomes exaggerated beneath the influence of an acquired wellbeing, and of heredity. A similar law governs the development and decadence of that organism we call language. A style of decadence is one in which the unity of the book is decomposed to give place to the independence of the page, in which the page is decomposed to give independence to the phrase, and the phrase to give place to the independence of the word' (1883: 25).[12] Years later, Havelock Ellis established a comparison between the decadents' over-emphasis on details and the excessive individualism in late Victorian society (Ellis 1932: 52).[13] Overall, the concern with the *pars pro toto* found a fertile ground in the theorizing of decadence, featuring in the writing of influential critics like Friedrich Nietzsche and Arthur Symons (Murray and Hall 2013). As Regenia Gagnier has stressed, the problem was not limited to stylistic debates but had socio-political implications (Gagnier 2010: 2).

This book reads the emphasis on the subordination of the whole to the part in conjunction with Linda Nochlin's claim that 'fragmentation, mutilation and destruction' constitute the founding tropes of modernity (1994: 10). Drawing on Nochlin's insight, it explores how, in the texts examined, masks function as fetish objects and manifestations of the uncanny. As fragments, masks fall into the field of synecdoche. Through the juxtaposition with broken sculptures and severed heads, they are embedded in a metonymic logic. These are not only the core features associated with decadent style, but also the operating mechanisms of fetishism. By using masks as figurations of alterity that combine the decadent preoccupation with degeneration with the Freudian notion of the return of the repressed and the experience the uncanny as 'a foreign body within oneself, even the experience of oneself as a foreign body' (Royle 2003: 2), these texts also anticipate or embody modernist sensibilities.

Book Structure and Outline of Chapters

While there is lively interest in the scholarship on masks in the context of cultural and literary studies, this monograph is the first to examine the fascination with masks from a comparative perspective and in the context of nineteenth- and early twentieth-century thought. Hans Belting's *Face and Mask* (2017) takes a broad approach and covers the history of the mask from ancient festivals to digital cyber faces. Existing comparative studies in the context of modernism (see Harris Smith 1984, Sheppard 2001) focus on performances. Other works place the *fin-de-siècle* fascination with masks within a single area study, or are concerned with single authors or specific artistic practices (see McQuillen 2013, Clayton 1994, Mariani 2008). This monograph is at once wider and more defined: it examines selected case studies across disciplines within a European context, all of which relate to a concern with degeneration and decline. On a different level, the book engages with recent debates in decadence and early modernist studies. The fascination with masks challenges the abrupt separation between authors associated with the 'half-mock interlude of decadence' (Symons 1899) and those considered exponents of symbolism, and thus part of early modernism. Moreover, examining *fin-de-siècle* accounts of masking involves a reflection on queerness, a feature that, as Vincent Sherry has argued, often prevented decadent texts from entering the modernist canon (2015: 3). Texts by Richard Le Gallienne, Max Beerbohm, Gabriele D'Annunzio and Jean Lorrain are therefore placed alongside the works of modernist authors like Hugo von Hofmannsthal and Andrei Bely. By including literary traditions in which decadence, as a critical category, either overlaps with symbolism (as in Russia), or is seen as constitutive of modernism (as in Italy and Germany), the book highlights the cosmopolitan dimension of decadence and foregrounds the mechanisms of influence and appropriation that pervade the writing produced in what Matthew Potolsky has called the 'decadent republic of letters' (Potolsky 2013). To show how pervasive masks were in the culture of the time, chapters juxtapose canonical works with texts that have not yet received critical attention, thereby adding a set of new voices to transnational debates about *fin-de-siècle* fiction. In 2013, Alex Murray and Jason David Hall concluded the introduction to *Decadent Poetics: Literature and Form at the British Fin de Siècle* by pointing out that the 'geographical and historical dimension' of decadence remains largely unexplored (2013: 21), and expressed the wish that other scholars take up this endeavour. Since then, Regenia Gagnier and Michael Saler have broadened the meaning of decadence by focusing on the wider circulation of these texts (see Gagnier 2015, Saler 2015). While my focus remains primarily on Europe, by embracing a comparative approach and going beyond the French/English territory, this book participates in this task.

The first chapter, 'From Objects to Things: Masks and the European *fin de siècle*', provides an overview of the debate that developed around masks in the last decades of the nineteenth century, and explores the shapes that masks assumed across disciplines and cultures. The role of masks at the crossroads of physiognomy and ethnography fleshes out connections between medical tools, artistic objects, and anthropological artefacts. Building on Heidegger's differentiation between objects and 'things' (Heidegger 1971: 174–82), the chapter discusses the shift of function that took place as the mask, in its many configurations, was separated from its original context of use and became associated with the paradoxes that Antoine Compagnon sees as characterizing modernity: the unfinished, the fragmentary, the insignificant and the self-referential (Compagnon 1990: 36).

Chapter 2, 'Mask Makers: From Ensor to Rodin, via Japan', explores narratives of mask-making across media. It focuses on four case studies in which masks appear at the boundaries of physiognomic and ritualistic practices: the grotesque masks by James Ensor, the Carnival and Nō masks featuring in the plays by Fernand Crommelynck and Kido Okamoto, respectively, and the 'masks of horror' through which Auguste Rodin attempted to capture the expression of agony of the Japanese dancer Hanako as she performed a hara-kiri scene. By comparing distinct Western and Eastern artistic practices, the chapter draws a connection between the Western fascination with the exotic and the interest in folkloric traditions within Europe, and demonstrates that mask-making functioned as a gendered practice that bordered on cultural appropriation.

Subsequent chapters are concerned with the mask as a trope in literary texts. Chapter 3, 'Masking Dorian Gray: Fetishism and Ego-mania in Beerbohm and Le Gallienne', examines the cult of personas, masks and disguises among British decadents in relation to transnational debates about Decadence and against the background of social, medical and legal debates on homosexuality. By reading Max Beerbohm's *The Happy Hypocrite* (1896) and Richard Le Gallienne's *The Worshipper of the Image* (1899) as parodies of Oscar Wilde's *The Picture of Dorian Gray* (1890–91), it rediscovers texts that have so far been considered marginal and derivative as important sources to highlight the role of the mask in the expression of the non-normative. It argues that, in parodying *The Picture of Dorian Gray* at a time in which it had become impossible to ignore the association between Wilde's novel and his homosexuality, these texts comment on their authors' stance towards the decadent movement, and contribute to the articulation of alternative gender and sexual models that were taking shape in Victorian culture.

The next two chapters explore the link between masks, fragments and severed heads in the work of Gabriele D'Annunzio and Jean Lorrain. D'Annunzio was a renowned womanizer while Lorrain was openly homosexual, but the work of both writers appears strikingly similar in their treatment of masks as fetishes and in the association of fetishism and sexual inversion. Chapter 4, 'Fragments: Gabriele D'Annunzio and Medusa's Head', focuses on the relation among mask-like faces, sculptural fragments and the Greek myth of Perseus and Medusa in D'Annunzio's novel *Il Fuoco* [*The Flame*] (1900) and the plays *La città morta* [*The Death City* 1896], *La Gioconda* (1898) and *La Gloria* (1898). Drawing on Alfred Binet's reflections on fetishism, as well on the insights of feminist theorists that build on Lacan's theory of the gaze, it examines the association between masks, broken sculptures and human fragments as it uncovers the mask's role as a tool to articulate alternative masculinities. The following chapter, 'Masks-Phobia: Jean Lorrain', focuses on the short stories collected in Lorrain's *Histoires de masques* (1900) and the novel *Monsieur de Phocas* (1901) to examine masks in relation to a system of signification. It argues that Lorrain draws on an imagery of masks rooted in romanticism and symbolism, as his texts pay homage to E. T. A. Hoffmann, Marcel Schwob and James Ensor. In addition, it shows how, in his fiction, the instability of the mask as sign is placed into relation with the inconsistency of sex and gender as fixed categories. By examining masks as devices to explore the return of the repressed, the chapter also questions the extent to which these pre-Freudian texts parallel the psychoanalytic approach.

Chapter 6, 'Masquerades: The Child, the Criminal and the "Savage"', develops a comparison between Hugo von Hofmannsthal's *Andreas* (1912–32) and Andrei Bely's *Petersburg* (1913). It explores how these novels use masks and doubling to reflect anxieties about a changing European landscape, while engaging with the paradigm of degeneration. In both narratives, masks stand in close relation to mirrors and portraits. The fear and fascination with the South and the East coincide with an act of introspection: just as in the works of the expressionists, masked and mask-like figures are equally reminiscent of a 'primitive' other and a divided, alien self. Moreover, in both novels masquerade acquires a political connotation and is brought into relation with the crisis of an expansionist power: Austria-Hungary for Hofmannsthal, who uses Andreas's journey to reflect on the height and decline of the Hapsburg Empire; Tsarist Russia for Bely, who establishes a parallel between the compulsion to disguise and the social unrest and terrorism besieging St Petersburg. Drawing on Hofmannsthal and Bely's shared interest in psychology and psychoanalysis, the chapter demonstrates that masks function as an emblem that conflates savagery and neurosis, primitivism and pathology.

By underlining the common thread throughout these works, I have no ambition to be exhaustive; there are many other works that could have been included in the study, from the early works of Luigi Pirandello to the *oeuvre* of W. B. Yeats, Rainer Maria Rilke and Arthur Schnitzler. I nevertheless hope that, in unearthing the interplay of medical, anthropological, sociological and aesthetic discourses, this book will contribute to debates about gender and ethnicity in decadence and modernist studies and initiate a dialogue on masks as key tropes in *fin-de-siècle* culture.

Notes to the Introduction

1. This study limits the discussion to texts written before the First World War, before the discourse of degeneration took a different direction and acquired explicitly racial connotations.
2. Both books were republished in expanded editions. The fourth and final edition of *Genio e follia* was re-titled *L'uomo di genio in rapporto alla psichiatria, alla storia ed all'estetica*, and issued in 1894; the fifth, expanded version of *L'uomo delinquente* was issued in 1897.
3. Nicole Hahn Rafter and Mary Gibson have documented how, in the five editions of *Criminal Man*, Lombroso broadened his inquiries to groups that were increasingly becoming a source of concern in late nineteenth-century Europe: women, southern Italians, Africans, children, the lower classes, brigands and anarchists (Gibson and Hahn Rafter 2006: 15). In establishing parallels and comparisons between these groups, Lombroso's findings exemplified the connections that in these years were being drawn between these subjects (see Horn 2003: 12).
4. David Phillips (1982) and Anne-Gaëlle Saliot (2015) have documented the afterlife of the cast in art and literature. Today, the cast is so well known that dummies used to train lifeguards reproduce its features, and it even has its own Facebook and Wikipedia page (Saliot 2015: 18).
5. I have slightly modified James Strachey's translation. The German text reads: 'wenn ein Symbol die volle Leistung und Bedeutung des Symbolisierten übernimmt' (1947: 258).
6. Under the influence of Derrida and Lacan, feminist scholars, among whom are Sarah Kofman (1985), Elisabeth Grosz (1993), Emily Apter (1991), Teresa de Lauretis (1994) and Louise Kaplan (2006), have challenged Freud's understanding of female sexuality in terms of 'lack' and the assumption that the fetish's task is to maintain the patriarchal order, and have introduced the possibility of female fetishism.
7. Freud stressed that the fetishist is aware of sexual difference, but at the same time keeps his original belief intact by shifting his focus to the substitute. The fetishist's unconscious thus reaches a compromise that helps him to overcome his revulsion for the female body and, in Freud's view, 'saves' him from becoming homosexual (Freud 1978a: 147–59).
8. Freud explains a young man's attraction for 'shiny noses' as the consequence of a mistranslation, in which the English 'glance at the nose' (with the nose substituting the 'lost' penis) is rendered as 'Glanz auf der Nase' [shine on the nose] (Freud 1978a: 152).
9. For a commentary on this passage, see Spackman 1996: 94; and Hertz 1985: 161–93.
10. For Freud, the decapitated head of Medusa inspires a fear of castration, but the snakes departing from the Gorgon's head function as a representation of the stiff penis and as a reassurance against this fear (2003: 85).
11. See Heidegger 1997: 65–68.
12. Regenia Gagnier notes that Bourget was probably informed by Désiré Nisard, who in 1838 had argued that the emphasis on detail at the expense of the whole pointed to the degenerated state of French culture (see Gagnier 2010: 2).
13. Years later, he reformulated the comparison in his introduction to the 1923 translation of Huysmans' *À Rebours*.

CHAPTER 1

From Objects to 'Things': Masks and Mask-Making in *fin-de-siècle* Europe

In a lecture delivered in 1950, titled 'Das Ding' (1950), Martin Heidegger elaborated on the distinction between *Gegenstände* and *Dinge* [objects/things]. He argued that 'objects' are taken for granted, connected to their everyday use, whereas 'things' are embedded in a network of relations with the world and with human subjects (Heidegger 1971: 174–82). Drawing on Heidegger, Bill Brown has noted that the transformation of objects into 'things' occurs when objects are faulty, take on a different use, or are separated from their original function:

> We begin to confront the thingness of objects when they stop working for us: when the drill breaks, when the car stalls, when the windows get filthy, when their flow within the circuits of production and distribution, consumption and exhibition, has been arrested, however momentarily. The story of objects asserting themselves as things, then, is the story of a changed relation to the human subject and thus the story of how the thing really names less an object than a particular subject–object relation. (Brown 2001: 4)

This chapter introduces the debate that developed around masks in the cultural landscape of the *fin de siècle*; it examines the mask's position at the crossroad of physiognomy, anthropology and ethnography, its increasing influence in artistic and theatrical practices, and recurrence as a motif in philosophy and literature. By drawing attention to the liminal status of masks, it fleshes out the blurred boundaries between anthropological artefacts, anatomical tools and artistic objects. In the *fin-de-siècle* imagination, as Europeans re-examined conceptions of portraiture through the encounter with non-Western cultures, masks were increasingly separated from their original context of use. In their multiple shapes and configurations, they were associated with the unfinished, the fragmentary, the insignificant and the self-referential, paradoxes that Antoine Compagnon sees as exemplifying the contradiction of modernity (1990: 26). As changeable, ever-shifting tropes without a fixed referent, they confronted artists and writers with their 'thingness', the capacity to reflect the relationship to the observer and the surrounding world.

Masks in the Museum: Death Masks and Ethnographic Busts

In his introduction to *Masks, the Art of Expression* (1994), a collection of anthropological essays on masking traditions across the world, John Mack defines the mask as an object designed to cover the human face and to bring about a new identity, and identifies its essential feature in its capacity for transformation. He ascribes a very different function to the Egyptian and the Roman traditions of funerary masks, in which the mask is a tool of portraiture. An exception to the rule, the funerary mask does not transform, but rather preserves the appearance of the masker: 'As the body deteriorates, the mask remains as a record of appearance, rather as a photograph survives more or less intact whilst over time the physical appearance of the subject portrayed alters' (1994: 16). Hans Belting develops this insight further as he observes that death masks, whether made out of wax or plaster, reproduce 'human faces as fac-similes whose authenticity is guaranteed by the actual body, with which they came into physical contact' (2017: 97).

In the Western world, the popularity of the mask as a form of portraiture is closely linked to physiognomy and the related (pseudo-)sciences of phrenology and pathognomy. Physiognomy was based on the belief that faces can be read as maps, each feature involving a specific meaning. Phrenology, a nineteenth-century development of physiognomy, endeavoured to decipher character according to the shape of the skull, while pathognomy focused on the study of facial expressions. However, the boundaries between these practices were not always neatly defined, and the study of expression frequently overlapped with the analysis of facial features. Johann Caspar Lavater (1741–1801), the Swiss pastor associated with physiognomy as a modern science, placed great emphasis on death masks. In his *Essays on Physiognomy* (1781–1803), he argued that the soul was legible most clearly on human features at the threshold of life and death, and that the death masks had therefore the capacity to captures the true, authentic expression of the face (Lavater 1781: 160). In the nineteenth century, G.-B.-A. Duchenne, Sir Charles Bell and Charles Darwin all used physiognomy to investigate the expression of emotions. The increased contact with non-European civilizations and the interest in defining national cultures further encouraged these endeavours. By the 1880s, the Italian anthropologist Paolo Mantegazza, in *Fisionomia e mimica* [*Physiognomy and Expression*] (1881), defined the human face as 'a book in which all must read, every day and every hour' (1881: 5). Mantegazza did not limit himself to the study of universal features, but relied on the evidence gathered in his travels to Africa and America to examine the extent to which expressions differed across the world's races. While acknowledging that signs of expression are muscular, he assigned typical features to each race, associating Europeans with 'intelligent expression', Chinese and Japanese with 'apathetic expression', Maoris with a 'ferocious expression', and Africans, who, like many of his contemporaries, he saw as the lowest in the evolutionary scale, with 'Simian expression' (1881: 233). As Mantegazza's book illustrates, anthropology inspired new fields of investigations to physiognomists. In turn, physiognomy continued to play a crucial role in anthropological inquiries (Cowling 1989: 24).

The extent to which physiognomy, ethnography and anthropology spoke to one another is exemplified by collections displayed in panoptica, forms of entertainment that offered to the general public 'a mix of visual striking objects with cultural, scientific and medical pretenses' (McIsaac 2016: 531). Inspired by Marie Tussaud, in 1869 Louis Castan and his brother Gustave Castan founded in Berlin *Castan's Panopticon* (1869–1922), a waxwork museum that aimed to offer 'an ever-changing picture of the progress of culture through the three-dimensional representation of persons and things' (Letkemann 1973: 319). The collection featured a miscellany of curiosities, historical and anatomical objects, including statues of the Prussian Royal family, ethnographic artefacts, life-sized waxworks of serial killers and anatomical Venuses.[1] The death masks on display offered a 'last portrait' of historical figures such as Napoleon Bonaparte, Mary, Queen of Scots, and Kaiser Wilhelm I, celebrities like Goethe, Beethoven, Dostoevsky, and Ibsen, but also criminals condemned to execution. Next to these, the panopticon displayed colourful ethnographic masks and busts intended to illustrate the diversity of the world races. The original casts were taken by anthropologists, and were then entrusted to Louis Castan to create a mould, through which the masks became reproducible objects. Castan was also in charge of finishing off the faces and colouring them in ways that reproduced the tone and texture of skin. In 1883, he took over the completion of 164 casts taken by the ethnologist Otto Finsch during his journey to the South Seas. An adviser to the New Guinea Company, Finsch was involved in the German colonization of South Asia, and used casting as a method to study the variety of races in the newly acquired German territories. The casts assigned to the Castan brothers represented 109 indigenous men, 33 women and 13 children (Friederici 2014: 14). Because of their realism and the direct connection to the models, they were of particular interest to anthropological institutes and ethnographic museums.[2] In 1890, the anthropologist Otto Schellong entrusted to Castan the completion of 39 casts taken from the indigenous people of Papua New Guinea. The collection was put on sale in 1900, a year after the Imperial Government took over the administration of Papua New Guinea (Friederici 2009: 9).

The value of the life mask as an ethnographic artefact, however, was beginning to decline around that time. Despite the high degree of realism, these masks were deemed too distant from their models, as they were altered and re-touched. Schellong recalls in his journal how even Otto Finsch claimed that, with 'the right colour palette and a few wigs', he would be able to transform 'any German countryman into a type from Papua Nova Guinea' (Friederici 2009: 13).

The *Edinburgh Phrenological Society*, which assembled one of the largest collections of death masks in Europe throughout the eighteenth and nineteenth centuries, prided itself on owning over 300 death masks and busts of celebrities, inmates of prisons and asylums, and subjects affected by medical conditions. In addition, the collection featured several ethnographic busts. Among these are the heads of Jochina and Phan, which can still be seen in the Anatomical Museum of the University of Edinburgh. Jochina, a man from the Botocudos tribe from Eastern Brazil, was part of a family of 'savages' travelling to Edinburgh for a live exhibition. He probably died on his way to or upon arrival to the city, and a cast was made of

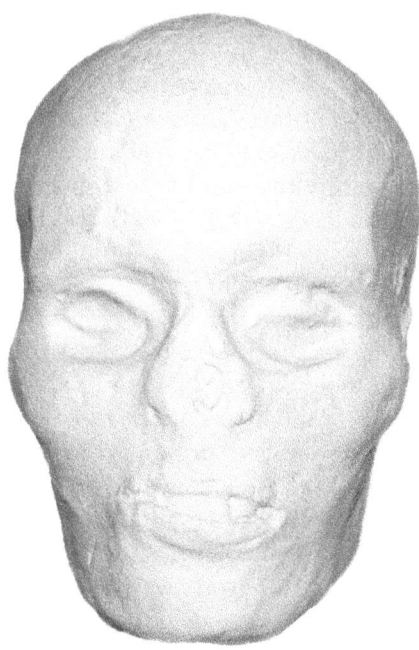

FIG. 1.1. Death Mask of Jochina, indigenous man from Brazil, Catalogue no. 6856, Anatomy Collection, The University of Edinburgh, photo by Ruth Pollit. By kind permission of the Anatomical Museum, University of Edinburgh

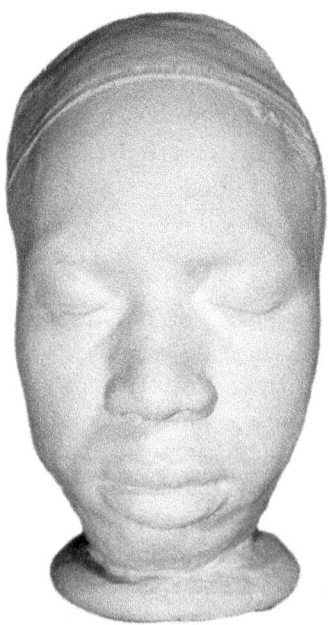

FIG. 1.2. Death Mask of Phan, indigenous woman from Madagascar, catalogue no. 6906, Anatomy Collection, The University of Edinburgh, photo by Ruth Pollit. By kind permission of the Anatomical Museum, University of Edinburgh

his feature after the wooden plugs in the ear and lip were removed. The white cast displays void orbits, as the head was already partially mummified. Phan, in contrast, arrived to Edinburgh in 1827 as a living specimen, where her head and features were measured by the Phrenological Society, who expressed great surprise to find 'favourable development' in a non-European. These two heads exemplify how live and death casts, despite involving completely different procedures, gave rise to similar results. Both captured the Other for the curiosity of the European spectator, reducing the model to a fragment. Both avoided the subject's gaze. In an essay published in 1891, Schellong noted this as a positive feature, since it encouraged viewers to focus on physical traits.[3]

Other collections, such as the 280 death masks displayed at the Vienna museum, documented historical dynasties and the celebrities that thrived under their rule. Hans Belting argues that, at the end of the nineteenth century, the death mask 'became a totemic object that permitted the creation of a nostalgic cult of the timeless, authentic face' (2017: 78). This cult, in his view, exemplifies a change in the modern cult of death, which shifted from the grave into an archival context.

Ernst Benkard's best-seller *Das Ewige Antlitz* [The Eternal Face], originally published in German in 1926 and translated into English as *Undying Faces* (1929), exemplifies the popularity of death masks throughout the nineteenth century. This photo-book featured photographic reproductions of the death masks of the collection of the Schiller National Museum at Marbach, including the renowned *Inconnue de la Seine*. As Benkard argues in the introductory essay, the death mask, as an object, exemplified the ill-defined zone between anatomical evidence and aesthetic practice (1929: 19). The photo-book contains an essay by the German artist Georg Kolbe, who, offering his view of a skilled practitioner, explained the process through which death masks are made and stressed the limited time available for the artist to capture human features between the last breath and the onset of rigor mortis.

Despite the availability of photographs, death masks survived as tools of research in criminal anthropology, the latest and most influential development of physiognomy. The most famous exponent of this field of inquiry was a colleague of Mantegazza's, the Italian anthropologist Cesare Lombroso, whose research into the nature of criminals and the relationship between genius and madness became highly influential in Europe. Lombroso's method relied on phrenology and physiognomy: he assumed that the study of somatic features and the measurement of the cranium denoted psychological traits, and provided his readers with an accurate description of the criminal type, characterized by 'jug ears, thick hair, thin beards, pronounced sinuses, protruding chins, and broad cheekbones' (Lombroso 2006: 53). In the first edition of *Criminal Man*, he noted that these features resembled those of 'Australian Aborigines and Mongols' (Lombroso 2006: 57), as well as of primitive humanity. He also argued that criminals tended to be weaker than normal men, insensitive to pain, and that biological regression pushed them to decorate their skin with drawings and symbols as was customary in prehistoric societies. To gather material for his research, Lombroso relied on photographs of inmates held in prisons and asylums, but he also commissioned ethnic skulls from

Fig. 1.3. Death Masks, *Deutsches Literaturarchiv Marbach*, by kind permission of DLA Marbach

Fig. 1.4. Death Masks, *Deutsches Literaturarchiv Marbach*, by kind permission of DLA Marbach

explorers in the southern hemisphere (Mazzarello 2011: 97). Many of these objects ended up in the museum that he opened at the University of Turin in 1884 with the dual purpose of introducing the general public to criminal anthropology and to provide an education for criminologists. A criminal's skull, displayed as a scientific relic, featured at the centre of the collection, while thirty wax masks of criminals provided a visual illustration of his theory of atavism.

Since the early 1880s, Lombroso had encouraged his students to produce plaster casts and wax masks of the subjects on which they performed autopsies (Montaldo 2013: 98). The wax masks exhibited in his museum had been created by Lorenzo Tenchini, a professor of anatomy at Pavia's university, a wax modeller who applied the phrenological studies of Franz Gall to anthropological studies. Like Lombroso, Tenchini believed that the signs of deviancy could be recognized by facial traits, and prided himself on having devised a special method for moulding death masks that permitted the 'exact reproduction of facial features, to the point that the hair system is preserved intact as it was on the body' (Musumeci 2009: 71). Lombroso probably first saw the masks at the 1885 Universal Exhibition in Paris, in the context of the first congress of criminal anthropology, where they were exhibited at the *Palais des beaux arts*. Each mask was accompanied by the skull of the criminal and its desiccated brain, complemented by a note describing the category of criminal to which the deceased belonged. After the second congress on criminal anthropology, which took place in Turin in 1906, Lombroso wrote to Tenchini asking to purchase the entire collection for his museum.

The application of a layer of wax over the plaster and the way in which the criminals' facial hair was preserved and attached to the masks made them unusual as works of art. As the German sculptor Georg Kolbe argued, death masks, at this time in history, were an accepted type of portrait, but supplementing them with 'hair and other adornments' risked turning the artworks into 'monstrosities, violations and false counterfeits of life' (1929: 45). From Tenchini's correspondence with Lombroso, we know that he was very attached to his masks and reluctant to part with them; he also claimed that they could not be reproduced, since the original texture of the skin would be lost. In the end, Lombroso succeeded in acquiring part of the collection and catalogued the masks as scientific evidence. The boundary between collection and fetishism was thus marked by 'classification and display' in opposition to 'accumulation and secrecy' (Stewart 1984: 163). At the end of his life, presumably to make a contribution to the study of genius, Lombroso decided to donate to the museum his very own face, where it can still be seen, preserved in a jar of liquid.

Overall, the practice of face masks entailed a fundamental ambiguity. On the one hand, death masks produced accurate portraits of exceptional men and artists, thereby providing an instrument for the study of 'genius'. On the other hand, the same practice was used to reduce the features of those suffering from medical conditions, prisoners, and the mentally ill to icons of deviancy. Most importantly, the display of historical portraits next to ethnographic life masks and busts documented the extent to which the historically remote and the geographically distant were compared, interpreted and understood in similar terms.

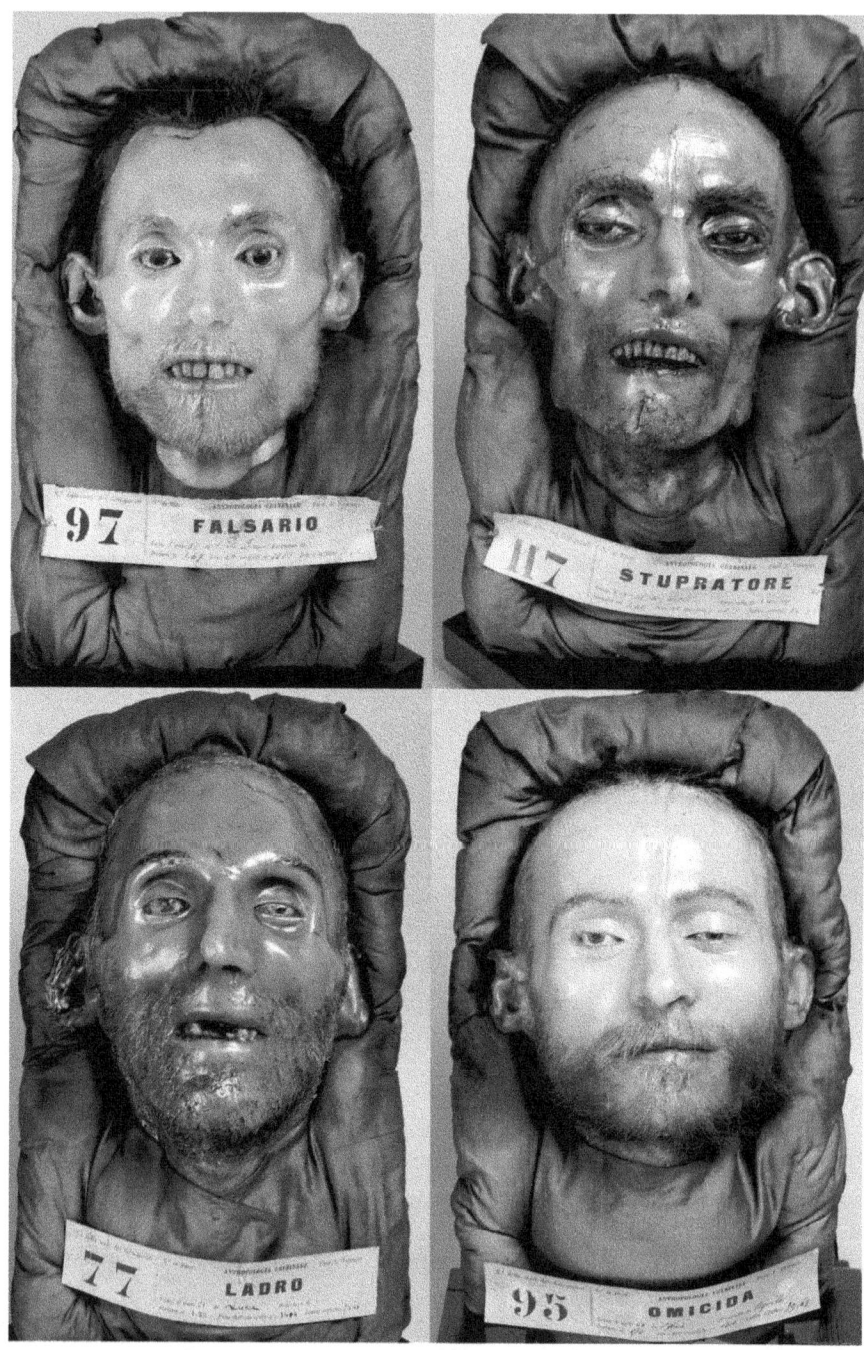

Fig. 1.5. Lorenzo Tenchini, wax masks mounted on wood: no. 77, 'thief', no. 95, 'murderer', no. 97, 'forger', no. 117, 'rapist'. Photograph by Paolo Giagheddu, by kind permission of the Museum of Criminal Anthropology 'Cesare Lombroso', University of Turin

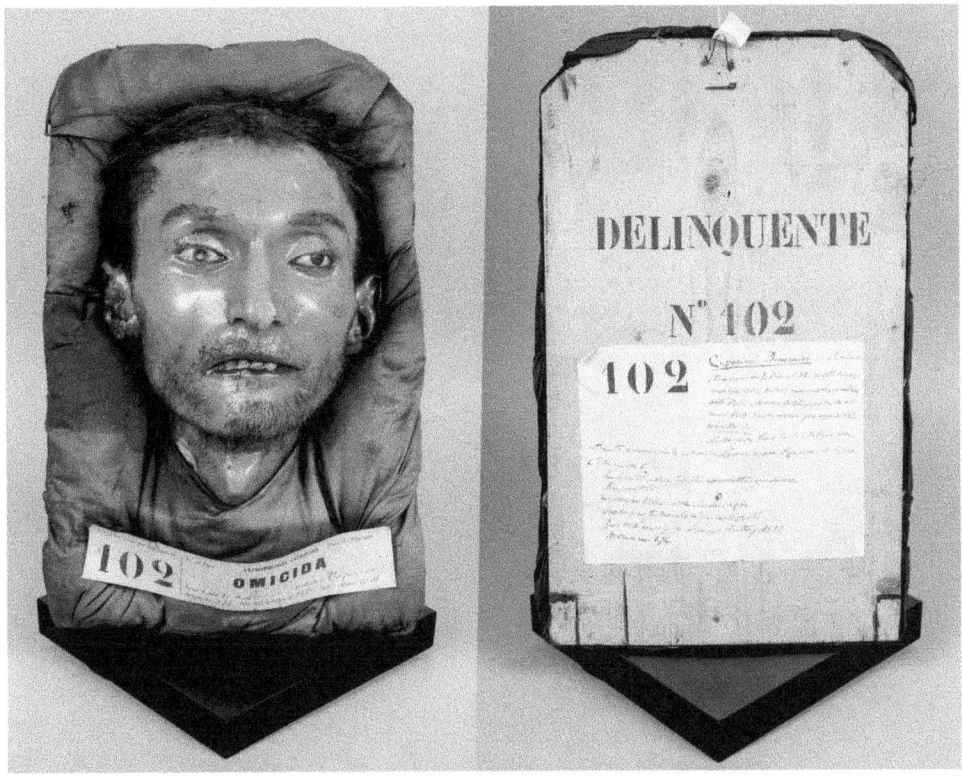

Fig. 1.6. Lorenzo Tenchini, wax masks mounted on wood, no. 102, 'murderer', front and rear. Photograph by Paolo Giagheddu, by kind permission of the Museum of Criminal Anthropology 'Cesare Lombroso', University of Turin

Masks, Fragments and the Cubist Gaze

In an article entitled 'Masks', published in 1903 in the influential journal *Art et Décoration*, Paul Vitry, curator of the Louvre Museum, contended that a pivotal change had occurred in European art, and that masks had become the object of new artistic research. After examining the proliferation of decorative masks by the contemporary sculptors Auguste Rodin, Antoine Bourdelle, José De Chamoy, Jean Carriès and Jules Dalou, Vitry identified in these masks the influence of ancient Greek, Gothic and Japanese art. He underlined three ways in which the mask, as an object, had been productively used in history: as an architectural detail in the Middle Ages, as a funerary object in ancient Egypt and Greece, and as a theatrical prop in ancient Greek performances and in Japanese theatre. While in these periods, he argued, the mask had an architectonical, practical or religious function, the contemporary decorative mask had detached itself from any of these sources: 'Does the lover of things Japanese or the curious person who hung, between his prints and books, a few Japanese masks with a huge grin, often think of this mask as a prop for the stage or for sacred dances? Certainly not, no more than any Parisian, going to the opera, thinks about religious origins of stage performances' (Vitry 1903: 345).

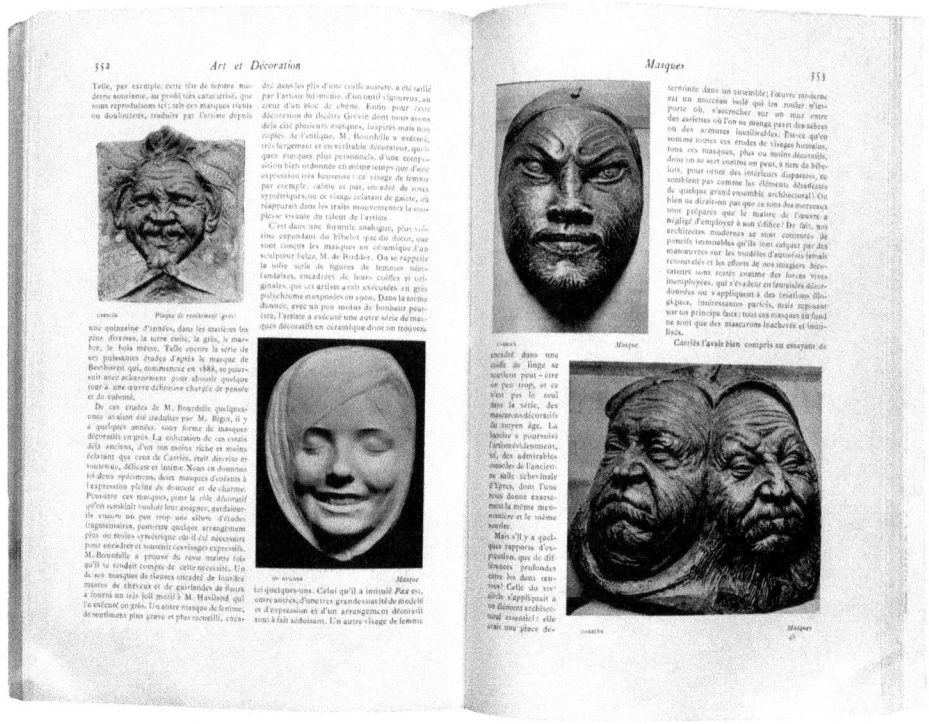

Fig. 1.7. *Art et Décoration* 1903, vol. 14, pp. 352–53

The masks that inspired Vitry's reflections were two- or three-dimensional ceramic, plaster, clay and glass portraits. Some of them, such as Carriès's ceramic 'masks of horror', were inspired by the demon-masks of Japanese Nō. Others, such as De Rudder's, were plaster masks reminiscent of Gothic art. While Vitry recognized the artistic value of these works, he remarked that they looked unfinished. These sculpted faces, he explained, would be wonderful if they were used to complement a work of architecture, as was the practice in Gothic art, but exhibited as autonomous pieces they gave the impression of being incomplete and lacking a fulfilling context. In Vitry's view, a correspondence between artistic artefacts and their original function would be possible only in primitive eras characterized by healthy artistic and cultural growth, which he saw as represented by ancient Greece; but this consonance was no longer conceivable in a contemporary European setting. Reflecting on the feeling of alienation evoked by these pieces, he remarked that they exemplified the tendency of the contemporary work of art to take shape as an isolated piece, a fragment no longer connected to the whole: 'The modern *oeuvre* is an isolated piece that can end up anywhere, hung on a wall between plates no one ever eats from, and unusable sabres and suits of armour' (1903: 353). Vitry's conclusion was that art was undergoing a process of degeneration of which masks had become the emblem. Switching to a lighter tone, he wondered whether the development of racing cars might not offer an opportunity to return the mask to a practical function, and in this spirit referred to two drivers' masks exhibited at the *Louvre* in 1901. In these objects, Vitry saw the desirable bond between a utilitarian object and an aesthetic artefact.

A decade later, the German artist August Macke, who was associated with the group *Die Blaue Reiter*, published in a journal edited by Wassily Kandinsky and Franz Marc an essay entitled 'Die Masken' [Masks] (1912), which today is considered a manifesto of the relationship between modernism and primitivism. Like Vitry, Macke considered Western art in decline, but argued that a process of renewal could be triggered through close contact with distant traditions. Whereas Vitry differentiated the contemporary mask from the masks of Ancient Greece, of the Middle Ages and of contemporary Japan, and regarded it as an empty evocation of them, Macke saw continuity in the use of masks through time and history. He compared folk paintings and drawings by German children to the collections held in Munich's Ethnology Museum, the first German museum to exhibit non-European art, and recognized mask-like features in the works of Paul Cézanne, Aubrey Beardsley and Paul Gauguin. 'The grotesque embellishments found in a mask', he wrote, 'have their analogies in Gothic monuments and in the almost unknown buildings and inscriptions in the primeval forest of Mexico' (1965: 89). Overall, his thesis was that cross-breeding between Europe and the Orient had the potential to engender a third, new style. Unlike Vitry, who saw in contemporary masks an emblem of decadence and alienation, Macke regarded the rediscovery of the mask as a sign of artistic and cultural rebirth. In the rest of his essay, works by modernist artists including Ernst Ludwig Kirchner, Henri Rousseau and Pablo Picasso were juxtaposed or compared to masks.

Between Vitry and Macke came the discovery of African Art. In 1907, Picasso, after studying African masks at the Trocadero museum in Paris, painted mask-like features on two of the prostitutes in 'Les Demoiselles d'Avignon', thus reproducing the aesthetic principles of North African sculpture on a two-dimensional surface. A few years later, the German Expressionists Erich Heckel, Max Pechstein and Karl Schmidt-Rottluff applied the same principles to sculpture, creating what they considered hybrids between Western and Eastern art. Picasso and the cubists, James Clifford has argued, had little interest in African art per se, but saw in masks an embodiment of the views they were defending in their own artistic research (1988: 192). The consonance between Cubist practice and African art was eloquently articulated by Carl Einstein in *Negerplastik* (1915). In his introductory essay, Einstein defied the nineteenth-century prejudice that saw Africans as less evolved and argued that African culture should be taken seriously. He suggested that Western art suffered a decline by neglecting the three-dimensional in favour of pictorial illusionism, and saw in cubism a way out of this impasse. What interested him most in African art was the distance from portraiture: the power of abstraction that the Cubists were after, he remarked, was naturally found in African art. Fascinated by the idea that a work of art can function as a fetish, he stressed how, in Africa, sculptures were worshipped as in the civilizations of antiquity. He also remarked

FIG. 1.8. Photograph of artefacts reproduced in *Negerplastik*, München: K. Wolff, 1920, pp. 90–91

that in these art works the parts took on a life of their own, freeing themselves from the whole — a mechanism that he saw embedded in ritualistic, religious practice.

Einstein dedicated an entire chapter to the African art of mask-making, noting that, just like tattooing, it functioned as a powerful practice of self-objectification. For him, African masks were 'impersonal' (1915: xxvi), filled with 'intensity of expression' and 'freed from any psychological insight' (1915: xxvi). 'I would like to call the mask frozen ecstasy', he wrote, and he concluded that 'in masks speaks the power of the cubist gaze' (1915: xx). As Clifford suggests, Einstein's essay contained elements of an 'ethnographic surrealism', in that it forced readers to re-envision the familiar through confrontation with otherness (1988: 15). Even though Einstein was appreciative of African sculpture, he also placed it in non-historical time. The logic that underpinned the 'discovery' of tribal art, and the way in which African artefacts were exhibited, inevitably reproduced Western colonial assumptions (Clifford 1988: 197).

In contrast to African masks, Japanese masks, which started circulating in European markets from the 1860s, were recognized as artistic masterpieces, compared to ancient Greek masks and linked to the very roots of the Western tradition. The French art historian Luis Gonse argued that masks exemplified Japanese skills in portraiture and that, in being at the same time sacred artefacts, they bridged Western and Eastern traditions (Gonse 1883: 76). Western artists like Claude Monet, Camille Pissaro, Octave Mirbeau, James McNeill Whistler, Paul Gauguin and Vincent Van Gogh were all deeply influenced by *Japonisme*. The popularity of exotic masks also inspired Western artists to experiment with masks as artistic

Fig. 1.9. Jean Carriès: Horror Mask, c. 1891,
Mask in enamelled ceramic, Musée d'Orsay, Paris

artefacts. Jean Carriès, for instance, created a series of porcelain masks inspired by Japanese Demon masks, including a 'Masque dit race jaune' [mask known as yellow race] (1888–92) and a 'Masque d'horreur' [horror mask] (1891). Between 1907 and 1912, Auguste Rodin shaped a series of masks of the Japanese dancer Hanako that strove to render the expression of agony that she enacted when performing suicide onstage. From the 1880s, the Belgian painter James Ensor filled his works with East Asian masks, which he juxtaposed to the carnival masks of Flanders and to images of death. Ensor's work had an important influence on the German Expressionists: the German-Danish artist Emil Nolde, in his 'Masks Still Life' series, was inspired equally by James Ensor's masks and by the artefacts exhibited at the ethnologic collection in Berlin. In her analysis of Nolde's 'Masks Still Life I', Jill Lloyd compares the work of the two artists:

> Whereas Ensor used masks to reveal the grotesque reality behind the façade of political society, Nolde's masks were simply hung against the painterly blue background, which isolates them in time and space. In this way he stressed their status as objects, but paradoxically they are objects animated by human emotions — laughing, exclaiming, pensive. Although they refer back to Nolde's long-standing interest in mask-like faces [...] this is the first painting where the masks occupy a peculiar middle ground between the world of objects and subjective emotions. They are like relics of a theatrical event still imbued with the stylized emotions of performance. (Lloyd 1991: 175)

Lloyd's description underlines the masks' liminality, their capacity to function across media and to defy historical time. In underlining the masks' distance from theatrical props, and their new function as portraits of the inner self, Lloyd also emphasizes their particular status as objects, or rather the transition from objects into 'thing' in their capacity to reflect human subjectivity.

Nietzsche and the Mask

Mask imagery is crucial in the thought of Schopenhauer, who in *Die Welt als Wille und Vorstellung* [The World as Will and Idea] (1844) argued that objects only exist in relation to subjects, or perceivers. For Schopenhauer, individuals cannot see beyond images and learn the true nature of thing; in the phenomenal, visible world, they live separately from one another under a mask, but are all part of the universal will.[4] *The World as Will and Idea* was highly influential for the symbolists, who were inspired by the book to reflect on the relationship between spiritual reality and the surrounding world (McQuillen 2004: 26).

When he set out to work on *Die Geburt der Tragödie aus dem Geiste der Musik* [The Birth of Tragedy from the Spirit of Music] (1872), Nietzsche was a declared follower of Schopenhauer. It is to him that he dedicated the fourth essay in the *Unzeitgemässe Betrachtungen* [Unfashionable Observations] 1974), titled 'Schopenhauer als Erzieher' [Schopenhauer as educator]. From Schopenhauer, Nietzsche acknowledged in this essay, he learned that the goal of life is not happiness, but the establishment of a nobler culture and the production of genius. Like his teacher, Nietzsche questioned the objective foundation of reality, the notions of a single truth and of a unified

Fig. 1.10. Emil Nolde, 'Masks' 1911, oil on canvas, 73 × 77.5 cm.
Photo by Chris Bjuland and Joshua Ferdinand. By kind permission of
The Nelson-Atkins Museum of Art, Kansas City, Missouri

self. Schopenhauer's influence can also be traced in Nietzsche's conception of the will, in the articulation of the duality of Apollonian and the Dionysian, and in his engagement with masks as misleading symbols of individuality.

Throughout his writing, Nietzsche used the mask to articulate a concern with decadence, and to address the possibilities of recovering.[5] As a prop, the mask plays a pivotal role in *The Birth of Tragedy*, in which Nietzsche traced the origin of Greek tragedy to Dionysian rites, and noted that the chorus, in which he saw a form of ritual, turns into theatre when the god Dionysus is represented by a masked actor. He further argued that all the heroes of the Greek stage are a mask of Dionysus, the original tragic hero. However, the mask also features as the emblem of the death of tragedy: Nietzsche accused Euripides, to whom he attributed the degeneration of this form of art, of having created characters dominated by single traits, and argued that the decline of Greek theatre was exemplified by the 'masks with one expression' typical of the new Attic comedy (Nietzsche 1967: 183). Furthermore, the mask is the metaphor implied in the dynamic opposition of the Apollonian and the Dionysian, identified, respectively, as the principles of dreams and individuality, and of intoxication and primordial unity. Nietzsche introduces Apollo as the god of '*Schein*', of appearance and illusion, and the Apollonian as the veil, the mask that hides Dionysian chaos (1967: 37). A form of mask, the Apollonian veil functions as a screen that protects the individual from direct knowledge: 'When after a forceful attempt to gaze on the sun we turn away blinded, we see dark-colored spots before our eyes, as a cure, as it were. Conversely, the bright image projections of the Sophoclean hero — in short, the Apollonian aspect of the mask — are necessary effects of a glance into the insides and terrors of nature; as it were, luminous spots to cure eyes damaged by gruesome night' (1967: 67).

Insofar as it mediates between the Apollonian and the Dionysian, the mask is linked to the creative principle of art. Its positive connotation is confirmed in *Jenseits von Gut und Böse* [*Beyond Good and Evil*] (1886), in which Nietzsche extolled the mask as a means of self-fashioning that challenges a single, stable identity: 'There is not only deceit behind a mask — there is so much goodness in cunning. [...] Every profound spirit needs a mask: more, around every profound spirit a mask is continually growing' (1972: 51). In the second essay of the *Unfashionable Observations*, however, Nietzsche used the mask as a metaphor to represent the lack of harmony that characterized late nineteenth-century humanity who, overwhelmed by science and rationality, had become hesitant and fearful. In this text, the mask became a form of protection that traps a fluid, changeable self into rigid social roles: 'No one runs the risk of bearing his own person, but instead disguises himself behind the mask of the cultivated man, the scholar, the poet, the politician. If we take hold of these masks, believing that they are serious and not just part of a farce — since all of them affect such seriousness — then suddenly we find ourselves holding in our hands nothing but rags and colourful tatters' (1995: 117). Nietzsche here anticipated writers like Luigi Pirandello, Jean Lorrain and Rainier Maria Rilke, as well as James Ensor, by asserting that there is nothing behind the mask. In line with this, in an essay written a year after the *Birth of Tragedy*, 'Über Wahrheit und Lüge im aussermoralischen Sinne' [*On Truth and Lies in a nonmoral sense*] (1873), he defined the mask as a tool for dissimulation, play-acting and social convention, but also as a substitute, a powerful alternative to a 'twitching and changeable human face' (2009: 27).

To explain the conflicting meanings attributed to the mask, the philosopher Gianni Vattimo distinguished between Nietzsche's use of 'mask' and 'disguise'. This duality mirrors the double meaning attributed to the Dionysian, which stands for a fearful reality from which the individual tries to escape and for a source of creativity and artistic impulses (Vattimo 1974: 22). For Vattimo, the complementarity of the Dionysian and Apollonian is resolved in a reduction of the Apollonian to the Dionysian, and the problem of *The Birth of Tragedy* becomes the liberation of the creative energy that the Dionysian represents. In the positive meaning of the mask,

Vattimo sees a free poetic, creative force, evocative of the need continuously to create metaphors. In its negative meaning, the mask turns into a disguise, a social role that traps the fluidity of the self, leading to the enactment of a fixed role. The essay 'On Truth and Lies' features an eloquent representation of the transition from 'mask' to 'disguise':

> What then is truth? A movable army of metaphors, metonymies, anthropomorphisms, in short, a sum of human relations which have been poetically and rhetorically intensified, transferred, decorated and which, after lengthy use, seem firm, canonical and binding to a people: truths are illusions that are no longer remembered as being illusions, metaphors that have become worn and stripped of their sensuous force, coins that have lost their design and are now considered only as metal and no longer as coin. (Nietzsche 2009: 257)

As a form of creative dissimulation, the mask is associated with the multiplication of tropes as a productive impulse. This practice comes to an end when the mask stagnates, hardens, is taken for granted and interpreted as truth. It is then that it loses its original meaning, as it begins to function like a metaphor that is taken literally, or 'a symbol takes over the full function and meaning of the thing that it symbolizes' (Freud 1955: 244), thereby turning into a disguise.

Masks on Stage: Atavism and Rebirth

Nietzsche's interest in Greek tragedy reflected the preoccupation of anthropologists who, in the last decades of the nineteenth century, were engaged in exploring the origins of theatre through rituals. In foregrounding the intent to retrieve a lost, ritualistic dimension, the use of the mask on stage symbolizes the continuity between decadents and early modernists. The mask is, for example, the underlying metaphor in Gabriele D'Annunzio's *La città morta* [The Dead City] (1898), a tragedy written for Eleonora Duse and Sarah Bernhardt, actresses known for playing psychological roles. But masks also feature in Alfred Jarry's *Ubu Roi* (1896), an avant-garde piece in which abstract, puppet-like beings represent contemporary society as seen through the eyes of a child. In both cases, masks echoed ancient Greek tragedy, symbolized the fall into Dionysian chaos as a rebellion against established morality, and embodied atavism and regression. As Susan Harris Smith has demonstrated, masks continued to function as seminal devices for all the artistic movements in the early decades of the twentieth century — from futurism to dadaism, from symbolism and surrealism to expressionism (1984: 6).

Theatre practitioners like Alfred Jarry, Vsevolod Meyerhold, Nikolai Evreinov, Jacques Copeau, W. B. Yeats, Antonin Artaud and Aleksandr Tairov shared Nietzsche's belief that contemporary theatre had degenerated and envisioned the mask as a return to theatricality. All these artists looked beyond the boundaries of European culture for traditions in which masks played an active role. Chinese and Balinese theatre, Japanese folk dances, the Italian *commedia dell'arte* became sources of inspiration, while forms of drama as different as Ancient Greek tragedy and Nō theatre were frequently compared or analysed in light of one another (Aaltonen 2000: 27).

The importance of the mask in relation to decadence and the avant-garde dream of renewal through the encounter with the Other is exemplified in the vision of Edward Gordon Craig (1872–1966), the British director, mask collector and mask maker. Heavily influenced by Nietzsche's thought, Craig derived from the Nietzschean notion of the *Übermensch*, the new, 'non-degenerate' man, the idea of the Über-marionette, a special actor whose physicality would not interfere with the work represented and who, by using masks, would spark the rebirth of contemporary theatre. Masks also featured as recurring topics in the journal *The Mask*, published in Florence since 1908, to which Craig contributed as an editor and collaborator under a variety of pseudonyms. Like Nietzsche, Craig insisted on the ritual roots of drama. He traced the origin of theatre in the use of the mask and regarded contemporary theatre as a decayed form of art that, by insisting on realism, had lost its symbolic potential. In 'A Note on Masks' originally published in 1909 and later included in the collection *The Theatre Advancing* (1919), Craig argued that the mask should be taken seriously. He recalled its religious role in ancient Greece and in Japanese, Indian, African and Amerindian art, claimed that drama had begun degenerating when the mask was neglected, and assured that it would regenerate when the mask would be brought back to the stage: 'The mask will return to the theatre. Of that I grow ever more and more assured; and there is no great obstacle on the way, although there is some danger attached' (Craig 1919: 105). In the same article, Craig suggested that oriental and ancient masks could function as source of inspiration for a theatre no longer tied to the dramatic text. However, the new 'world mask' should not be a copy or a revival, but an original, independent creation, the work of a great artist. 'They need not fear that we shall ask them to sport the mask,' he wrote, 'but they must just see how it becomes us and what fun and what fancy we can make within its shadow' (1919: 109–10).

Overall, Craig saw in the mask a mystical object that could inspire the restoration the sacred on stage. Acting on his suggestion, Yeats decided to place a mask on the character of the Fool in *The Hour-Glass* and began to reflect on the use of masks for his cycle on Cuchulain, inspired by ancient Gaelic sagas and designed to be performed as a Nō dance (Le Boeuf 2009: 201). Moreover, Craig's vision anticipated experiments by the Russian avant-garde, as well as the work of the Bauhaus and the German Expressionists (Bablet 1981: 111). A few years later, the dadaists gathered at the Café Voltaire in Zurich used masks 'reminiscent of the Japanese or ancient Greek theatre, yet wholly modern' that, like antique masks, were meant to represent 'characters and passions that are larger than life' (Ball 1996: 64). In neutral Zurich, during the First World War, the mask became a magical tool that led to a loss of the self, a symbol of the essence of theatre and an objective correlative through which, as Ball wrote, 'the horror of our time, the paralyzing background of events, is made visible' (Ball 1996: 64–64).

The Mask as Decadent Trope

The protagonist of Joris-Karl Huysmans' *À Rebours* [Against Nature] (1884) became a prototype for the decadent hero: the last scion of a degenerate aristocratic line, he withdraws from Parisian society, self isolates in his mansion and dedicates his life to exploring sensations. Hailed by Arthur Symons as the 'breviary of decadence' (1899: 139), *À Rebours* played a pivotal role in the *fin-de-siècle* imagination and was an important influence for Oscar Wilde's *The Picture of Dorian Gray* (1891) and Jean Lorrain's *Monsieur de Phocas* (1901). A lesser-known work by Huysmans, however, best illustrates the paradigmatic role of masks in decadent fiction.

The closing tale of the collection *Le Drageoir aux épices* [A Dish too seasoned], originally published in 1874, *L'Émailleuse* [The Enameller] opens with a description of the extravagant outfit of the poet Amilcar, who visits his friend, the painter José, in the boarding house to which he has recently moved. José looks ill and tired, and explains his condition as the result of an infatuation: 'Je suis amoureux d'une Chinoise... Oh! si tu savais comme elle est belle. Un teint d'orange mûrie, une bouche aussi rose que la chair des pastèques, des yeux noirs comme du jayet!' [I am in love with a Chinese girl... Oh! If you only knew how beautiful she is. A complexion like a ripe orange, a mouth as red as the inside of a water-melon, eyes as black as jet!] (Huysmans 1921: 75).

Overwhelmed by José's excitement, Amilcar concludes that his friend has gone mad and leaves to search for a doctor. As soon as he is alone, José makes a hole in the wall to spy into the adjacent room, where his beloved resides. He is left bewildered by what he sees: the girl has the same gaze of the mysterious woman who haunts him, but appears suddenly different, at once familiar and unfamiliar: 'C'était elle et ce n'était pas elle, c'était une Française qui ressemblait, autant que peut ressembler une Française à une Chinoise, à la fille jaune dont le regard l'avait bouleversé. Et pourtant c'était bien le même œil câlin et profond, mais la peau était terne et pâle, le rouge de la bouche s'était amorti; enfin, c'était une Européenne!' [It was she, and it was not she. It was a French woman who resembled, as much as a French woman could, a Chinese. This was the yellow girl whose glance had bowled him over. And yet, it was the same deep-set and cajoling eye; but the skin was pale and tarnished, and the red of the mouth was not so intense; in short, it was a European woman!] (Huysmans 1921: 80).

Upset by the discovery, José hurries downstairs to question the receptionist, but the latter bursts out laughing and, holding up a mirror to her wrinkled face, teases him and contrasts her own features to those of the young girl: 'Comment, pas Chinoise! Ah çà! est-ce que j'ai une figure comme elle, moi qui ne suis pas née en Chine?' [What do you mean, not Chinese! *ah çà*! Do I have a face like hers, I who wasn't born in China?] (Huysmans 1921: 80). A few minutes later, José hears a voice asking for Ophélie and finds himself in front of an old woman with a bucket of oil paint. Intrigued, he returns to his own room and resumes spying through the hole. In the circle of light that opens in the darkness, he sees the girl standing in front of a mirror in the company of the old woman, who has taken out of her suitcase a collection of little boxes, pads and brushes and now sets out to begin her work:

> Soulevant la tête d'Ophélie comme si elle la voulait raser, elle étendit avec un petit pinceau une pâte d'un jaune rosé sur la figure de la jeune fille, brossa doucement la peau, pétrit un petit morceau de cire devant le feu, rectifia le nez, assortissant la teinte avec celle de la figure, soudant avec un blanc laiteux le morceau artificiel du nez avec la chair du véritable; enfin elle prit ses estompes, les frotta sur la poudre des boites, étendit une légère couche de bleu pâle sous l'œil noir qui se creusa et s'allongea vers les tempes. La toilette terminée, elle se recula à distance pour mieux juger de l'effet, dodelina la tête, revint vers son pastel qu'elle retoucha, resserra ses outils et, après avoir pressé la main d'Ophélie sortit en reniflant.
>
> [Raising Ophelia's head, as though she were about to shave her, she spread over the young girl's face a reddened-yellow paste, then gently brushed the skin, kneaded a little morsel of wax in front of the fire and proceeded to correct the nose, matching its hue with that of the rest of the face, and soldering, with a milky-white substance, the artificial morsel to the flesh of the true nose. Finally, she took the pads, rubbed them on the powder in the boxes and spread a light layer of pale blue under the black eyes, which became hollow and elongated in the direction of the temples. The toilet finished, she stepped back a distance, the better to judge the effect, tilted her head and came back to her colours, which she retouched here and there, then gathered up her tools and, after having pressed Ophelia's hand, departed, sniffing.] (Huysmans 1921: 81)

José chases the old woman down the stairs and demands an explanation. She introduces herself as an enamel painter and, in exchange for a drink, reveals the mystery: an old man has agreed to leave Ophélie all his fortune on the condition that she let herself be painted and that he should never see her unmasked. This man, the enamel painter continues, used to live in Tibet and had once been married to a Chinese woman who abandoned him. On his return to France, he found in Ophélie, a destitute Parisian prostitute, something that reminded him of his wife. Deeply shocked, José considers throwing himself in the Seine — thereby fulfilling the destiny of Ophelie's namesake Ophelia — but when the girl appears and offers her company in exchange for an expensive gift, he immediately sobers up. The poet Amilcar, amused, dedicates to Ophélie a satirical sonnet in which he compares her to a water lily.

L'Émailleuse engages with two types of masquerade: aesthetic costume and ethnic impersonation. The first is embodied by Amilcar, the dandy, a 'creature perfect in externals and careless of anything below the surface, a man solely dedicated to his own perfection through a ritual of taste' (Moers 1960: 13). By committing to self-fashioning, the dandy refuses values associated with masculinity like efficiency and productivity, and adopts traits associated with femininity, taking care first and foremost of appearances. Rita Felski has argued that, in doing so, that dandy exposes femininity as a system of signs that are not necessarily attached to a natural body, thereby upsetting binary perceptions of gender (1995: 96). The second masquerade, the ethnic impersonation, was a frequent custom in *fin-de-siècle* France: the art critic Louis Gonse was known for posing with Nō masks and Japanese outfits, the writer Jean Lorrain regularly showed up to balls and social events dressed as an Arab or Turk, while the artist Antoine Bourdelle posed in a photograph as a Chinese man as late as 1925. In this type of masquerade, markers of ethnicity are appropriated by the white performer.

Aesthetic costume and ethnic impersonation are closely related, as both express the superiority of the impersonators, who subvert gender and ethnic norms, over women and non-Europeans, whose femininity and ethnic difference are 'natural' and who are not allowed to appropriate the signs of masculinity and whiteness. Through a parody of these practices, Huysmans' tale foregrounds the decadents' obsession with artificiality, the link between make-up and the mask, the role of the mask as double and its relation to the mirror. The mask of Ophélie consists of oil paint, wax and other artistic media that the enamel painter carefully blends in with the skin. A mask of artifice, it combines organic and inorganic material and changes the familiar into the unfamiliar, the common into the spiritual. By becoming one with the face upon which it rests, the cosmetic mask undoes the opposition characteristic of the mask and the face, as the two are no longer antithetical elements, but merge into a third entity. A modern Pygmalion, the painter José falls in love with 'un tableau ... un déguisement de bal masqué!' [a picture ... a masked-ball disguise!] (Huysmans 1921: 81). The real Ophélie, a prostitute/ actress, does not compare to the work of art that had been the cause of Jose's obsession, however, she shares with her Oriental *doppelgänger* a marginal status. Devoid of agency and personality, she is at once a portrait of the old man's deceased bride and a blank canvass onto which José projects his desire. When Ophélie washes off her mask, she appears dreadfully vulgar: for decadents and aesthetes who fetishize femininity, the 'natural' woman represents the emptiness of modern bourgeois society (Felski 1995: 107).

The tale foregrounds the role of the mask as a fetish. The Chinese mask turns Ophélie into an idol, an object of worship; moreover, the mask is a fetish in a Freudian sense, as it becomes a substitute, an object that satisfies the aesthete's desire. Furthermore, it functions as a commodity that can be bought and sold, and that is therefore embedded in the logic of capitalism that is so repellent to the dandy. As fetish, it highlights the decadent obsession with detail, the inverse relation of the part to the whole that Bourget identified as a crucial feature in decadent style (Bourget 1883: 25). Huysmans' mockery of Orientalism is ultimately self-mockery, since the opening piece of *Le Drageoir aux épices* is a 'Japanese Rococo' that fetishizes the facial features of a Japanese girl. The short story thus unveils the self-referential dimension of decadent fiction, and exemplifies the extent to which decadent writers parody and quote one another, moving 'within a recognizable network of canonical books, pervasive influences, recycled stories, erudite commentaries, and shared tastes' (Potolsky 2013: 5).

The cult of cosmetics and artificiality had an important predecessor in Charles Baudelaire's 'Éloge du maquillage' [In Praise of Cosmetics]. In this essay, Baudelaire defended the value of artifice and argued that cosmetics were endowed with a spiritual quality that the child and the 'savage' understood immediately in their instinct for ornamentation (Baudelaire 1885: 101).[6] These considerations relied on nineteenth-century anthropological paradigms that compared the development of the species to the growth of the individual, and on the rooted analogy between women, children and contemporary 'savages', who were associated with pre-history and the pre-modern. In his studies, the anthropologist Cesare Lombroso extended the analogy to criminals, arguing for the need of ornamentation as a sign of atavism. These concepts were borrowed by the modernist architect Adolf Loos (1870–1933), who used them — to the opposite end of Baudelaire — to engage in a battle against the decorative style of the Viennese secession. Like the art critic Paul Vitry, Loos complained that, in contemporary society, aesthetic artefacts no longer had a practical function, and called for the removal of ornaments from utilitarian objects. Applying the concept of atavism to the aesthetic sphere, he established a link between the need for ornamentation and arrested development in cultural evolution.[7]

A similar logic underpinned the writing of Max Nordau, for whom dandyism was closely related to degeneration. In his international best-seller *Degeneration*, Nordau argued that Western Europe had been corrupted by decadents and aesthetes 'unfit for the labor of common life' and that decadent style, with its complex vocabulary and syntax, reflected the over-stimulation and mental strain caused by new media and by daily exposure to technology (Nordau 1993: 301). Nordau saw in the writing of the decadents an extension of their persona. For him, the preference for the artificial over the natural, thematically articulated in decadent fiction, found a correspondence in the decadents' urge for masking and self-fashioning, which betrayed their cosmopolitan outlook and anachronistic taste: 'The common feature in all these male specimens is that they do not express their real idiosyncrasies, but try to present something that they are not. [...] The impression is that of a masked festival, where all are in disguise and with heads too in character. There are several occasions where this impression is so weirdly intensified, that one seems to be moving amongst dummies patched together at haphazard, in a mythical mortuary, from fragments of bodies, heads, trunks, limbs, in headless pall-mall, clothed at random in the garments of all epochs and countries' (Nordau 1993: 10). The subordination of the whole, marked in decadent texts by the over emphasis on words and sentences, manifested itself in the urge to collect, to purchase 'aimless bric-a-brac', objects severed from their original context of use and to any ends of utility, which Nordau saw exemplified in the 'fierce or funny Japanese masks' (1993: 10) these artists hang in their houses.

Conclusions

In Nietzsche's thought, the mask featured as a negative trope for the decay of Western civilization, but also as the emblem for its recovery through 'healthy barbarism'. For Paul Vitry, the mask, at the turn of the century, lost the connotation it had acquired throughout different phases of history as a religious artefact, theatrical prop and architectural detail, and became an emblem of decadent features lingering in contemporary Western art. Nordau followed the same logic as he foregrounded the cult of masks, make-up and costume in aesthetes, decadents and symbolists as symptoms of degeneracy. A decade later, August Macke used the mask as a symbol of the rebirth of Western culture through the influence of primitivism. These contradictions are less surprising if, following Renato Poggioli, we define decadence as 'the feeling at once oppressive and exalting, of being the last of a series' and modernism as 'the opening of a new series' (Poggioli 1968: 75). As Poggioli noted, these definitions represent two opposite sides of the spectrum, and are therefore closely related: 'The implicit distinction is a secondary one, limited to recognizing that, while a futurist mentality tremulously awaits an artistic palingenesis, preparing for its coming practically and mystically, the decadent mentality resigns itself to awaiting it passively, with anguished fatality and inert anxiety' (Poggioli 1968: 75). In this light, the mask symbolizes both decadence and the emerging modernist sensibilities, nostalgia for Hellenism, the Middle Ages, the Gothic and longing for a 'new primitiveness' and a 'return to barbarism'.

Linda Nochlin has argued that the *fin-de-siècle* obsession with the fragment on the one hand involved an association with mutilation and dismemberment, but that on the other, by sanctioning the destruction of the past and its traditions, it led to the transformative process that is seen as constitutive of modernism (1994: 8–11). As a visual illustration of anthropological theories, as a prop and as a tool of portraiture, the mask, in *fin-de-siècle* Europe, was closely related to the fragment. It was also associated with the unfinished, a principle both criticized as symptomatic of decline and hailed as productive, and with the insignificant and the self-referential, which featured as poetic tenets praised by the decadents and criticized by their detractors. Across disciplinary fields, a shift of function occurred as the mask, turned from utilitarian artefact into a trope for the paradoxes involved in modernity, and into a master-signifier that overtook the place of several signifieds. This shift also marked the mask's transition from object to 'thing'.

Notes to Chapter 1

1. The permanent collection was complemented by live shows of dancers, ventriloquists, hunger artists and people suffering from physical deformities, as well as by the so-called *Völkerschauen*, re-enactments of non-European ways of life by subjects wearing stereotypical costumes, realized with the support of the anthropological society presided over by Rudolf Virchow.
2. The masks were purchased by the Anthropological Museum in Paris, the Anthropological Institute in Florence, the Russian Academy of Science in St Petersburg, the Ethnological Museum in Berlin and even by the Australian Museum in Sidney (Friederici 2014: 12).
3. 'The face-mask represents something dead, but it appears convincing through sculpture, it also offers at first glance the natural proportions, which in photographs must be reconstructed by the imagination of the onlooker. In addition, the mask does not display the expression of the eyes, so that the mere physicality of the face gets more attention' (Schellong, cited in Friederici 2009: 5).
4. By prioritizing the will to live, and placing the species before the individual, some aspect of Schopenhauer's thought resonated with Darwin's ideas of evolution and the notion of the survival of the fittest.
5. While Nietzsche distanced himself from nineteenth-century thought by challenging the idea of progress, he echoed the preoccupation with regression by deploying a rhetoric of sickness and pathologies. Moreover, he considered Western civilization under threat and called for a 'healthy barbarism' (see Aschheim 1993: 646).
6. 'Les races que notre civilisation, confuse et pervertie, traita volontiers de sauvages, comprennent, avec un orgueil et une fatuité fait risibles, comprennent, aussi bien que l'enfant, la haute spiritualité de

la toilette. Le sauvage e le baby témoignent, par leur aspiration naïve vers le brillant, vers les plumages bariolés, les étoffes chatoyantes, vers la majesté superlative des formes artificielles, de leur dégoût pour le réel, et prouvent ainsi, à leur insu, l'immatérialité de leur âme' [Those races which our confused and perverted civilization is pleased to treat as savage, with an altogether ludicrous pride and complacency, understand the lofty spiritual significance of the toilet. In their naïve adoration of what is brilliant — many-coloured feathers, iridescent fabrics, the incomparable majesty of artificial forms — the baby and the savage bear witness to their disgust for the real, and thus give proof, without knowing it, of the immateriality of their souls] (Baudelaire 1885: 101).

7. These beliefs were articulated in his lecture 'Luxury carriages' (1898), in which Loos compared the development of the individual and that of the social body of the nation, and went as far as anticipating the Freudian link between the primitive and the unconscious: 'The less advanced a nation, the more extravagant its ornament, its decorations. The Red Indian covers every object, every boat, every paddle, every arrow over and over with decoration. To prefer ornamentation is to put oneself on the level of the Red Indian. But we must seek to overcome the Red Indian within us' (Loos 1998: 77). In the seminal essay 'Ornament and Crime' (1908), he parodied the Lombrosian association by including provocative statements such as: 'The child is amoral. To our eyes, the Papuan, too. The Papuan kills his enemies and eats them. He is not a criminal. But when modern man kills someone and eats him he is either a criminal or a degenerate' (Loos 1964: 19) and 'ornament is a phenomenon of backwardness and degeneration' that 'inflicts a serious injury... on cultural evolution' (1964: 21).

CHAPTER 2

Mask-Makers:
From Ensor to Rodin, via Japan

By 1900, masks, which had been absent on the Western stage for centuries, enjoyed a revival as theatrical props. The turn of the century also saw renewed interest in the masked rituals that survived within Europe, such as the tradition of carnival. As Western artists started experimenting with mask-making, an intense dialogue developed between theatre and the visual arts. This chapter focuses on four case studies in which masks play a crucial role: the paintings in which James Ensor juxtaposes East Asian masks, Flemish carnival masks and skulls; the plays *Le Sculpteur de masques* [*The Sculptor of Masks*] by Fernand Crommelynck (1907) and *Shuzenji Monogatari* [*The Tale of Shuzenji*] by Kido Okamoto (1908); and the series of decorative masks that Auguste Rodin shaped from 1907 to 1911 after the Japanese actress Hanako. It argues that these works engage with a common trope of Western gothic fiction, the idea of a portrait that becomes a masterpiece at the expense of its model, or as life ebbs away from it,[1] but that, as masks substituted painting, this trope acquired a new connotation as a gendered practice and as a form of cultural appropriation. Drawing on Edward Said's insight that the discourse of orientalism, as developed in nineteenth-century thought, was also applied to marginal elements of Western societies (1979: 207), on Lacan's theory of the gaze and on Laura Mulvey's feminist development of gaze theory (1999: 833–44), it examines the implication of a shift of function as masks, from emblems of Flemish or Japanese folklore, were abstracted from the original performative context — whether the carnival parade or Japanese Nō — to become inscribed in physiognomic practices. Detached from its usual function, placed at the crossroads of portraiture and ritual, the mask offered a fertile ground to express the mastery of the gaze, as well as the artist's confrontation with alterity and the encounter of perceptions of modernity and the archaic.

Flanders and the Far East: James Ensor, 'Prince of Masks'

James Ensor (1860–1949) had a strong interest in the folklore and traditions of Ostend, the Flemish town in which he was born and spent most of his life. A popular sea resort, Ostend was also renowned for its carnival celebrations, which included masquerades, parades and drinking games. Ensor began engaging with masks in the 1880s. In early works, he used masks as elements of still lives or within the context of the Flemish carnival. The first canvas in which he placed masks on his main figures, *The Scandalized Masks* (1883), captures the looks that two revellers exchange as an old woman, dressed as a witch, steps into a dark room and meets the gaze of a man seated in front of an empty bottle. Scholars have interpreted the figures as portrayals of Ensor's father, an Englishman who had become an alcoholic, and his Belgian maternal grandmother, who enjoyed taking part in the celebrations of carnival:

> Ma grand'mère m'affublait souvent de costumes bizarres... Elle adorait les mascarades. Je la vois encore pendant une nuit de carnaval dressée devant mon petit lit. Elle était costumée en paysanne coquette et son masque était affreux, J'avais peut-être 5 ans, elle en avait plus de 60. Mon enfance a été peuplée de rêves merveilleux et la fréquentation de la boutique de la grand'mère toute irisée de reflets de coquilles et des somptuosités des dentelles, d'étranges bêtes empaillées et des armes terribles de sauvages m'épouvantaient.
>
> [My grandmother often dressed me up in strange costumes... She adored masquerades. I still see her standing in front of my little bed one night during carnival. She was dressed as a coquettish peasant and her mask was dreadful, I was maybe 5 years old, she was over 60. My childhood was populated with amazing dreams and times spent in my grandmother's shop, iridescent with shimmering shells and sumptuous lace, strange wild beasts and terrible, savage weapons which frightened me.] (Ensor 1999a: 105–06)

In his grandmother's eclectic shop, Ensor could see masks designed to be worn for carnival, as well as Chinese and Japanese masks brought by Ensor's brother-in-law, a Sino-German art dealer (Legrand 1971: 79). By the late 1870s, when Ensor studied at the Belgian academy in Brussels, Japanophilia was at its height. Japanese art was a frequent topic of discussion in artistic circles, and Nō masks were exhibited by the *Compagnie Japonaise* in the Rue Royale in Brussels (Tricot 2008: 161). Like many of his contemporaries, Ensor copied Japanese prints, especially by Hokusai, developing sinuous lines and filling his paintings with oriental themes. He also studied Chinese porcelain and East Asian masks, both of which feature in his still lifes.

Ensor's art took an important turn in 1888. Before that date, Ensor had used masks in a realist context, either as objects or carnival props. Afterwards, he conflated mask and face to develop an 'expressionistic world of mask-men' (Schoonbaert 1989: 15). *The Entry of Christ into Brussels* (1888), a painting rich in religious and political references,[2] exemplifies this shift. Here Ensor offered an overview of the city's streets filled by a Mardi Gras parade; masks, indistinguishable from faces, mock the members of Belgian society, while Jesus features as an alter ego for the unheeded artist. With this work, Ensor began deconstructing the dichotomy of mask and face, which would be replaced by the dyad of masks and skulls.

As art historians have pointed out, Ensor's depiction of the masses and his use of caricatured heads finds a parallel in that of English caricaturists such as James Gillray and William Hogarth (Tricot 1997: 100–17), and of French satirists like J. G. Grandville, Honoré Daumier and Gustave Doré (Hostyn and Florizoone 2000), whose works Ensor knew well. For Ensor, after 1888, the mask was no longer a device to transform, as in carnival, but, following physiognomics practices,

FIG. 2.1. James Ensor, *Scandalized Masks*, 1883, oil on canvas, 135 × 112 cm, Royal Museums of Fine Art Belgium, Brussels

Fig. 2.2. James Ensor, *Still Life with Chinoiseries*, 1906, oil on canvas, 78.5 × 98.5 cm, photo by Rik Klein Gotink, by kind permission of KMSKA, Antwerp

highlighted the inner features of the 'dreadful humanity' and the 'enormity of deformations' of the society that surrounded him (Ensor 1999a: 192).

This artistic development took place after Ensor's paintings had been refused at several exhibitions in Brussels, and at a time in which he was experiencing tensions with the avant-garde group 'Les XX'. Moreover, this was a difficult time in Ensor's personal life, in which he was pressured to abandon painting and lost his father and his grandmother (Legrand 1971: 79). In a letter to Jules Dujardin, written on 6 October 1899, Ensor described how the mask expressed the resentment that he perceived surrounded him, and how it gave him the opportunity to take revenge on both colleagues and critics:

> ... entouré d'hostilité au sein même de XX et critiqué partout sans mesure [...] Je pris plaisir à peindre des masques. Depuis le gout du masque ne me quitte plus. J'ai pu contempler ainsi philosophiquement les faces hypocrites, dissimulées, intéressées et fourbes des couards écrasés par mes méprisantes évolutions. La vie était heureuse, elle appelait logiquement la couleur outrancière et violente. Elle reflétait les critiques intéressées des confrères, l'ignorance, la mauvaise foi, l'incapacité des critiques, les attaques viles et mesquines des ex-imitateurs contribuèrent largement à me maintenir dans cette voie exceptionnelle de

FIG. 2.3. James Ensor, *Skeleton Looking at Chinoiserie*, 1885, oil on canvas, 101 × 61 cm, photo by Rik Klein Gotink, by kind permission of Museum of Fine Arts, Ghent

FIG. 2.4. *Skulls and Masks*, 1888, 129 × 91 mm, etching, photo by Hugo Maertens, by kind permission of Museum of Fine Arts, Ghent

lumière et d'outrance ou les imitateurs et pasticheurs cette fois n'osèrent plus me suivre.

[... surrounded by hostility within the XX and criticized everywhere without measure [...] I took pleasure in painting masks. Since then a taste for masks has not left me. I have thus been able to contemplate philosophically the hypocritical, deceitful, self-interested and cunning faces of the cowards crushed by my scornful ideas. Life was happy, it logically called for outrageous and violent colour. It reflected colleagues' biased criticism, the ignorance, bad faith, and uselessness of critics; the vile and petty attacks of former imitators greatly contributed to keep me on this exceptional path of light and excess where imitators and pastiche-makers, this time, did not dare to follow me.] (Ensor 1999a: 271)

In numerous speeches, Ensor continued to assert the association between masks, inner isolation, and the development of an expressionist style: 'traqué par les suiveurs, je me suis confiné joyeusement dans le milieu solitaire ou trône le masque tout de violence, de lumière et d'éclat' [stalked by followers, I have joyously shut myself up in the solitary domain where the mask holds sway, wholly consisting of violence, light and brilliance] (Ensor 1999a: 37).

In the same years, he began to juxtapose East Asian artefacts with skulls and skeletons. Retouching a painting finished three years earlier, which featured a character in a kimono against a background of Japanese prints, he painted a skull

FIG. 2.5. *The Astonishment of the Mask Wouse*, 1889, oil on canvas, 109 × 131 cm, photo by Hugo Maertens, by kind permission of KMSKA, Antwerp

over the figure's head and added an inanimate skull at the bottom left, whose empty sockets gaze back at the viewer. The title of the painting, *Skeleton Looking at Chinoiserie* (1885), underlines Ensor's frequent conflation of China with Japan. With the etching 'crânes et masques' [Skulls and Masks] (1888), he fleshed out the parallel between the masks' empty eyes and the skull's empty sockets. The following year, he painted *The Astonishment of the Mask Wouse* (1889), a dramatic scene in which a masked female figure, dressed in Chinese silk, confronts a character in an East Asian mask who intrudes from the right, against a background of inanimate Asian demon masks, carnival masks, and skulls.[3] Masks and skeletons populate the artist's studio in *Skeletons in the Studio* (1900): a skeleton lies on the floor, looking to the right; the other stands staring back at the observer. East Asian masks, including Japanese masks, hang on the wall and dominate the upper part of the painting.

Like *The Entry of Christ into Brussels*, Ensor's *Self Portrait with Masks* (1899) portrays the artist surrounded by a masked mob. The motif became popular in the fiction of the period, featuring in Hofmannsthal's *Andreas* and Jean Lorrain's *Monsieur de Phocas* — a novel in which Ensor features as a character, and to which he would dedicate a painting. In Ensor's self-portrait, Japanese demon masks, tribal masks,

FIG. 2.6. James Ensor, *Self Portrait with Masks*, 1899, oil on canvas, 120 × 80 cm, by kind permission of the Menard Art Museum, Komaki, Japan

FIG. 2.7. James Ensor, *Man of Sorrows*, 1892, oil on canvas, 21.5 × 16 cm, photo by Rik Klein Gotink, by kind permission of KMSKA, Antwerp

FIG. 2.8. James Ensor, *The Skeleton Painter*, 1896, oil on canvas, 80.7 × 70.5 cm, photo by Hugo Maertens, by kind permission of KMSKA, Antwerp

FIG. 2.9. James Ensor, *The Intrigue*, 1890, oil on canvas, 90 × 149 cm, photo by Hugo Maertens, by kind permission of KMSKA, Antwerp

mask-like faces with Asian, Indian or African features and Flemish carnival masks all share traits with the skeletons intruding in the parade. One of the ethnic masks has a broken nose, a tear that, instead of revealing the skin beneath it, displays a dark spot. Francine-Claire Legrand reads this 'injury' as a sign that the mask, no longer a shield for the face, has become an empty husk.[4] For Legrand, Ensor portrays the feeling of being held hostage by the masks that he has created, as well as the fear to become one of them (Legrand 1993: 18).

In *The Man of Sorrows* (1891) Ensor identified again with Christ's passion and incorporated the traditional attributes of the suffering Christ — the dripping blood, the crown of thorns — into the iconography of a Nō mask. In other paintings, such as *The Skeleton Painter* (1896), he gradually eliminated his own features through a process that Claire Moran has defined as 'self-skeletonisation' (2007: 239). Ensor's use of self-portraiture hinged on the effect that Lacan describes as the gaze, as the artist is reduced to an object through the gaze of the viewer: skulls look down at the painter-skeleton from above, masks stare at him from below, while his empty sockets stare back at the observer.

Scholars have often searched Ensor's biography in search of an explanation for his use of East Asian motifs. The painting *The Intrigue* (1890), in which a married couple stands surrounded by a crowd wearing carnival masks and East Asian demon masks, while death intrudes from the back and a Japanese doll is waved in the foreground, has been interpreted as a reference to the brief marriage of Ensor's sister Mitche with a Sino-German art dealer (Schoonbaert 1989: 17).[5] In 1899, Ensor painted Mitche's daughter Alexandra, then nine years old, sporting a Chinese costume between East Asian masks (*Portrait of the Artist's Niece in Chinese Costume*, 1899). As a young woman, he portrayed her again in a kimono against a background of demon-masks (*Portrait of my Niece Alexandra Daveluy*, 1927). As these works show, Chinese and Japanese motifs are frequently conflated in Ensor's art, and intimately connected to his personal life.

Ensor rarely distinguished between the familiar and the exotic, and claimed that all influences originated in Ostend. Concerned with defending his originality, he argued that Impressionists like Seurat, Signac and Renoir, and Expressionists like Gauguin and Van Gogh, whom he referred to as 'très chinois' (1999a: 129), brought back from the Orient nothing more than what he had already seen in his grandmother's boutique in his childhood: 'à Ostende, dans la boutique de mes parents, j'avais vu les lignes ondulées, les formes serpentines des beaux coquillages, les feux irisés des nacres, les tons riches des fines chinoiseries...' [In Ostend, in my parents' boutique, I had already seen the wavy lines, the serpentine forms of the beautiful shells, the iridescent fires of mother-of-pearl, the rich tones of fine *chinoiserie*...] (Ensor 1999a: 129). As an older man, however, he drew a sharp line between local and non-European masks. In a lecture given in 1937, titled 'Masque divers' [Different masks], he described the masks originating in Africa and East Asia as artefacts that have remained immobile through the centuries, associating them with criminality, savagery and debauchery, and regretted that these masks had made it to Europe. In contrast, he underlined the playful side of Flemish carnival:

> Que dire des origines troubles, louches, cachées, du masque d'Afrique. Que dire des péchés capitaux et des crimes couvés et commis sous le masque, couverts par le masque. Aux siècles d'esclavage, masque signifiait lâcheté, dissimulation, criminalité, crapulerie, égoïsme, exploitation, impunité, duperie, fuite, détraquement, cruauté, satanisme, morsures, griffes et féminités. Du masque au fard, il n'y a pas loin. Je condamne sans rémission le masque mal venu des enfers d'Afrique, d'Asie, d'Océanie, de Meurtricie, de Sommeille, de Cracozie. [...]
>
> Voyez, goûtez nos masques ostendais. Oui, ils évoluent aux quatre vents de l'esprit habillés de tendresse, corsés de joliesses, pourprés, azurés, nacrés, coquillés, huîtres, surmoulés, rayés, turbotés, barbus, stockfischés, schollés, gaminés, farcis de fantaisie, ils s'en donnent à cœur joie. Adorable mascarade, couleurs cinglantes, gammes et jardins d'amour, chants de bourdons, chocs de cristaux, cloches sur le peau. Oui, notre carnaval est chaud.
>
> [Consider the murky, shady, hidden origins of the African mask. Consider the capital sins and of the crimes brooded upon and committed under the mask, covered by the mask. During centuries of slavery, the mask meant cowardice, concealment, criminality, debauchery, egoism, exploitation, impunity, deception, flight, perversion, cruelty, satanism, mauling, claws and femininity. It is a short step from the mask to make-up. I condemn unequivocally the mask which unfortunately came from the hell of Africa, Asia, Oceania, from Murderland, Dreamland, from Cracozie. [...]
>
> Come and enjoy our local masks. Yes, they develop in all directions of the mind, clothed in tenderness, seasoned with beauty, crimson, azure, pearly, shell-like, oystery, over-moulded, striped, bearded, full of dried cod and turbots, childishly playful, filled with imagination, they enjoy themselves without restraint. An adorable masquerade of bold colours, scales and gardens of love, songs of the bumblebee, crystal shocks, veils for the skin. Oh yes, our carnival is hot.] (Ensor 1999b: 190–91)

As an attack on the appropriation of African masks by the Cubists and East Asian imagery by French and German Expressionists, the passage betrays Ensor's xenophobia and his desire to ground his own practice in the local. In associating femininity with debauchery and deception, it also underlines his ambiguous relationship to women, his belief in the decadent motto that 'there is a short step from the mask to make-up' (Ensor 1999b: 190).

For Timothy Hyman, Ensor absorbed carnival 'with his mother's milk' (1997: 77) and spoke its language more than any other artist. Hyman goes as far as to argue that Ensor, a keen reader of Rabelais, offers a visual equivalent to Bakhtin's conceptualization of carnival as a phenomenon that suspends social hierarchies and in which people merge into a collectivity.[6] However, while Ensor used masks as a tool of social critique and engaged with the loss of control brought about by the crowds, he did not portray carnival as a liberating force. On the contrary, his masks are dark and oppressive, linked to an imagery of death. In this sense, his poetics of masking is reminiscent of E. T. A. Hoffmann and Edgar Allan Poe, although, in a letter dated 1928 to the art critic André de Ridder, Ensor claimed that he did not appreciate the mixture of reality and imagination in the former, and that he felt for the latter only the 'sympathy of an imaginative Anglo-Belgian' (Ensor 1999a: 191).

The combination of masks and skulls, the merging of masks and caricature heads, the association of East Asian motifs and images of death are all strands of Ensor's work that are sometimes developed separately; other times, they overlap. Originating in frightening childhood memories, at once familiar and unfamiliar, local and exotic, Ensor's masks are an embodiment of the Freudian uncanny. Since the masks' empty eyes, just like the skulls' sockets, look back at the viewer, confronting them with disintegration and dissolution, they also exemplify the Lacanian gaze.

Fernand Crommelynck and the Flemish Carnival

In his artistic trajectory, Ensor transitioned quickly from the mask as decorative object to carnival prop to tool for caricature to hollow husk (Legrand 1971: 79). A similar process lies at the core of Fernand Crommelynck's *Le Sculpteur de masques* [The Sculptor of Masks]. Like Ensor, Crommelynck stressed the tension between the use of the mask as portraiture, strongly reliant on the physiognomic tradition, and its function as token of ritual. Unlike Ensor, however, he did not engage with exotic masks: his focus was on the rituals that survived within Western culture, more specifically the Flemish carnival. As the child of a French mother and a half-Flemish father whose family moved back and forward between Paris and Brussels, Crommelynck's perspective on Flanders is both that of an insider and an outsider. Many of his plays, including *Le Sculptor de masques*, are set in Flanders and focus on local folklore; however, the venue that he had in mind was from the outset the Parisian stage. For plays designed to be staged in Belgium, he had a very different agenda: during the time in which he acted as the director of the *Théâtre des Galeries* in Brussels, he insisted that only French plays be presented, and discouraged the inclusion of Flemish elements (Alsip 1971: 14).

A first version of *Le Sculpteur de masques*, a one-act play in verse, appeared in 1906 in the magazine *En Art*. After meeting and befriending James Ensor in Ostend in 1908, however, Crommelynck rewrote the piece in prose, this time as a three-act play. He had moved to Ostend to join his father, who had found him a job as correspondent for a local newspaper, and in this role he had the opportunity to observe several of Ensor's paintings, including *The Entry of Christ into Brussels* (1888), which made a strong impression on his imagination (Moulin 1978a: 49; Knapp 1978: 41). Bettina Knapp has argued that the impact of Ensor's art on Crommelynck was so profound that *Le Sculpteur de masques* was essentially a transposition of Ensor's paintings. Both artists, she stresses, were interested in the pre-Christian traditions that survived in Flanders and saw masks as primitive religious devices. For both Ensor and Crommelynck, the mask fulfilled a similar function as it underlined the hypocrisy of society and served as a screen for the mutable self: 'The mask hides or protects inner nature, a mystery to others — unreal, divine, or even demoniacal. As in the Japanese Nō drama, the mask separates the inchoate from the formed, the unconscious from the conscious' (Knapp 1978: 45). Moreover, it functioned as the harbinger of death, 'the spokesman for psychological and physical disease' (1978: 45). For Knapp, the ways in which Crommelynck, in his stage directions, described light falling on the masks recalls Ensor's sapient use of *chiaroscuro*, and the store of Crommelynck's mask maker is a recreation of Ensor's studio in Ostend.

Like Ensor, Crommelynck was interested in the loss of control that individuals experience in a crowd, in the capacity of the mask to conjure up the grotesque, and in the analogy between masks and skulls. Furthermore, while Ensor, in his portraits of women, associated femininity with the mask, and masks with death, Crommelynck conflated the two. In *Le Sculpteur de masques*, mask-making becomes a gendered practice, and the sculptures reflect the alterity of femininity as well as the otherness of death.

The play is set in a small town in Flanders, which Jeanne Moulin recognizes as Bruges (1978a: 18), with each act taking place in a different season, the third act being set in February, during the carnival celebrations. It revolves around the ambition of a mask-maker, Pascal, and the sacrifice of his wife, Louison, whose dying features he captures in a series of masks. As an artist, Pascal does not fit in with the rest of the community, who expect concrete results through labour and a direct contribution to society. Only the town's coffin-maker establishes a connection between mask-making and his own profession: 'Je travaille pour la douleur et vous travaillez pour la joie, oui... Mais nous sommes voisins... Oui, et ceux qui viennent chez vous viendront aussi chez moi' [I work for sorrow, and you work for joy, yes... but we are neighbours... yes, and those who come to you will also be coming to me] (Crommelynck 1967: 258). Pascal, who cannot bear sadness, chases him away. He also forbids the doctor to stop in front of his door, claiming that his home is the realm of eternal carnival.

Since Pascal models his masks after the features of the community, they function as a form of portraiture. The bird-catcher Cador, who, like Pascal, does not have a bourgeois occupation, takes on the role of the physiognomist as he associates each feature with a moral characteristic. Louison's sister Magdeleine quickly denies any resemblance, betraying an anxiety that there may be something indecent in the display of vices:

> ... Cador s'arrête devant les masques qui ornent les murs. Il rie si fort que Louison et Magdeleine se retournent.
> CADOR: Oh! Oh! Celui-ci, c'est le potier du quai de la Main Noire!
> MAGDELEINE: Mais non...
> CADOR: C'est lui, oui. Celui-là était tellement saoul en suivant la procession qu'il éteignait son cierge avec le vent de son nez!
> *Devant un autre masque*
> Ici c'est la petite Pauline qui pleure quand je l'embrasse et qui dit 'Mon Dieu!... Mon Dieu!...' Et voici Ochs, le vieux Ochs, si avare qu'il a peur de ses deux mains... C'est lui!

> [*Suddenly Cador stops in front of the masks, which are hanging on the walls. He laughs so loudly that Louison and Magdeleine turn around*
> CADOR: Oh! This one is the potter who lives on the river bank!
> MAGDELEINE: No, it's not...
> CADOR: It's him all right. He was so drunk when he followed the procession that he kept blowing out his candle with his own breath!
> *In front of another mask.*

Here's little Pauline who cries when I hug her and says: 'My Lord! My Lord!...'
It's her all right.. And there's Ochs, old Ochs, who's such a miser that he's afraid
of his own hands! ...it's him!] (Crommelynck 1967: 247)

By magnifying facial features, Pascal's masks also function as tools of caricature. The mask-maker gives his art the status of a science through the precision with which it allows him to map inner characteristics, and boasts about the superiority of mask-making over medicine: 'Dites à vos malades que je les guérirai! Je leur montrerai des choses qu'ils n'ont jamais vues [...] Je leur montrerai des choses inventées par des hommes qui étaient des hommes — et la vie leur reviendra!' [Tell your patients that I shall cure them! I'll show them things they've never seen before! [...] I'll show them things that men have invented, real men! And life will come back to them!] (1967: 253). He does not limit himself to reproducing the features of man, but dreams of modifying and multiplying them, finding legends and stories for each of his masks, rewriting the villagers' lives with biographies of his own invention. Symbolically, his project takes place during carnival, when the portraits are worn by the revellers in the parade and become a tool for transformation.

Claiming that inspiration feeds on strong passions, Pascal, the 'Dionysian artist-creator' (Knapp 1978: 35) asserts the right to everything that is filled with life. In this spirit, he seduces Louison's younger sister, Magdeleine. When Louison sees them together, she faints and falls ill. Her condition rapidly worsens, but she refuses to address the source of her grief, thereby torturing both her sister and husband with guilt. After helping Louison up after a fall, Pascal grasps her face and imagines its imprint on his hands, 'comme le visage de Jésus sur le linge de sainte Véronique' [like the face of Jesus on Saint Veronica's veil] (Crommelynck 1967: 301), a comparison that underlines Louison's role as a victim and marks the beginning of a process that reduces her to a mask. At the end of the second act, Pascal confesses to Magdeleine about his violent impulses towards his wife: 'Parfois, je la hais! J'ai envie de la détruire, d'être sur elle, à guetter sa mort, avec mes deux mains à son cou!' [Sometimes I hate her! I feel like destroying her, like keeping my hands around her neck, waiting for her to die!] (1967: 293). Louison disappears in the third act, but she is replaced and multiplied by the masks secretly carved by her husband. When he is certain of his wife's imminent death, Pascal discloses the masks modelled on Louison and uses them to terrify Magdeleine, who draws back in fear. At the end of the first act, Pascal had pointed to Louison, collapsed on the floor after seeing him on his knees in front of her sister: 'Mais c'est Louison! ... C'est Louison! Je te dis que c'est elle!' [It's Louison! ... it's Louison! ... I tell you it's her!] (1967: 263). In the third act, similar words are used to indicate the masks scattered on the work bench. 'C'est elle, il n'y a pas à dire non. C'est elle. Son visage de tristesse, son visage de silence!... C'est Louison, oui ... Son visage de doute, de soupçon; son visage de douleur ... C'est bien elle ...' [It's her, no mistake about it. It's her. Her face wreathed in sadness, her face wreathed in silence... It's Louison, all right... Her face full of doubt and suspicion; her face filled with pain... it's her, all right] (1967: 307).

Since artistic conventions at the beginning of the twentieth century demanded that portraits should have a neutral expression, Pascal's carvings can be more accurately defined as studies of emotions. By multiplying Louison's features, these simulacra effectively substitute his wife, assuring the preservation of her features beyond death. However, the reduction to a disembodied face confers a macabre connotation to the artefacts. The violence inherent in mask-making is reinforced by the enactments of beheading that take place in the carnival parade, and by the presence of skulls among the masks (1967: 312–18). When the people in town become aware of the adultery, they compare Pascal to Bluebeard, the fairy-tale character who murders his wives, and they either avoid the house, contributing to the family's isolation, or vandalize it to express their disapproval. As Louison lies dying, drunken revellers burst in, discover the artefacts and carry them away along with other masks to wear during the Mardi Gras parade. Magdeleine hysterically announces her sister's death, but Pascal remains unperturbed. Louison, he claims, has come back to life as her effigies are worn by revellers:

> MAGDELEINE *paraît et disparaît*: Pascal! Morte, Pascal! Morte!
> PASCAL, *très calme*: Tu dis ça, toi... mais je sais bien qu'elle est partie danser ... [il rit]. Elle est partie avec Cador; je viens de la voir partir... Elle dansera toute la nuit ... Je l'ai vue, je te dis, moi ... Il ne faut pas rire ...
>
> MAGDELEINE: *Appears, then disappears.* Pascal!... Dead... Pascal!... She's dead!
> PASCAL: *Very calm.* You just say that, but I know that she went to the dance ... *He laughs.* She went with Cador; I just saw her leaving... She'll dance all night... I saw her, I tell you, I did... Don't laugh .... (1967: 320)

Crommelynck's play, unlike Ensor's paintings, does not involve the exotic artefacts that were exciting the imagination of Western artists. Yet the capacity of Pascal's wooden masks to function as portraits and as ritualistic objects, their ability to conjure intensity of expression, are the same features that Parisians found impressive in Japanese masks. Like Nō masks, Pascal's sculptures are used in ritual dances and handled carefully, as objects endowed with power. The character's dreams of writing a story for each of his masks also finds a parallel in Nō performances, in which masks are used to evoke characters divided into fixed categories and appearing in a number of plays.[7] Moreover, Crommelynck's play called for an acting style that, not unlike the acting that Sada Yacco's troupe introduced to Western audiences in 1900, magnified gestures and alternated mobility with climactic poses. In his stage directions, Crommelynck underlines that Pascal has 'the expressive face of an actor', but that his features sometimes freeze, becoming 'totally expressionless' (1967: 253). When the play premiered in Paris, at the *Théâtre de Gymnase*, on 1 or 2 February 1911, Armand Bour, who was playing Pascal, announced that it inaugurated the so-called 'théâtre expressive' [expressive theatre]. This claim initiated a debate that soon took over the debate about the subject matter of the play. A journalist reviewing the play for *Le Cri de Paris* on 5 February 1911 protested: 'Le mot impressive n'est pas dans *Littré* ... c'est un mot belge. Il n'a d'ailleur aucun sense' [the word *impressive* is not in the dictionary... it's a Belgian word. Anyways it does not make sense] (Moulin 1978b: 44).

While the style of the play and the fascination with masks was in line with the Parisian enthusiasm for exotic performances, Crommelynck's focus remained on the pre-Christian, pre-modern traditions of Flanders. As a French–Belgian artist writing in French, he contributed to the construction of the mythology around Flemish culture that in these years took place in the work of Francophone writers. He also capitalized on the exotic flavour that Flemish traditions had for metropolitan audiences. Furthermore, the drama echoed the discourse that French symbolists like Jean Lorrain developed around masks, associating them with caricature and embodiments of repressed desires.

Building on Freud's theory of the fetish, Laura Mulvey suggests that in visual representations there are two strategies to challenge the threat posed by femininity: the woman is either used as a scapegoat, a sacrificial victim, or becomes a fetish, thereby turning into a reassuring, rather than threatening presence. In the first case, the woman disappears; in the second, she becomes an icon, an ideal image (Mulvey 1999: 64–67). In *Le Sculpteur de masques*, Crommelynck uses both strategies. Whereas Pascal represents the Dionysian artist, the bearer of the gaze, the women in the play are all objects of the gaze; moreover, Louison is a martyr figure who literally disappears. On the other hand, by substituting fragmentary portraits for a living woman, Pascal turns femininity into a reassuring presence. Seemingly portraits of Louison, an embodiment of her different expressions, the masks capture first and foremost Pascal's sense of guilt. Worn by the villagers in the carnival celebrations, Louison's features are placed on male bodies, and the carnival mob obliterates not only political and social status, but also gender difference. Brought to life by the dancers, the effigies stare back at Pascal. On stage, they also look back at the spectator. It is at this moment that the sculptures cease to be portraits and, in providing faces for strangers, enter the sphere of ritual. As the object of desire returns the look of the observer, the gaze captured in the mask's eyes is closely reminiscent of the look of Ensor's masks, and as in Ensor's paintings, it associated with disintegration and dissolution.

Kido Okamoto and Nō Masks

While European artists were influenced by Japanese art, *fin-de-siècle* Japanese intellectuals were confronting the political and cultural changes brought by the opening up of Japan to the West, the fall of the shogunate and the Meiji Restoration (1868). Meiji artists exposed to Western culture adopted the cosmopolitan fashions of European capitals and strove to develop a culture that was 'modern and yet Japanese' (Esenbel 2015: 262). Politicians and theatre managers set out to modernize Japanese dramaturgy and to create a national drama capable of impressing audiences coming from abroad and encouraging patriotism at home. Since the aristocratic Nō was almost extinguished, and bunraku, the puppet theatre, was not deemed dignified enough to represent the nation, the choice fell on kabuki, the popular theatre (Wetmore 2006: 179). With the aim of rehabilitating it as a respectable art, the government, in 1872, imposed censorship on all erotic and cruel scenes, and demanded historical accuracy and a more realistic acting style (Shionoya 1986: 101). Kabuki had always been a theatre of entertainment, and the reformers' attempt to turn it into an instrument for education had limited success. However, artists and actors continued to devise strategies to modernize it, introducing contemporary subject matter and adapting stage conventions (Rimer 2016: 11–12). The result was shin-kabuki, or 'new kabuki', dramas written by modern playwrights within the kabuki's apparatus, often shortened to adapt to modern dramaturgy.[8]

Kabuki was a highly stylized form of theatre, featuring conventional character types, climactic poses, quick role changes, and mask-like make-up. Although it originated with female performers, women had been banned from the stage since 1629, replaced by *onnagata*, male actors specializing in female roles. The repertoire was constituted by centuries-old plays, originally written to suit the style of great former actors. In the early twentieth century, authors who were not part of the kabuki establishment, like Kido Okamoto and Shōyō Tsubouchi, started to write for the stage, and drama began to be considered a form of literature. Kido Okamoto (born Keiji Okamoto, 1872–1939) was the son of an interpreter at the British Legation in Tokyo. He grew up in a transnational environment, learning English from his uncle and Chinese from his father, and participated in the courses and activities held at the Legation. From an early age, he was an avid reader of Western literature. A practising journalist, in 1908 he collaborated with Otojirō Kawakami, who had performed in the United States and Europe with his wife Sada Yacco. Through Kawakami, he started writing plays for the famous kabuki actor Ichikawa Sadanji.[9] He also became aware of the success that Kawakami's troupe had enjoyed in Paris. Following Loïe Fuller's advice, Kawakami had modified kabuki plays by shortening them, emphasizing erotic scenes and grotesque aspects and placing at the centre of the action a *seppuku*, the ritual suicide by disembowelment, regularly enacted by Sada Yacco. *Shuzenji Monogatari* [The Tale of Shuzenji] premiered in Japan, but was nevertheless informed by these experiences.

Although it Japan, at that time, it was difficult to publish dramatic literature, Okamoto succeeded in publishing *Shuzenji Monogatari* in the literary journal *Bungei Club* in 1909. The play was performed in 1911 at the Meijiza theatre in Tokyo: Sadanji played the role of Yashao, the mask-carver; while the roles of Yashao's daughters, Kayede and Katsura, were played by two *onnagata*. The play was so successful that it became the model for shin-kabuki plays. It was performed about twenty times in Japan between 1911 and 1940, and as long as Sadanji lived, he was the only actor to play the leading role. Like traditional kabuki, the play foregrounded the virtuosity of the leading actor and had extreme variations in tempo. Unlike traditional kabuki, it was much shorter and did not feature background music (Powell 2016: 41).

Shuzenji Monogatari was inspired by a mask and built on the events associated with the Shuzenji temple, where Yoriiye, the second shogun of the Minamoto family, was exiled and assassinated on the orders of his maternal grandfather, in 1204. In 1908, during a visit to Shuzenji, Okamoto had the opportunity to observe the wooden mask that is said to have been carved after Yoriiye was poisoned in his bath. In a lecture held in March 1925, he described it as a mask for ancient Nō performances and recalled how it reminded him of two legends. The first was the story of Yoriiye's concubine, who accompanied the ex-shogun to the temple

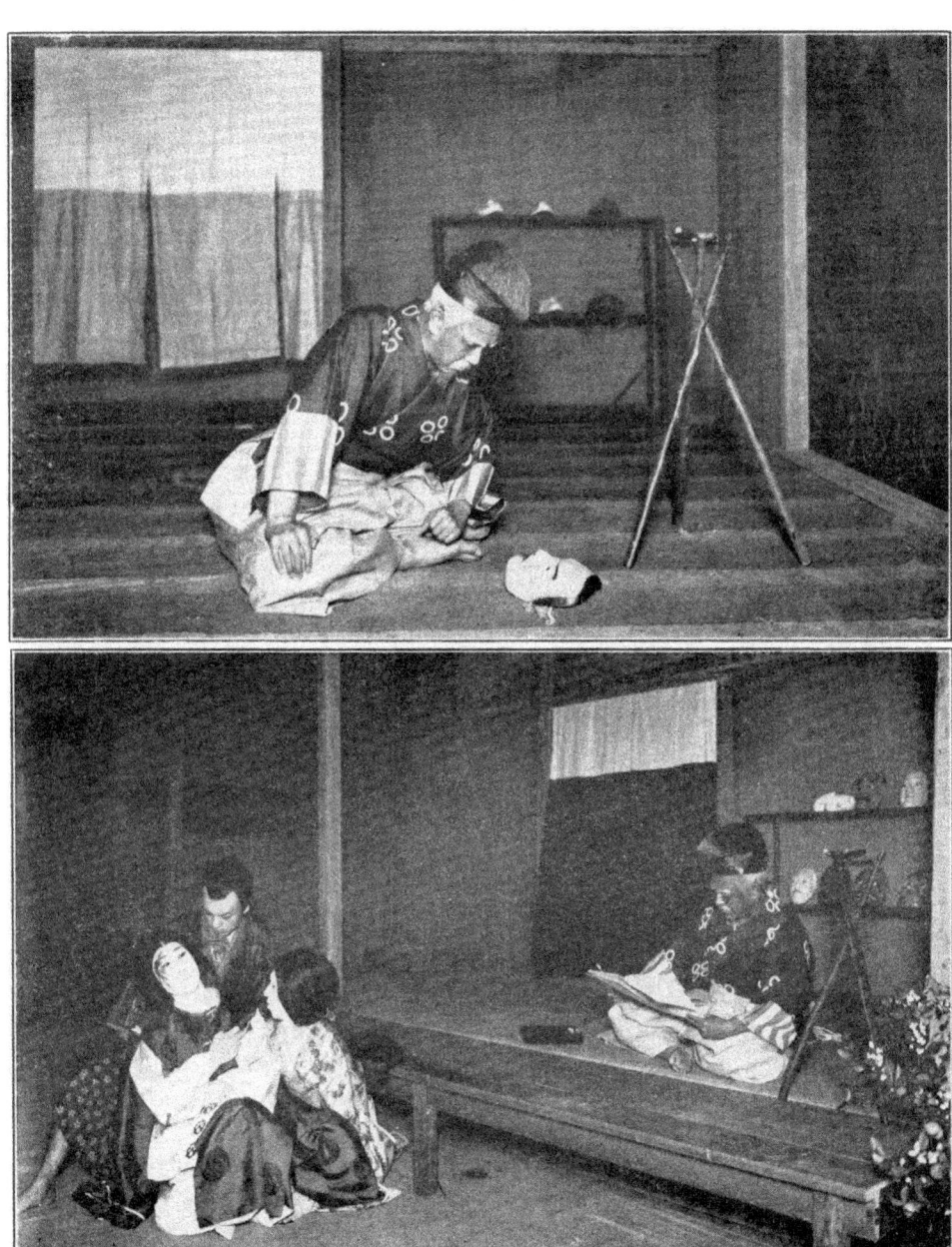

Fig. 2.10. Two photographs of the Tokyo's production of *Shuzenji Monogatari*, included in the 1928 edition by Samuel French

of Shuzenji, and of how she was able to escape on the night that Yoriiye was assassinated. The second was the story of Ukyo Kongo, a Nō actor whose beautiful wife became ill as he was travelling. Upon his return, he found her in her death throes, and without wasting any time he immediately took a brush and a pen and began to sketch her portrait as she passed on to the afterlife. According to Okamoto, these legends provided him with the plot. Before beginning to write, he returned to Tokyo, researched mask-making in the thirteenth century, and discovered that there had been ten famous mask-carvers at the time of Yoriiye. He was, however, unable to identify the maker of Yoriiye's death mask. Among the ten names, he picked 'Yashao' because he liked the resemblance with 'Yasha', the name of an evil spirit (Okamoto 2006: 128). In an article written on the occasion of the Tokyo premiere, in 1911, he returned to the origin of the play:

> *Shuzenji Monogatari* is entirely fictional, inspired by the mask of Yoriiye that belongs to the temple of Shuzenji. The mask of Yoriiye was probably a possession of Yoriiye. When I look at this mask as a bequest left by a tragic figure like Yoriiye, I feel deeply for him; the mask conjures up the image of deities from ancient Greece who are said to have worn the masks of tragedy. It seems to me that the mask has been carved with the unfortunate fate of Yoriiye's life. This is where I got the idea for the mysterious drama in which the mask-maker Yashao carves a mask that foretells the fate of the tragic shogun. (Okamoto 2006: 131–32)

By associating masks with the origin of tragedy, Okamoto implicitly references Nietzsche's *The Birth of Tragedy*, which was well known among *fin-de-siècle* intellectuals in Japan. Moreover, the comparison of Nō masks and ancient Greek masks was common in Western studies of Japan.

Shuzenji Monogatari opens with a description of Yashao's shop, where his two daughters are at work and Nō masks are 'arranged on the shelves, and hung on the walls' (Okamoto 1928: 1). Yashao's older daughter, Katsura, complains about her task and questions mask-making as an honourable profession, while the younger sister, Kayede, proudly defends her father's trade. The ex-Shogun Yoriiye, exiled to Shuzenji, has given Yashao the task of carving a mask of himself to be handed down to future generations but, after several months, Yashao is still dissatisfied with his work. Impatient with the delay, Yoriiye comes to Yashao's house and threatens him with death if he does not deliver the mask. Yashao excuses himself by arguing that the carving of a mask requires inspiration, and that a mask can be considered finished only when it is imbued with life: 'I make masks, giving life to a rough block of wood, giving it the semblance of man, woman, angel, man-eating yasha, infusing into it the spirit of goodness, wickedness, righteousness, or unrighteousness. When the whole energy of mind and body is concentrated in both arms, and the spirit poured like water into the lifeless wood, the mask is shaped. The work is begun, but whether the power persists cannot be told' (Okamoto 1928: 7). Yashao's daughter Katsura intervenes, and she promises the mask to the shogun. When the carving is taken out of the box, the Shogun and his helpers are favourably impressed by the resemblance, but Yashao repeats stubbornly that the portrait is a mask of death: 'It is not the visage of a living man! The eyes are fixed in hatred, a wraith or ghost, as if cursing' (Okamoto 1928: 11). The Shogun does not pay attention to the warning and invites Yashao's elder daughter, who is impatient to leave her father's house, to follow him as his concubine. The second act, in which Yoriiye addresses Katsura with a display of emotion that was new on the kabuki stage (Powell 2016: 41), portrays their romance and discloses the attack prepared by the shogun's opponents.

In the third act, as news of the fighting at Shuzenji reaches the mask-maker, Katsura, now dishevelled and wounded, shows up at her father's home. Holding in one hand a halberd, in the other the mask of the ex-shogun, she tells her father how, as the troops arrived and the shogun was in his bath, she wore the mask, impersonating him, and was able to give Yoriiye time to escape: 'I covered my face with this mask to deceive the enemy, and suffer death in my lord's stead. In the dim light, I ran to the court, weapon in hand, and cried out, "Here is the grand shogun Yoriiye!" Running out of the palace grounds, all followed me, thinking me to be Yoriiye!' (Okamoto 1928: 24).

As she is fainting, supported by her father and sister, the Temple priest arrives and announces that the Shogun has been assassinated. Kayede laments that her sister has sacrificed herself in vain, but Yashao laughs at death, relieved that his ability as a mask-maker is no longer questioned. After rejoicing that his work has the capacity to foretell destiny, he endeavours to create another perfect mask: 'You must endure a little longer', he urges his dying daughter, as he rushes for brushes and paper. 'I must have the features of a dying woman! Endure a little longer, however it may pain you!' (Okamoto 1928: 26). The play closes with the mask-maker intent on drawing the features of the dying Katsura. Thus the daughter who had most criticized Yashao's art becomes the source of inspiration for his masterpiece. In this way, the play shifts the focus from the death mask of a man to that of a (still living) woman.

Kei Shionoya notes that Okamoto made Yashao speak with a slightly archaic register to signal that he embodied the virtues of old Japan (Shionoya 1986: 115). However, Yashao's aspiration as an artist was a new feature in a context in which mask-making had always been the domain of artisans. Like the protagonist of Crommelynck's play, Yashao is a Dionysian artist-creator, a Nietzschean figure willing to put art above everything else. Moreover, whereas women's self-abnegation and lovers' suicides were common subjects on the kabuki stage, the display of death agony for its own sake was not so common and reflected expectations of Japanese theatre shaped in the West (Foley 1988: 78). Like Kawakami, Okamoto shortened his play and foregrounded a scene of death agony, although Katsura's role was still played by an *onnagata*. Moreover, Katsura's impersonation of Yoriiye has important gender implications. The masquerade takes place off stage, and Katsura is no longer wearing the mask when she enters her father's home — in fact, her features are effaced by the hair that falls in front of her face. The audience was therefore invited to imagine a complex gender performance, a male actor impersonating ideal femininity (the *onnagata* in the role of Katsura) in turn impersonating a male character (the shogun Yoriiye). In this light, the portrait of the dying Katsura also captured the features of a woman punished after cross-dressing in a public performance.[10]

Okamoto's play was so successful that by 1937 the tale was incorporated into the second volume of *We Japanese: The Customs, Manners, Ceremonies, Festivals, Arts and Crafts of Japan*, presented by the authors, Frederic De Garis and Atsuharu Sakai, as 'the best-ever popular encyclopaedia of Japanese Culture', which undertook to bring to global readerships 'true aspects of the Japanese nation' (De Garis and Sakai 2002: 5). In this collection, the tale of the Shuzenji temple featured in prose, presented as an old legend and with no reference to Okamoto. Curiously, Sakai, who was in charge of the second volume, chose to omit the ending, which he apparently considered un-Japanese. In Sakai's version, Yashao mourns his daughter, but takes comfort in the fact that that she died honourably defending the Shogun. The story closes with a meditation on the power of the mask to foretell the future, rather than with the mask-maker sketching his dying daughter (De Garis and Sakai 2002: 303).

Besides enjoying success in Japan, where it is still performed today, *Shuzenji Monogatari* successfully travelled abroad. In 1925, the French scholar Albert Maybon selected it as an example of new kabuki in his treatise on Japanese theatre (Maybon 1925). In 1927, Kuninosuke Matsuo translated it into French, and in the same year the play premiered in Paris at the Champs-Elysées, as part of the international festival organized by Firmin Gémier, under the title *Le Masque* [The mask]. While all the actors were French (Gémier played the role of Yashoe) the performance was the first Japanese play staged in France with a Japanese director (Keisuké Omori). The English version, titled *The Mask-Maker*, followed suit, and the play was published in 1928 by Samuel French, in a 'version adapted and prepared for stage production' by the kabuki scholar Zoë Kincaid, in the translation by Hanso Tarao. While in Japan dramatic literature was beginning to be considered as worthy of literary merit, it is as a text designed for performance that shin-kabuki plays reached the West. The Samuel French edition did not include an analysis of acting or stage devices, but it featured two photographs from the Tokyo production, the first foregrounding Sadanji Ichitawa contemplating the mask he had made for the Shogun; the second capturing him sketching the face of his dying daughter — which, covered in make-up, already looks like a mask. While in the first picture Yashao's masks lie flat on the shelves in the background, in the second they are displayed upright, and stare back at the audience.

In the introduction to the drama, Kincaid underlines that Okamoto's play reflects the importance of masks in Japanese culture, where 'craftsmen who carved masks have always been regarded with reverence' and where 'the mask from ancient times has been regarded as divine, something belonging to the gods' (Kincaid 1928: 4). Kincaid further stresses the crucial role that masks have traditionally in Nō, where the actor 'regards his mask-treasures as he would his life' and 'bows respectfully before his mask when it is taken out of a lacquer box or brocade bag to be worn during a performance' (1928: 4). Okamoto's play contained all the ingredients to become a success in the West: it was short enough, it foregrounded the duality of the mask as portrait and performative prop, and it offered the opportunity to admire in one performance Nō masks, a kabuki show, and the suicide scene that Western audiences expected from Japanese theatre. The translation of the title is indicative of the extent to which the theme of mask making intrigued Western audiences. If, in the Japanese version, the story revolves around the legend of the Shuzenji Temple, in the French and English version it is first and foremost a story about a mask.

Rodin, the 'Mask of Horror' and the Japanese Dancer

The French sculptor Auguste Rodin was close to Edmond de Goncourt, the main proponent of Japanese art in the 1980s, and personally acquainted with many artists influenced by *Japonisme*, including Claude Monet, Camille Pissarro, Octave Mirbeau, James McNeill Whistler, Paul Gauguin and Jean Carriès. He owned a copy of Van Gogh's 'Père Tanguy', which was considered a manifesto of Japanophilia, and he attended Universal Exhibitions. Like the art historians Edmond Pottier and Louis Gonse, Rodin saw in Japan a refined civilization that offered many points of comparison with ancient Greece, as well as an example of what the West had been like before the advent of modernity (Blanchetière 2008: 104). In 1900, he affirmed that the drawings he exhibited at the *Pavillon de l'Alma* in Paris were 'snapshots varying between Greek and Japanese' (Buley-Uribe 2007: 109).[11] Bénédicte Garnier, however, notes that Rodin's Japanese collection never attained the breadth and scope of his collection of Greek, Roman, and Egyptian art (2007: 24). Rodin bought Japanese items unsystematically and was not able to distinguish historical items from artefacts produced for export. Moreover, he hardly engaged with Japan as subject matter in his own work, with the exception of the series of sculptures modelled on the Japanese actress Hanako.

Like many Parisians intellectuals, Rodin discovered Japanese theatre through Sada Yacco who, under the direction of Loïe Fuller, was performing at the Parisian Universal Exhibition in 1900. At that time, Rodin was studying the body in movement, and the combination of dance and histrionic expressions displayed by Sada Yacco in 'La Geisha et le Chevalier', especially her performance of suicide, impressed him to the extent that he attempted, unsuccessfully, to schedule an individual meeting with her. The troupe, advised by Fuller, had modified the kabuki repertoire to meet the expectations of the French, who, in Kawakami's view, 'adore tragedy that ends in death or suicide and are fascinated by the display of horror' (Shionoya 1986: 40). Sada Yacco was extolled by French critics, who compared her to divas like Elenora Duse and Sarah Bernhardt. However, she was also compared to an 'inert doll', a 'small intelligent animal', and associated with a 'primitive consciousness'.[12] These comments echoed the features that in France were associated with Japanese character: sensuality, *petitesse*, infantilism, and ferocity (Shionoya 1986: 28). As the art historian Edmond Pottier noted in the article 'Grèce et Japon' (1890), these stereotypes been shaped in the eighteenth century by the writing of Montesquieu, who had described the Japanese as 'des gens opiniâtres, capricieux, déterminés, bizarres, décourageant la rigueur de lois par l'atrocité de leurs mœurs, et prêts à s'ouvrir le ventre pour la moindre fantaisie' [stubborn, capricious, determined, bizarre people, prone to discourage the rigour of the law through the atrocity of their customs, and ready to open their bellies on the slightest fantasy] (Pottier 1890: 14). At the time in which Sada Yacco was performing in France, theatre critic Jules Lemaître still portrayed Japanese as 'eternal children' and emphasized the immobility of their culture (Lemaître 1898: 38).

Like Sada Yacco, Hanako, a stage name for Hisa Ōta, had been 'discovered' by Loïe Fuller and her fame built on the success of her predecessor.[13] A geisha trained in traditional Japanese dance, Hanako had embarked for Europe with a group of actors recruited to perform at an exhibition in Copenhagen in 1902. She had then joined the company *Arayama*, which travelled across Europe, with moderate success. Fuller met Hanako at the Savoy Theatre in London, where she saw her in 'Hara-kiri', a play advertised as 'a production more essentially Japanese than any yet seen in this country — not even excepting the performance of Madame Sada Yacco' (Sawada 1984: 30). She offered her artistic advice to the company, on the condition that Ota Hisa, who had so far been performing a minor part, could take on the leading role. Deeming the geisha's name unpronounceable, she then changed it to 'Hanako', beginning the construction of a Japanese persona for the European imagination. At the Colonial exhibition in Marseille, in 1906, the company, in addition to the signature piece 'Hara-kiri', performed two new plays, 'La Vengeance d'une geisha' and 'Galatée', drawn from the kabuki play *Jingoro Hidari*, in which Hanako played the role of a doll (Sawada 1984: 46). Rodin had travelled to the exhibition to draw the Cambodian dancers, and, led by Fuller, had the opportunity to watch both plays. Deeply impressed by Hanako's portrayal of suicide, he asked to meet her off-stage and sketched her dressed as a doll. Next to Hanako's figure, he drew a Japanese mask (Minami 2002: 17).

In the same year, Fuller interrupted her engagement with the company *Arayama* and started a second collaboration with Hanako and a smaller group of actors. She wrote from scratch a series of 'Japanese dramas' that capitalized on the clichés that Western audiences associated with Japanese culture: tragedies like 'La Martyre', 'La Poupée japonaise', 'La Petite Japonaise' and comedies like 'L'Ophélie japonaise', most of which ended with the suicide of the protagonist. Kathy Foley has argued that Hanako, as Asian female, was 'more "other"', and exemplified the perfect object for seduction, evoking both female sensuality and the consequences that this display deserved in the European romantic tradition (1988: 79). In his biography of her, Sawada recalls how Hanako, aware of the triviality of these shows, would often panic at the suspicion that there might be Japanese spectators in the audience (Sawada 1984: 56). Nevertheless, Fuller presented the shows as authentic Japanese theatre, belonging to the great theatrical tradition and choreography of Japan. Hanako's acting in 'La Martyre' is recorded by a review published in *L'Illustration* on 3 November 1906, titled 'Death of Osedé:

> A sensational drama last Saturday evening at 9:30 p.m. in the presence of Paris's best audience. Madame Hanako committed suicide by disembowelling herself. But it was suicide. An emulator of Sada Yacco, Hanako is a tiny Japanese gifted with a graceful form, lively eyes, a rebellious nose, feline movements.

> The comedy in which she displays her varied talents as a saucy flirt, a mime, a dancer, turns into a tragedy when Osodé (the heroine's name), the prey of gloomy sorrow, suddenly changes her behaviour: she takes hold of a knife and she slowly thrusts it into her flesh, her eyes convulse, her nostrils palpitate, her face pales and blood spreads over her white tunic. She then collapses to the floor and dies. It is almost ... too realistic. At least for those audience members whose nerves are too weak to tolerate such a performance. (Savarese 1988: 68)

As Nicola Savarese has noted, Hanako's emphasis on suffering contributed to the paradoxical interpretation of kabuki as a 'realistic' form of theatre (Savarese 1988: 68).

Rodin was fascinated by Hanako's ability to mimic death agony, and repeatedly invited her to pose in his atelier. From his diary, we know that Hanako started visiting him in 1907, although the sessions were often interrupted by her acting duties, and that she continued posing for him every summer until 1911 (Blanchetière 2007: 131). Although during that time Rodin's research was centred on the body in motion, he was not interested in Hanako's dancing, but in capturing in a static portrait the appearance of suffering that that she was able to act out in her performances. Rodin's biographer Judith Cladel describes Hanako's posing as follows: 'Hanako did not pose like other people. Her features were contracted in an expression of cold, terrible rage. She had the look of a tiger, an expression thoroughly foreign to our Occidental countenances. With the force of will which the Japanese display in the face of death, Hanako was able to hold this look for hours' (Cladel 1918: 162). In contrast, Sawada reports a testimony of Hanako that stresses how she found the posing sessions, in which she was asked to maintain the same expression for fifteen minutes, very demanding: 'à l'aide d'un miroir, je travaillais l'expression de mon regard, avant de poser, mais monsieur Rodin n'était jamais satisfait, même lorsque je pensais avoir trouvé cette expression d'agonie qu'il recherchait' [using a mirror, before posing, I worked on the look in my eyes, but Monsieur Rodin was never satisfied, even when I thought I had found the expression of death agony that he sought] (Sawada 1984: 64–65).

The obsession with Hanako's range of expressions resulted in fifty-eight busts, heads and masks in clay, bronze and glass paste, now classified by the Musée Rodin into different types. The sculptures known as types A (shaped in 1907), B, C and D (shaped in 1908) capture the expression of suffering that Rodin had seen on stage. These portraits focus on Hanako's strabismus (squint), marked by the dots in her eyes and by her frowning eyebrows; her mouth is open, underling her expression of anguish. While A types can be described as decorative heads, B types are oval-shaped faces with empty eyes, no ears or hairs, that Rodin referred to as 'masks'. Types C and D build on the research developed in type B, with additional details (see Blanchetière 2007: 131).

From Sawada's biography, we know that Rodin referred to type D as 'Tête de l'angoisse de la mort' [head of the anguish of death] (Sawada 1984: 71). Monique Laurent suggested that, in reducing Hanako's features to a mask, Rodin intended to study a range of emotions, which he saw conjured in masks as used in Japanese theatre (1979a: 28). From Rodin's diary, we know that, between 1910 and 1912, when he was working on this project, he purchased four Japanese masks for his

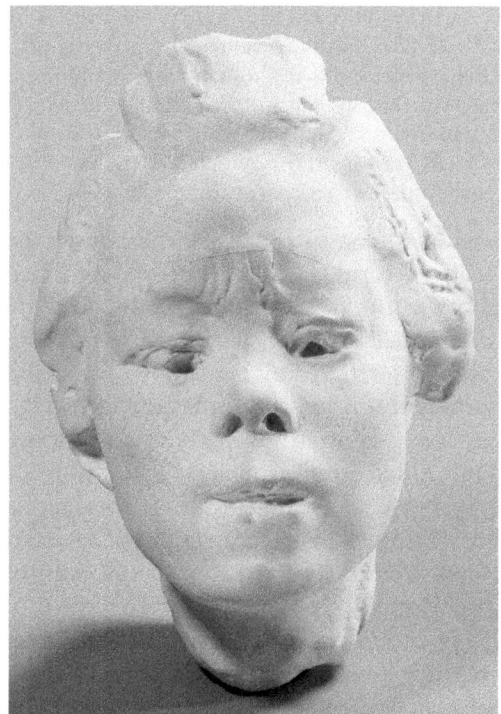
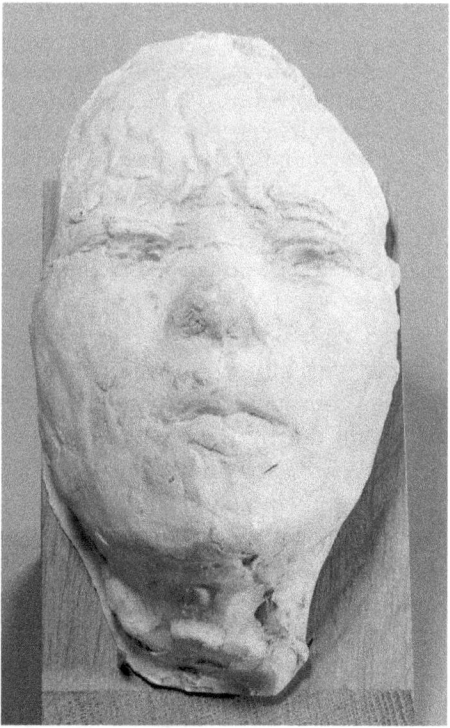
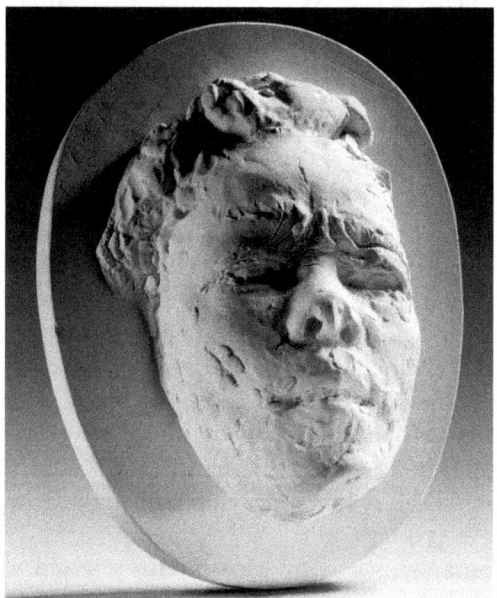

FIGS. 2.11, 2.12. Auguste Rodin. *Mask of Hanako*, type A, 1907, plaster,
19 × 12.5 × 14 cm; type B, 1907–11, plaster, 20.5 × 11.6 × 8.7 cm. Rodin Museum, Paris
FIG. 2.13. Auguste Rodin. *Mask of Hanako*, type C, 1907–08, plaster,
26 × 20.4 × 12 cm, Rodin Museum, Paris

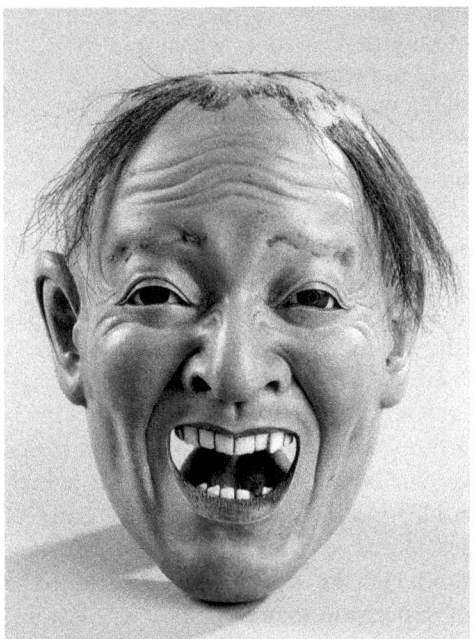 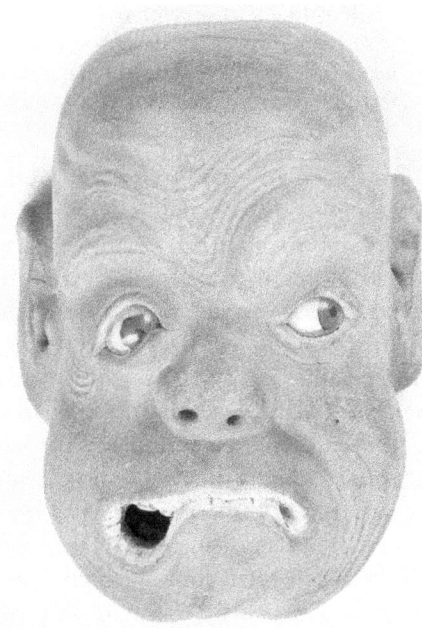

FIG. 2.15. *Mask Deformed by a Grimace*, nineteenth century, wood, 13 × 18 × 8 cm, Collection 'Antiquities', Japan, photo by Jerome Manoukian, Rodin Museum, Paris.
FIG. 2.14. *Laughing Mask*, c. 1875, wood, 18.5 × 14.5 × 9 cm, Collection 'Antiquities', Japan, photo by Jerome Manoukian, Rodin Museum, Paris.

collection. The most ancient one is a bugaku mask dating back to the eleventh century, crafted to be worn at court dances. The other three, known as 'Masque au visage hilare' [mask of a laughing face], 'masque au visage furieux' [mask of a furious face] and 'masque au visage déformé par une grimace' [mask of a face deformed by a grimace], are nineteenth-century artefacts made for export and intended for decorative use. They are shaped after traditional Nō masks, but complemented with glass eyes and, in the case of 'Masque au visage hilare', human hair.

Garnier argues that there is a direct connection between the intensity of expression conjured by these masks, Rodin's appreciation of Sada Yacco and Hanako's performances, and the portraits that he made of Hanako (2007: 82). Certainly, Rodin's use of the mask as a form of expression can be brought into relation with his appreciation of the fragment. Recalling the sessions with Hanako, Judith Cladel chose to underline the moment at which the head is cut off from clay and becomes a complete figure:

> I watched Rodin model the head of Hanako, the Japanese actress. He rapidly modeled the whole in the rough, as he does for all his busts. His keen eye and his experienced thumb enable him to establish the exact dimensions at the first sitting. Then the detailed work of modeling begins. The sculptor is not satisfied to mold the mass in its apparent outlines only. With absolute accuracy he slices off some clay, cuts off the head of the bust, and lays it upside down on a cushion. He then makes his model lie on a couch.

> Bent like a vivisector over his subject, he studies the structure of the skull seen from above, the jaws viewed from below, and the lines which join the head and the throat, and the nape of the head to the spine. Then he chisels the features with the point of pen-knife, bringing out the recesses of the eye-lids, the nostrils, the curve of the mouth. (Cladel 1918: 161–62)

In Cladel's account, the sculpted head lies 'on a cushion', while the artist approaches the Japanese model, who is likewise lying on a couch, 'like a vivisector'. The narrative involves an interchangeability between the cast and the model, both of whom are (literally or metaphorically) ready to be dissected by the artist-anatomist. The perception of these masks as fetish objects was encouraged by the display chosen by Rodin, who arranged some of the type B masks on an oval surface, a setting reminiscent of his versions of the 'Tête de Saint Jean-Baptiste sur un plat' (1887) on which Rodin had worked in the 1880s (Laurent 1979b: 32).

The theme of the severed head is similarly evoked by the four masks in glass-paste that belong to the series 'meditating woman', associated with type E, in which glass-paste gives the sculpture a waxy, translucent look that recalls the texture of human skin. According to Sawada, the idea for these masks originated during a break between sessions, in which Rodin and Hanako went for a walk and the sculptor was struck by the actress's peaceful expression (Sawada 1984: 45). Rodin, who considered this mask one of his best attempts, laid one of them on a pillow in a room of his studio at the Hôtel Biron, next to the glass-paste heads of his life-long partner, Rose Beuret, and of his former student and lover, Camille Claudel. François Blanchetière notes that, as an old man, he frequently visited these masks and seemed to draw from them a sense of comfort (2008: 109).

In her biography, Cladel underlines the uncanny feelings conjured by the mask:

> I have one of these studies before me now. It has been cast in a composition of coloured glass, and the vivid flesh coloring lends reality to work. This mask is not disfigured by rage. The bloodless head, with its fixed stare, lies on a white cushion, and no one can escape its disquieting influence. Some people shudder when they see it. 'One might think it the head of a dead person', they say.
> ...I cannot say that it resembles death; on the contrary, it is so lifelike that it is almost supernatural. One might call it a condemned person, a being so terrified by the approach of death that all the blood has rushed to the heart. It is a spirit frozen in fear, the eyes looking into the unknown, the large nostrils scenting death. The bulging forehead, the high, Mongolian cheek-bones, and the flat nose make the face run towards the mouth, with its remarkable expression. Obstinate, although conquered, it will draw its last breath without a cry.
> Meanwhile life seems to throb in every cell. This head, so like a being that has been put to death, has the soft, pliant flesh of a ripe fruit (Cladel 1918: 162)

Although the decorative head portrays Hanako's expression during a moment of rest, not the agonizing gaze that she produced in her performances, the display chosen by Rodin was similar to the treatment reserved for death masks, with the difference that the eyes of Hanako are wide open and stare back at the observer, a look that Blanchetière compares to the petrifying gaze of the Gorgon (2008: 109) and that Cladel associated with awareness of imminent death. Hanako's features, in this sculpture, are less marked as Asian than in the heads and masks that portray her dying gaze: her lips are red, the glass paste confers a white, translucent look. Nevertheless, Cladel identified the frightening effect in racial terms, emphasizing the head's 'bulging forehead, Mongolian cheek bones, flat nose'. She then described the entirely different connotation that the same head took up at night, when it lost its foreignness and became an emblem of the familiar:

> How gentle and touching it seems now! It is no longer bloodthirsty and savage, that exotic expression which repelled me has quite disappeared. These features, expressing the innermost self under a stress of emotions, revealed a poor creature that has loved and suffered. It is a pitiable face that has been molded by life. I have seen that sad, tired expression of anguish in one whose strength is gone, but who still makes an effort to understand misfortune in order to strive against it. I have seen it on my mother's face... (Cladel 1918: 164–65)

Lit by a candle, the head was no longer 'exotic, bloodthirsty and savage' but had acquired a sacrificial look that reminded Cladel of her own mother. In this setting, Cladel abandoned gender-neutral language and associated the head's expression with a specifically female look. From a threatening artefact, the head turned into an innocuous fetish. While Fuller's productions conjured a Japanese Salomé, Rodin's sculptures, by reducing Hanako to a severed head, conflated the punishment that the female seducer deserves according to the clichés of European romanticism with the threat of decapitation that Salomé represents. Decorative heads, masks, and severed heads blend metonymically Rodin's series, taking over each other's field of signification. In all these sculptures, the head of Hanako looks back at the observer.

All the fifty-three sculptures of Hanako are fragments. Rodin did, however, portray Hanako's full body in a series of drawings produced in 1907, during a session in which she agreed to pose for him naked. These are quick sketches, and were not designed to serve as a plan for sculpture. Although the emphasis is on the dancer's ability to hold a pose, some of the drawings already indicate the transformation of her features into a mask. In an interview with the journal *The World* released in 1907, Rodin described the experience of studying Hanako's physique. He compared Hanako's size to the height of a table, and confessed that, upon seeing 'the small size and the exotic traits', he 'first thought of a monkey' and expected that her body would reveal 'some particularities'. After seeing the actress naked, however, he acknowledged that her charm rested in her movements. He concluded that Hanako was indeed a 'real doll, but with a reserve of intelligence and energy' and that the Japanese had 'secrets that we cannot penetrate' (Judrin 2002: 20).

As Hanako's biographers underline, Rodin treated Hanako as a member of the family, with kindness and respect (Sawada 1984: 75). Laurent points out that Rodin never considered her an ethnic model, nor regarded her as exotic, and argues that he was interested in the inner energy emanating from the actress (1979a: 25). However, he associated the type of theatre Hanako was engaged in with tormented sexuality and emphasized her small size, comparing her to a doll and a monkey. Moreover, like his contemporaries, he associated Japan with the pre-modern. Although he considered Japan a great civilization and had great appreciation for Hanako's art, he

70 MASK-MAKERS

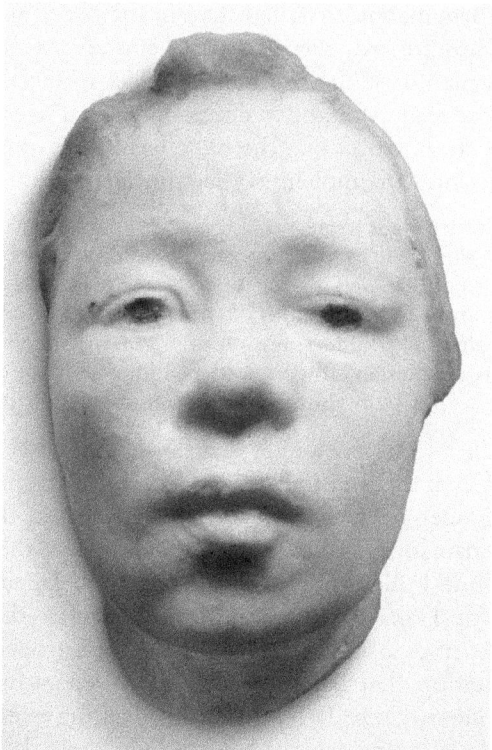

FIG. 2.16. Auguste Rodin, *Mask of Hanako*, modelled *c.* 1907; executed 1911, *pâte-de-verre* (ground glass refired in a mould), 21.9 × 12.1 × 8.9 cm, by kind permission of the Philadelphia Museum of Art, Philadelphia.

thus participated in the anthropological discourse that saw non-European societies as living in a different historical moment (see Fabian 1983: 37). While the study of ancient Greece inspired him to create a new genre, and to conceive of the fragment as a work in its own right, his impression of Hanako's performances led him to shape a series of masks that embody alterity in ethnic and gender terms.

Conclusions

Ensor's paintings of masks, Crommelynck and Okamoto's theatrical props, and Rodin's sculptures of Hanako constitute very different artistic practices, each grounded in a specific cultural context. However, they are brought together by the new meaning that mask-making acquired, at the turn of the century, as a consequence of the encounter of Western and non-Western traditions. By foregrounding the mask's ability to portray and maximize facial features, these works underline the extent to which mask-making, at the turn of the century, was still anchored to physiognomic and phrenological practices, which in turn continued to function as pillars of caricature. On the other hand, by inserting the carved portraits in the folkloric representations of carnival, or by establishing a connection to Japanese performances, these works conceptualized mask-making within the sphere of ritual. In doing so, the artists reclaimed a ritual function for the mask and a shamanistic role for the artist, who was increasingly marginalized in industrial, capitalist societies.

If points of conjunction between Ensor and Crommelynck can be identified in a shared culture background, the similar treatment of mask-making by Crommelynck and Okamoto is surprising. The common thread between these plays relies on the renewed interest in ritual masks in Western aesthetics, as well as on the Japanese attempt to modernize kabuki by integrating elements of Western dramaturgy. By using an Eastern model inspired by kabuki performances, Rodin similarly aimed to rejuvenate Western sculpture. His decorative heads and masks, so reminiscent of severed heads, effectively projected the alterity of femininity onto the axis of ethnicity.

In all these case studies, the mask holds a dual status as reassuring and threatening. The sculptor enjoys capturing and objectifying human features, but, as the model looks back at the observer, the pleasurable look becomes terrifying and conjures the experience of the Lacanian gaze. Moreover, the carvings reduce mobility to stillness, the model to a fragment. As studies of emotions, the masks do not convey much information about the women they are shaped on, but reflect the vision and fantasies of the male artist. As fragments, they evoke the violence implicit in their creation, and are associated with skulls and severed heads.

In 1883, Edmond Pottier proclaimed: 'l'ère du bibelot, de la curiosité mercantile, est close: celle de l'influence artistique commence' [the era of the trinket, of mercantile curiosity is over: that of artistic influence begins] (1883: 107). Underlining the bi-directionality of the influence, Otojirō Kawakami commented on the fine tuning between Japanese and French taste, and described France as 'un pays brutal dont le climat est presque semblable à celui du Japon' [a brutal country in which the climate is almost similar to that of Japan], 'the best country from which Japan could draw an example if in need of foreign plays' (Shionoya 1986: 111). Far from being passive agents, women like Fuller and Hanako and Asian theatrical agents like Kawakami and Okamoto were actively involved in shaping the gender and racial constructs at the core of the works examined, albeit within the framework of hegemonic conventions and unequal power dynamics.

With its three-dimensionality, its status as lifeless object with the capacity to become imbued with life, the mask embodied the expectations that the turn of the century directed toward the foreign. By combining the decadent preoccupation with regression with the Freudian notion of the return of the repressed, it evoked the experience of the uncanny as 'a foreign body within oneself, even the experience of oneself as a foreign body' (Royle 2003: 2). As a facsimile and a substitute for the face, it functioned as the ultimate fetish that addressed the artist's encounter with otherness: death, femininity, the Japanese woman.

Notes to Chapter 2

1. See, for example, in Edgar Allan Poe's 'The Oval Portrait' (1842) or Nathaniel Hawthorn's 'The Birth-Mark' (1843).
2. Ensor exhibited the painting only in 1929, when he was already an established artist.
3. For a thorough analysis of this painting see Tricot (web publication) <http://jamesensor.vlaamsekunstcollectie.be/en/sources/online-publications/who-is-hiding-behind-the-mask-in-the-astonishment-of-the-mask-wouse>.
4. A similar message is conveyed by the skeleton featuring in *Skeleton Arresting Masqueraders* (1891), which is wearing a half-mask, leaving the dyad mask/skeleton exposed. This painting, too, features a mask from the Japanese Nō in the background.
5. The title, 'L'Intrigue' refers to refers to a tavern ritual in Ostend, in which masked men, during carnival, drink at other people's expense (Tricot 2008: 166). Since the marriage of Ensor's sister took place in 1892, scholars have speculated that the artist changed the date on the painting, pretending to have produced it two years earlier to avoid a direct reference (Schoonbaert 1989: 17).
6. Bakhtin develops his conceptualization of Carnival in *Rabelais and his World*, originally published in 1965.
7. Ten years later, W. B. Yeats wrote of a similar project in the preface to *Four Plays for Dancers*, a work strongly influenced by Nō: 'I shall hope for a number of typical masks, each capable of use in several plays. The face of the speaker should be as much a work of art as the lines that he speaks or the costume that he wears [...]. Perhaps in the end one would write plays for certain masks' (Yeats 1921: v).
8. Other reformers created new forms of theatre, such as *shimpa*, the 'new school' of melodramatic plays championed by Otojirō Kawakami, *shingeki*, the 'new drama' based on Western model, and *shinko-kugeki*, historical dramas famous for the frequent use of swordplay (Powell 1990: 5).
9. Okamoto's plays are mostly historical dramas set in the Edo period and frequently involve the theme of double suicide, with the protagonists killing one another onstage (Shionoya 1986: 115). Today, Okamoto is mostly known for his crime fiction series 'The Curious Casebook of Inspector Hanshichi', which transposed a Western genre into the Japan of the Edo period.
10. A few years earlier, Japanese government authorities had allowed women to perform on stage on the condition that they did not, under any circumstance, dress up as men (Shionoya 1986: 107). Okamoto did not break the law, as he used *onnagata* for the female roles; moreover, crossdressing, in his play, takes place offstage. Nevertheless, through the gender performance, the play engages with taboos and discussions related to women's roles on stage.
11. In the last two decades, Rodin's relationship to Japan has been the subject of several exhibitions, including 'Rodin et l'extrême orient' (Paris, 1979); 'Rodin et le Japon' (Paris-Tokyo, 2001), 'Rodin: Le Rêve japonais' (Paris, 2007).
12. Jean Lorrain described her as a 'frail and rare living trinket' with a 'narrow and pink face, enamelled with make-up', and spoke enthusiastically about her 'puerile chirping and doll-like singing' (Shionoya 1986: 45). Paul Klee, who in 1902 had the opportunity of seeing her perform in Italy, was impressed by the 'primitive conscience' of the actress, her climactic poses, and the 'barbaric music' that accompanied her dancing (Shionoya 1986: 48).
13. Hanako's story first featured in a series of articles by Donald Keene in 1962, then gathered in 'Hanako' (1971). Sawada's biography of the artist appeared in 1997. Savarese (1988), Foley (1988), Blanchetière (2007, 2008), Judrin (2002) and Minami (2002) have contributed to the reconstructions of Hanako's performances.

CHAPTER 3

Masking *Dorian Gray*: Fetishism and Ego-Mania in Beerbohm and Le Gallienne

The last decades of the nineteenth century saw important developments in the articulation of modern sexuality in the medical and legal spheres. According to Michel Foucault, it was at this time that homosexuality was first conceived in the West in terms of a social identity (2003: 42). In 1882, Krafft-Ebing's *Psychopathia Sexualis*, which introduced the word 'homosexuality' into the English language, was translated from German. Havelock Ellis and John Addington Symonds's *Sexual Inversion*, the first medical textbook on homosexuality published in English, appeared in 1897. In the legal field, the *Criminal Law Amendment Act* of 1885 classified all male–male sexual interactions as illegal. Throughout the century, same-sex practices had been considered illicit, but now homosexuality was beginning to be associated with a distinctive personality and sensibility (Foucault 1978: 43). Wilde became the first public personification of the homosexual (Sinfield 1994; Felski 1995: 103), while his trial was used to 'legitimate male sexual practices by proscribing expressions of male experience that transgressed those limits' (Cohen 1987: 801).

This chapter explores the interest in masks, disguises and self-fashioning in *fin-de-siècle* English literature in the context of transnational debates around decadence and degeneration and against the background of medico-legal debates about homosexuality. It develops a comparison between *The Picture of Dorian Gray* (1890–91) and two fictional pieces published in the aftermath of Wilde's trial, Max Beerbohm's *The Happy Hypocrite* (1896) and Richard Le Gallienne's *The Worshipper of the Image* (1899), texts in which the mask functions as a fetish object intimately linked to the protagonist's narcissism. Since both Beerbohm and Le Gallienne's works involved borrowing from *The Picture of Dorian Gray* and presented an inversion of the novel's thematic construction, they can be considered forms of textual appropriations that, by involving parodic elements, highlight the extent to which writers associated with Decadence influenced, rewrote and quoted one another (Potolsky 2013: 5).[1]

Both Beerbohm and Le Gallienne have been labelled 'second-hand writers' and their works have been dismissed as anachronistic and derivative (Brack 1978: 178).

The Happy Hypocrite and *The Worshipper of the Image*, however, are interesting in the light of, and not despite, their 'parasitic' elements, as allusions to *The Picture of Dorian Gray* offer insight into the understanding of gender and sexual identities that was developing around the time of Wilde's trial, as well as into the authors' stance on decadence. By using the mask to conjure up an association between decadence, narcissism and sexual inversion, Beerbohm and Le Gallienne's texts echo, and to a certain resist, the production of normative and 'deviant' identities in contemporary literary, medical and legal discourses. Masks are used in conjunction with decadent imagery to conjure up a multiplicity of desires that go beyond a heterosexual framework. As fetishes and as embodiments of 'ego-mania', they stand in close relation to the Decadent cult of posing, artificiality and parody, as well as to the over-emphasis on the part at the expense of the whole. They also share a connection with a range of experiences, from dandyism to the articulation of same-sex love, which challenged late Victorian sexual and gender norms and were perceived as a threat to the wholesomeness of the nation.

Masks and Mirrors in *The Picture of Dorian Gray*

By following the themes and styles introduced by Baudelaire and Huysmans, and featuring the motif of the animated portrait, *The Picture of Dorian Gray* combined a French-inspired style of decadence with gothic fiction. However, the novel was read differently by different readerships, and for some, it functioned as a coded text. The plot has become familiar. The artist Basil Hallward paints a portrait of Dorian Gray that betrays his adoration for the young man. Upon seeing the portrait, Dorian falls in love with his own beauty and makes a wish that his painting should age in his stead. From this moment, the work of art, which Dorian keeps hidden in his attic, records the passing of time and his increasing moral degradation, whereas Dorian's own features remain unchanged. Under the influence of Lord Henry, Dorian begins to practice a 'new hedonism' based on the cultivation of experience for its own sake. Like the protagonist of Huysmans' *À Rebours*, he dedicates his life to exploring sensations, and divides his time between aesthetic pleasures and excursions in disguise to London's East End. When, haunted by the fear that his secret may be exposed, he attempts to destroy the portrait, the work of art is restored to its 'exquisite youth and beauty', while the servants find on the floor a body 'withered, wrinkled, and loathsome of visage' (Wilde 2005: 357).[2]

Mirrors and masks play a crucial role in Wilde's aesthetics, where they address conceptions of the self, social roles, as well as the relationship between nature, life and art (Dickson 1983: 5; Thornton 1989: 269; Dyer 2005: 64; Whiteley 2017: 5–9). Overall, Wilde embraced the mask, and in 'The Decaying of Lying', claimed that anything interesting lies in artifice and façades, rather than beyond it (Wilde 2007c: 72–103). In *The Picture of Dorian Gray*, mirror and masks are frequently used in relation to Dorian's portrait: the painting is 'the most magical of mirrors', designed to reveal to Dorian 'his own soul' (Wilde 2005: 258), whereas Dorian's own face, which remains unchanged though the years, is only a 'mask of youth' (Wilde

2005: 339). While the painting acquires human qualities, and 'has a life of its own' (Wilde 2005: 266), Dorian's features remain ageless like a 'mask of glass' (Wilde 2005: 218). Lord Henry gives Dorian a silver mirror adorned with cupids, which Dorian uses to compare his youthful reflection to the aging features of the portrait. He also introduces him to a yellow book that could be, or is at least modelled after, Huysmans' À Rebours; Dorian recognizes himself in all except one aspect of the protagonist, since '[h]e never knew — never, indeed, had any cause to know — that somewhat grotesque dread of mirrors, and polished metal surfaces, and still water, which came upon the young Parisian so early in his life' (Wilde 2005: 276). In taking on the role of the dandy, and turning his life into a work of art, Dorian embraces the notion of identity as a form of artifice. In the course of the narrative, he becomes a fan of masked balls and keeps a closet full of 'curious disguises' (Wilde 2005: 301). Masking, however, assumes a gloomy connotation as he frequents shabby taverns under a false name and in disguise and, after committing a murder, feels 'the terrible pleasure of a double life' (Wilde 2005: 314). Towards the end of the novel, Dorian's relationship to mirrors also takes on a darker shade: he feels uneasy observing his features distorted in the reflecting surfaces in opium dens, and he eventually smashes the mirror that Lord Henry has given him with a gesture that prefigures the destruction of the portrait.

Masking and parody also pervade the novel at a stylistic level. Chapter eleven, which deals with Dorian's activity as a collector, his fascination with exotic and esoteric objects severed from their context of use, imitates À Rebours, deploying researched vocabulary and indulging in elaborate descriptions, in the manner of the French decadents. Moreover, the aphorisms found throughout the novel function as a subtext that subverts the moral message of the ending. Jonathan Dollimore has noted that Wilde's contemporaries perceived a connection between his transgressive aesthetics and his sexual transgression (1991: 67), and has argued that, in focusing on the de-centered and the different, Wilde anticipated postmodernists' rejection of the unified subject. Building on Dollimore, Felski has stressed that Wilde's denial of the natural self, and of natural sexuality, functioned as an inspiration for those who did not conform to heteronormativity (1995: 103). Wilde's embrace of fluid identities (Dollimore 1991: 71), however, contrasts with the emphasis that the novel places on the face as a legible 'map' of virtues and vices. Dorian's belief that the painting functions as a 'visible symbol of the degradation of sin' (Wilde 2005: 250) is backed by moral physiognomy, which had an extensive influence in Victorian culture. Basil summarizes the notion that physical appearance functions as an index to character when he comments: 'Sin is a thing that writes itself across a man's face. It cannot be concealed. [...] If a wretched man has a vice, it shows itself in the lines of the mouth, the droop of his eye-lids, the moulding of his hands even' (Wilde 2005: 293). Following this assumption, the first changes in the portrait take place after Dorian's involvement with the actress Sybil Vane.

Dorian finds Sybil in a 'wretched hole of a place' in London's East End, among 'horrid old Jew[s]' and 'tawdry girls' (Wilde 2005: 212, 214, 239), and develops a fascination with her stage personas. 'To-night she is Imogen!' he describes her to

Lord Henry, 'and to-morrow she will be Juliet'. To the question: 'When is she Sybil Vane?' Dorian answers without hesitation 'Never' (Wilde 2005: 216). On the evening when Dorian proposes to her, she has impersonated Shakespeare's Rosalind 'disguised as a pretty boy'. For Richard Dellamora, Dorian is attracted first of all by her cross-dressing, and by her ability to give shape to the playwright's masculine genius, while his authentic feelings towards women are betrayed by his fascination with the roles in which Sybil is murdered or driven to suicide by a lover (1988: 29). After Sybil's suicide, a 'touch of cruelty in the mouth' (Wilde 2005: 245) spoils the expression of the painting. Following the same logic, the portrait begins to drip blood after Dorian murders his friend Basil, the only person who has been allowed in the attic and has shared his secret. Through this murder Dorian, who has so far been the embodiment of the dandy-aesthete, turns into the prototype of the aesthete-criminal.

The idea of the criminal as an aesthete had been popularized by Thomas De Quincey's 1827 essay 'On Murder, Considered as One of the Fine Arts', which had a strong influence on subsequent literary representations of crime. Wilde engaged with this discourse in the essay 'Pen, Pencil and Poison', originally published in 1889 and later included in his collection of essays *Intentions*. In this piece, he described the life and works of the poet, painter and poisoner Thomas Griffiths Wainewright, and considered the effect of crime on his art. Scholars have traced a correlation between this playful essay and Wilde's novel (Danson 2006: 100).[3] However, whereas in his essay, Wilde concludes that 'Crime in England is rarely the result of sin. It is nearly always the result of starvation' (2007a: 119), in his novel he identifies the motivation for crime in inheritance and underlines Dorian's position as the last heir of a degenerate lineage. Just like the protagonist of Huysmans' *À Rebours*, Dorian wanders through the gallery of his country house contemplating the portraits of his ancestors. He questions essentialist notions of identity as he dismisses the 'shallow psychology of those who conceive the ego in man as a thing simple, permanent, reliable, and of one essence'. However, he stresses the crucial role of family history as he considers man 'a complex multiform creature that bore within itself strange legacies of thought and passions, and whose very flesh was tainted with the monstrous maladies of the dead' (Wilde 2005: 288). Each of the portraits turns into a mirror as he notices his resemblance to his wicked ancestors, and wonders what 'strange poisonous germ crept from body to body till it reached his own' (Wilde 2005: 288).[4]

The novel remains ambiguous about whether homosexuality features, or not, among Dorian's sins. When it appeared, however, the press reviews did not hesitate to draw a direct link between Dorian's moral degradation, triggered by his encounter with the yellow book, and criminalized sexual practices. *The Daily Chronicle* described Wilde's tale as 'unclean' and 'French' — 'a tale spawned from the leprous literature of the French decadents' (Beckson 1970: 72). *The St. James Gazette* judged the book a 'stupid and vulgar piece of work' and suggested that it made the author liable for prosecution (Beckson 1970: 68–69). *The Scots Observer* read it as a text of 'medico-legal' interest and went as far as connecting it with a recent scandal that involved a network of telegraph boys who also worked as male prostitutes. 'Mr Wilde has brains, and art, and style', the reviewer wrote, 'but if he can write for none but outlawed noblemen and perverted telegraph boys, the sooner he takes to tailoring (or some other decent trade) the better for his own reputation and the public moral' (Beckson 1970: 75).

Max Nordau, in *Degeneration* (1892), placed Wilde, the 'quasi-heraldic symbol of the aesthetes' (1993: 317), among the narcissistic 'ego-maniacs'. A convinced supporter of art's impact on society, he questioned Wilde's belief in the separation of art and ethics and refused to spend any time analysing fiction that he considered a mere copy of Huysmans' and Baudelaire's works. He focused instead on Wilde's eccentric lifestyle, particularly his pose as a dandy-aesthete. Starting from the assumption that that the 'natural' aim of clothing is to attract the attention of the opposite sex, he denounced Wilde's dandyism as a 'pathological aberration of a racial instinct' and as 'a purely anti-socialistic, ego-maniacal recklessness' (1993: 318). 'What really determines his actions', he wrote referring to Wilde, 'is the hysterical craving to be noticed, to occupy the attention of the world with himself, to get talked about' (1993: 317).

Building on Cesare Lombroso's analysis of artistic genius as a form of madness, as well as on Paul Bourget's analogy between the social organism and literary language, Nordau compared the work of the aesthetes and the decadents to the practice of the born criminal. Both, he reasoned, were guilty of excessive individualism at the expense of the social whole, and therefore constituted a threat to a healthy, organic society. For Nordau, the difference between the artist 'who complacently represents what is reprehensible, vicious, criminal, approves of it, perhaps glorifies it' and 'the criminal who actually commits it' was only a matter of degree. Just like criminals, aesthetes and decadents needed to be kept under control: 'It never occurs to us to permit the criminal by organic disposition to expand his individuality in crime, and just as little can it be expected of us to permit the degenerate artist to expand his individuality in immoral works of art' (Nordau 1993: 326).

Nordau's reasons for placing Wilde among the degenerates were narcissism and the exacerbated need for attention, rather than homosexuality. For him, non-normative sexual preferences were one among many symptoms, rather than the primary cause of the disease of the decadents. Nonetheless, *Degeneration*, which appeared in English in 1895, the same year in which Wilde was tried, contributed to popularize the belief that decadent literature was the output of degenerate minds. Moreover, it played a role in the association of Wilde's personal conduct with his artistic production, and encouraged the jury to search in *The Picture of Dorian Gray* for evidence of Wilde's homosexuality (see Hyde 1948).

The perception of a relation between narcissism and homosexuality outlived Wilde's trial, and found productive ground in psychoanalysis. In his 1914 reading of *The Picture of Dorian Gray*, Otto Rank listed the numerous references to the myth of Narcissus,[5] and concluded that Dorian's narcissistic attitude was intimately connected to 'his imposing egoism, his inability to love, and his abnormal sexual life' and that 'the intimate friendship with young men ... are attempts to realize the erotic infatuation with his own youthful image' (Rank 1971: 71). Rank was building on his own 'Beitrag zu Narzissismus' [Essay on Narcissism], published two years earlier, as well as on the work of Sigmund Freud, who, in the *Three Essays on Sexuality* (1905) and in the 1914 essay 'On Narcissism: An Introduction' (Freud 1978b), had characterized homosexuality as a particular kind of narcissism. Freud, in turn, was building on nineteenth-century sexology, especially the work of Havelock Ellis, who in his *Studies in the Psychology of Sex* (1897) had stressed the interplay of narcissism and sexual inversion. Wilde was familiar with Ellis's work, and had challenged traditional interpretations of narcissism in his poem in prose 'The Disciple', a rewriting of the Narcissus myth published in 1894, which Gregory Bredbeck reads as 'an intervention into the psycho-mythology of Victorian sexology' (1994: 48). In this poem, Wilde re-wrote the Greek myth through an inversion that shifted the focus from Narcissus to the pool of water that reflects him. For Bredbeck, inversion, as a rhetorical device, challenged inversion as a sexual concept, disrupting 'sexology's increasingly stringent efforts to reify identity as a universalized and intransigent phenomenon' (1994: 59). *The Picture of Dorian Gray*, however, took a more ambiguous approach, and Eve Kosofsky Sedgwick argues that it established a pattern through which narcissism became a screen for homosexuality: 'How does a man's love of other men become a love of the same? The process is graphic in *Dorian Gray* [...]. The novel takes a plot that is distinctively one of male–male desire, the competition between Basil Hallward and Lord Henry Wotton for Dorian Gray's love, and condenses it into the plot of the mysterious bond of figural likeness and figural expiation between Dorian Gray and his own portrait' (1990: 60). Steven Bruhm goes as far as suggesting that *Dorian Gray* announced 'the theory of narcissism that psychoanalysis will work out as the master-narrative for the twentieth-century queer man' (2001: 72). Other readings of the novel (see Glick 2001: 129–63) shift the focus from narcissism to the related concept of fetishism, stressing how anthropological and sexual fetishism interweave with the fetishism of commodity, the process through which, as Marx argues, objects lose connection with their use value (Marx 1963: 93).

Since *The Picture of Dorian Gray* had come to represent decadence in Britain, when Wilde was condemned, the label of 'degenerate' was applied, by extension, to the fiction associated with the movement. The rumour that Wilde had been arrested with a 'yellow book' under his arm — a French novel that, according to the customs of the time, was wrapped in yellow paper — led to vandalism at The Bodley Head, the publishing house led by John Lane that issued *The Yellow Book*, a literary quarterly in which many of the writers associated with decadence had found a home for their pieces. In the attempt to dissociate his business from Wilde, Lane removed him from the list of contributors for The Bodley Head and also dismissed Aubrey Beardsley, the illustrator of Wilde's *Salomé*. Nevertheless, many writers feared repercussions and looked for new publishers for their own work (MacLeod 2006: 6). Wilde's name became taboo in respectable circles, but the author continued to exert a strong influence on literary culture (Bristow 2010: 21).

The Enamel Mask: Max Beerbohm's *The Happy Hypocrite*

Max Beerbohm (1872–1956) attended the University of Oxford in the 1880s, when aestheticism was at its peak. For several years, he was under the influence of Wilde's writing, which had a considerable impact on his style. Wilde's persona also influenced his pose as a dandy. In 1893, when he was still a student, Beerbohm published an article titled 'Oscar Wilde by an American', in which, posing as an outsider, he praised *Salomé* as a great work, lamenting that it had been denied a stage licence. In the same year, he met Wilde in person and became acquainted with his circle of friends (Hall 2002: 28). Soon, however, he distanced himself from aestheticism and began to caricature Wilde. When Wilde complained about Beerbohm's drawings, Beerbohm responded by writing to Reginald Turner, who was a mutual friend: 'So long as the man's head interests me, I shall continue to draw it. He is simply an unpaid model of mine and as such he should behave' (Hall 2002: 73). In the essay 'A Peep into the Past', written in 1894, Beerbohm portrayed Wilde as overweight, elderly and outdated, mocked his 'womanly care and taste', and made fun of the 'constant succession of page-boys, which so startles the neighbourhood' (1972: 4). The piece had been designed for the first issue of *The Yellow Book*, but at the last minute Beerbohm replaced it with 'A Defence of Cosmetics', a satirical manifesto of decadence that parodied the aesthetic of Wilde and Walter Pater, while at the same time mimicking their style. The article caused a large public outrage. 'A Peep into the Past' was scheduled to appear in a subsequent number, but became unpublishable after Wilde was arrested.

Dennis Denisoff stresses that for Beerbohm, caricature, as a form of art, did not involve a moral judgement. On the contrary, Beerbohm maintained that, by forcing the audience to compare exaggeration with reality, parody contributed to empathy and understanding: 'if a caricature affected us at all towards its subject, it would affect us favourably towards it. Tragedy, said Aristotle, purges us of superfluous awe, by evocation, and comedy likewise purges us of superfluous contempt' (1953: 124). Building on Jonathan Dollimore's definition of camp as 'an invasion and subversion of other sensibilities' that 'works via parody, pastiche, and exaggeration', Denisoff contends that 'A Peep into the Past' and 'A Defence of Cosmetics' partake in this aesthetic (2006: 311). 'Notwithstanding the fact that Beerbohm suggests that he viewed as fallacious and elitist the position that people should direct all their attention to beauty alone', he writes, '[Beerbohm] nevertheless used camp to sustain aestheticist concerns regarding personal pleasure, sympathy, and identificatory diversity' (2006: 127).

'A Defence of Cosmetics' was issued at the time when Wilde was at the height of success as a writer and dramatist, and in the same year in which Sarah Grand, with 'The New Aspect of the Woman Question' (1894), criticized the theory that men and women belonged to different spheres and demanded that women be given the same opportunities as men. Implicitly drawing on Baudelaire's 'Éloge du maquillage' [In Praise of Cosmetics], the essay, subsequently re-published under the title 'The Pervasion of Rouge' in Beerbohm's collective works (1896), established a link between cosmetics and the mask and mocked the decadent's cult of artificiality. It also engaged with the premises of *The Picture of Dorian Gray*: the capacity of facial features to map character and emotions, and the interpretation of the surface as the reverse of the soul. Beerbohm challenged a theory of masks based on antithesis, upon differences between a natural and artificial self, and argued that, for artists and dandies, the mask *is* the self. He then outlined the consequences that the triumph of artifice would have for Victorian women, presenting the 'kingdom of rouge' as the latest development of a process of evolution. Women, he noted, had lately begun to demand the same rights as men, but the enamel mask would halt their efforts, since caring for their masks would become a priority, and any kind of action would cause 'powder [to] fly, enamel [to] crack' (Beerbohm 1896: 115). 'Artifice', he continued, 'is the strength of the world, and in that same mask of paint and powder, shadowed with vermeil tinct and most trimly pencilled, is woman's strength' (1896: 112). Comments such as these functioned as a parody of the decadents' cult of the artificial, but were also directed at the New Women, the 'horrific pioneers of womanhood' who, by practising sport, riding bicycles, writing and even demanding the right to vote, threatened to 'intrude into men's domain' (Beerbohm 1896: 113).

These ideas stand at the core of the parable *The Happy Hypocrite: A Fairy Tale for Old Men*, originally published in *The Yellow Book* in 1896, a year after Wilde's arrest, and later issued as a book, in 1914. Beerbohm acknowledged Wilde's influence, and sent the story to him along with his collected works when Wilde came out of prison. Wilde interpreted the piece as a reversal of *Dorian Gray*, and in 1897 wrote to Reginald Turner: 'I have just read Max's Happy Hypocrite, beginning at the end, as one should always do. It is quite wonderful, and to one who was once the author of Dorian Gray, full of no vulgar surprises of style or incident' (Hall 2002: 39). In a letter to Beerbohm, he added 'The implied and accepted recognition of Dorian Gray in the story cheers me. I have always been disappointed that my story had suggested no other work of art in others' (Hall 2002: 39).

The Happy Hypocrite is set in the Regency period, at the time when the cult of dandyism originated in Britain, and, like *The Picture of Dorian Gray*, it revolves around a transformation that brings about an identity crisis. Lord George Hell is a 'greedy, destructive, and disobedient' dandy who leads a life of excess without attempting to hide it (Beerbohm 1914: 11). His face, which is 'tarnished by the reflection of this world's vanity', is a testament to his sins (Beerbohm 1914: 24). One day, he falls in love with the young actress Jenny Mere and asks her to be his wife, but she refuses on the grounds that she can only marry a man 'whose face is wonderful as are the faces of the saints' (Beerbohm 1914: 25). To win Jenny's love, Lord George visits Mr. Aeneas, a famous mask-maker who has helped many distinguished men, including the dandy Beau Brummell, hide their adulteries, and asks for a mask that fulfils Jenny's request. The mask is made of fine wax, its texture closely resembles that of skin, and completely merges with the human face:

> [...] while Julius heated the inner side of the waxen mask over a little lamp, Mr. Aeneas stood over Lord George gently smearing his features with some sweet-scented pomade. Then he took the mask and powdered its inner side,

quite soft and warm now, with a fluffy puff. 'Keep quite still, for one instant,' he said, and clapped the mask firmly on his Lordship's upturned face. So soon as he was sure of its perfect adhesion, he took from his assistant's hand a silver file and a little wooden spatula, with which he proceeded to pare down the edge of the mask, where it joined the neck and ears. At length, all traces of the 'join' were obliterated. It remained only to arrange the curls of the lordly wig over the waxen brow.

The disguise was done. When Lord George looked through the eyelets of his mask into the mirror that was placed in his hand, he saw a face that was saintly, itself a mirror of true love. (Beerbohm 1914: 38–39)

Lord George marries Jenny wearing the mask, under the false name of 'George Heaven'. He abandons his extravagant look and criminal lifestyle, gives away all his wealth and leads a simple life with his wife. However, his ex-lover, a performer no longer in her prime with a French name ('La Gambogi'), has seen him purchase the mask and threatens to destroy their happiness. One day, she shows up at the cottage where he and Jenny are happily living together and orders him to unmask. After a fight, she succeeds in tearing the mask off; however, she discovers that 'his face was even as his mask had been. Line for line, feature for feature, it was the same. It was a saint's face' (Beerbohm 1914: 68).

Beerbohm is reticent about the vices of his protagonist: all we know is that they include indulgence in drinking and food, excessive expenses on clothing, arrogance, unkindness, dishonesty and debauchery, but the list, as Beerbohm stresses, is not comprehensive. Like *The Picture of Dorian Gray*, *The Happy Hypocrite* associates privilege and crime, the aesthete and the criminal. Both tales revolve around deceit and establish links between fraud, masks and disguises. The protagonists examine their faces in the mirror, contrasting youthful features to the 'tarnished' face, which they keep hidden, and lead a secret life in disguise and under an assumed name. Like Dorian, Lord George delights in costumes and adores the theatre; his beloved is a young actress who resembles Dorian's fiancée in her use of an infantile rhetoric and her passion for acting. Both Sybil Vane and Jenny Mere are working-class women; both see in the faces of their lovers a signifier of moral qualities, but also of class. Since Lord George and Jenny's marriage is built on deceit, it can be seen as exemplifying the principle that Lord Henry, in *The Picture of Dorian Gray*, finds at the core of all relationships: 'When one is in love, one always begins by deceiving one's self, and one always ends by deceiving others, that is what the world calls a romance' (Wilde 2005: 214). In both tales, the mask is increasingly associated with shame, and the threat that the fraud be publicly exposed is embodied by a witness who has worshipped the protagonists, is familiar with their past, and has either been kept at a distance or rejected (Basil/La Gambogi). Just as Dorian assaults Basil with 'the mad passion of a hunted animal' after the painter has seen the changes in the portrait (Wilde 2005: 300), Lord George threatens to drive *La Gambogi*, 'violently from the garden' before she attacks his face 'like a panther' (Beerbohm 1914: 77).

In other ways, Beerbohm's fairy tale functions as an inversion of *The Picture of Dorian Gray*. Whereas Dorian goes from innocence to a life of sins, Lord George follows the opposite route, from moral degradation to redemption. At the peak of his criminal life, Dorian alternates public roles with secret outings, whereas Lord George never conceals his behaviour, 'so that, in time, every one knew how horrid he was' (Beerbohm 1914: 12).[6] In *The Picture of Dorian Gray*, the mask (Dorian's face) becomes a mirror, in *The Happy Hypocrite* it is the mirror (Lord George's face) that turns into the mask. Most importantly, whereas Wilde's novel revolves around the friendship and reciprocal influence between three men, Beerbohm, in re-writing Wilde, removes the homosocial context and focuses on a heterosexual romance.

Beerbohm was drawn to homosexual milieus and was part of a circle of friends that was 'about as openly homosexual as you could find in the London of the 1880s' (Hall 2002: 34). He was close to Aubrey Beardsley, Robert Ross and Lord Alfred Douglas, whose involvement with Wilde led to his arrest, and was an intimate friend of Reginald Turner. His correspondence with Turner displays tolerance towards male–male sexual interaction, but also increasing irritation with Wilde's self-exposure and lack of precaution.[7] The letters written during Wilde's first trial, rather than serious concern for him, betray curiosity and amusement. Beerbohm returned from New York to attend Wilde's second trial, wrote enthusiastically to Turner of Wilde's speech about 'the Love that dares not tell his name'[8] and, according to Beerbohm's biographer, went as far as visiting the office of the police inspector who had arrested him. Here, he was mortified to see that his caricatures had been used as evidence: 'I hadn't realized till that moment how wicked it was. I felt as if I had contributed to the dossier against Oscar' (Behrman 1960: 85–86). As late as 1920, however, he declined an invitation to review Frank Harris's biography of Oscar Wilde, and commented that the association would involve a 'raking up of the old Sodomitic cesspool — the cesspool that was opened in 1895' (Beerbohm 1988: 118). Overall, Beerbohm was tolerant of homosexuality, but did not approve of its public display.

Neither Wilde's nor Beerbohm's tale explicitly violates sexual norms, but while *The Picture of Dorian Gray* engages with homosexuality through coded references and allusions, *The Happy Hypocrite* seems to displace sexual meaning altogether (Lane 1994: 943). However, by describing his protagonist as a mature, overweight man who dresses in Georgian costume, Beerbohm was effectively caricaturing Wilde. Moreover, *The Happy Hypocrite* assumes a different meaning if read in conjunction with the essay 'A Defence of Cosmetics' and with Beerbohm's letters to Reginald Turner, which he wrote intending from the outset that they be published (Beerbohm 1964: 49). In these letters, Beerbohm acknowledges that the source for Jenny Mere, the muse who inspires Lord George's transformation, was the sixteen-year-old music-hall actress Cissie Loftus, who also features in 'A Defence of Cosmetics'. In the correspondence, Beerbohm's infatuation with Cissie, whom he addresses as 'Mistress Mere', temporarily displaces the focus on Wilde. The attitude of the author towards Cissie Loftus, however, parodies Dorian's stance towards Sybil Vane in *The Picture of Dorian Gray*. Like Dorian, Beerbohm falls in love with Cissie by seeing her acting. He attends all her performances, draws her for *The Sketch*, and even goes as far as wandering through the neighbourhood where she lives with her mother (Hall 2002: 100). In a similar way to how Dorian seeks the approval of Basil and Lord Henry, Beerbohm fills his letters to Turner with details about 'Mistress Mere'. In *The Picture of Dorian Gray*, Dorian comments that Sybil's death seems to him a 'wonderful ending to a wonderful play', with 'the terrible beauty of Greek tragedy', and Lord Henry convinces him that her death has forever changed her into a muse (Wilde 2005: 253). In his own letters, Beerbohm wishes that the purity of his love be preserved by Cissie's death, and often fantasizes on how this could come about. On 14 August 1893, he writes: 'Picture her moving always between the walls of some nunnery [...] Sister Cecilia. It would be lovelier almost than if we married — unless she were to die in childbirth. I cannot imagine anything lovelier than that' (Beerbohm 1964: 47). On 19 August, his aunt's funeral became an occasion to imagine a similar scenario: 'All the time that they were reading the words of the service — "Earth to earth, ashes to ashes" — I tried to fancy that it was my young wife Cecilia, *aetat*; 17, who was being mourned and that whole scene belonged to the future. Oh how lovely it would be' (Beerbohm 1964: 53). On 23 September, he uses an image that recurs in *The Happy Hypocrite* — in which both Lord George and Jenny are literally struck by love's arrows — and wishes that 'Cupid had shot his arrow not to quicken my heart but to make rigid her limbs' (Beerbohm 1964: 70). He then compares his love for Cissie to Turner's feelings for 'Miss Cumberlidge', a fictitious figure that Beerbohm used to circumvent Turner's homosexuality: 'Forgive me, dear Reg, for meandering so far: I am sure there must have been times when you have wished Miss Cumberlidge to be petrified for an eternal moment' (Beerbohm 1964: 70). Since Beerbohm was familiar with Turner's sexual preference, and since the figure of Miss Cumberlidge was Beerbohm's invention, the comparison underlines the extent to which his obsession with 'Cissie/Mistress Mere' is based on make-believe. Just as Dorian falls out of love with Sybil when the actress, distracted by her love, loses focus in her performance, Beerbohm's infatuation ends abruptly when Cissie changes her acting style and performs with a mask of make-up:

> By the way, it is all over. I hate Cissy Loftus, or rather I can see her now with no emotion but regret — cold regret. I saw her last night and she had gone a step too far. She had piled a Pelion of rouge upon an Ossa of powder: her eyes shone again and she had even abandoned the little prologue about 'kind permission' and 'a few of our leading music-hall artists' ... the flowers were very lovely and were intended I am sure for Mistress Mere, not for the tawdry creature made in her image. (Beerbohm 1964: 72)

In 'A Defence of Cosmetics' written in the following year, Beerbohm writes again about Cissie, emphasizing how, after the first performances in which she had 'nothing to tinge the ivory of her cheeks', she suddenly presented herself with 'her pretty face rouged with the best of them' (1896: 121). He then stresses the absurdity of considering her performance 'a triumph of naturalness over the jaded spirit of modernity' (1896: 21) and argues that her charm had from the outset to do with artifice, cunning and travesty:

> [...] with her grave insouciance, Miss Cissie Loftus had much of the reserve that is one of the factors of feminine perfection, and to most comes only, as I have

said, with artifice. Her features played very, very slightly. And in truth, this may have been one of the reasons of her great success. For expression is but too often the ruin of a face; and, since we cannot, as yet, so order the circumstances of life that women shall never be betrayed into 'an unbecoming emotion', when the brunette shall never have cause to blush nor La Gioconda to frown, the safest way by far is to create, by brush and pigments, artificial expression for every face. (Beerbohm 1896: 21–22)

In this passage, Beerbohm places the enamel mask extolled in 'A Defence of Cosmetics' on Cissie Loftus. Like the death fantasy of the letters, the mask keeps Cissie's features 'beautiful and without meaning' (Beerbohm 1964: 10) and (temporarily) prevents her from turning into one of the 'awful New Women' that Beerbohm warns against in his essay and letters (1964: 104).

For Rank and Freud, stories centred on the double involved a moment of self-recognition in which the protagonist discovers that his desire cannot be fulfilled and that behind the love-object there is death, rather than love (Rank 1971). Insofar as it provides the protagonist with a different identity, the mask of Lord George embodies the double. However, there is also another, not quite explicit mask in the narrative, as *La Gambogi* hints when she says to Lord George: 'Your wife's mask [...] is even better than yours' (Beerbohm 1914: 66). Both Lord George and Jenny Mere, Beerbohm suggests, are wearing masks. This subtext complicates a reading in which the mask represents the expectations of the female protagonist ('the face of a saint' and 'an image of true love'). Like Lord George, Jenny Mere also wears a mask that merges with her face. It is the mask, rather than the human being, that in the tale becomes the object of desire, worship and devotion, and that in Beerbohm's essays and letters is placed into connection with death imagery.

Scholars have interpreted *The Happy Hypocrite* biographically, as indicative of Beerbohm's philosophy of the mask. 'Max early on knew what he wanted to be and created himself in that image', writes John Hall. 'Over the course of time (much like his own fairy-tale character, Lord George Hell) he grew to become his mask' (Hall 2002: 20). However, if we read Beerbohm's fairy tale in the context of the debates raised by Wilde's arrest, its parodic elements acquire ideological implications. Wilde's trials, as Cohen has argued, constructed the identity of the homosexual in antithesis to that of the bourgeois male, defining 'healthy, natural and true' behaviours in contrast to illicit sexual practices (Cohen 1987: 801). By turning the dandy-aesthete into a bourgeois, Beerbohm is apparently complicit in this logic. However, the focus on masks, combined with the emphasis on hypocrisy in the title, encourages the interpretation of the tale as a parody of late Victorian values and sexual norms. Beerbohm echoes Wilde's philosophy of masks, going farther than Wilde does in the novel by disregarding references to heredity and moral physiognomy, and by portraying identity as performative. The logical extension of this proposition is that there is no standard of behaviour or gender norm, but only a performed self. On the other hand, this theory does not extend to women. In the only instance in which Beerbohm imagines for Cissie Loftus a future other than an imminent death, he envisions her confined to his household:

> Why doesn't she act only for me night after night? You and a few polished admirers could come whenever you liked; she should receive no salary but have breakfast and lunch and dinner with me — supper as an occasional treat when she has been sweeter than ever, in which case we should never sup. If she wished it, she should have breakfast in bed sometimes, with iced tea and little pieces of toast shaped like letters of the alphabet, for she probably cannot spell yet — she left her convent too soon. In the morning she could help me draw caricatures for the paper. Either she must do this or go back to the convent. (Beerbohm 1964: 51)

While the fairy tale does not deploy humour in the same way, it ends with a similar scenario: Lord George decides that Jenny Mere will not continue performing, and will dance for him only, dedicating her life to marriage. Unlike the New Women of the 1890s, the protagonist of *The Happy Hypocrite* does not contest the notion of different spheres. In contrast to the menacing *Gambogi*, Jenny Mere gives up any public appearance and ambition, lives happily without any material good, and dedicates her life to her husband.

The New Women and the decadents, as Linda Dowling has demonstrated, were often attacked on the same grounds and accused of disrupting masculine and feminine attributes (Dowling 1979: 438). In Beerbohm's 'A Defence of Cosmetics', the decadents are the object of parody, the New Women the material through which parody is developed. The mask purchased by Lord George is fundamentally conservative, but still demonstrates the superiority of art over nature, performance over biology. The mask that Beerbohm placed on Jenny Mere, in contrast, does not bring about change. It functions as a device that forces women to refrain from action and that stops them from intruding into men's domain (Beerbohm 1914: 115), underlining Beerbohm's concerns about rejection of Victorian constructions of the feminine, and anxiety about increasing blurring of the boundaries of assigned gender roles.

A Disease with no Name: Richard Le Gallienne's *The Worshipper of the Image*

Like Max Beerbohm, the poet, essayist, journalist and critic Richard Le Gallienne (1866–1947), in his youth, worshipped Wilde as an idol. Originally from a middle-class family from Liverpool, he moved to London in the early 1890s, began collaborating with John Lane, and along with Wilde, W. B. Yeats and Lionel Johnson, frequented the Rhymers' Club. As a reader for The Bodley Head and as a reviewer with a weekly column in *The Star*, Le Gallienne had influence in London's literary world. As James Nelson acknowledges, he was 'a characteristic personality of the 1890s, who played a significant role at The Bodley Head during its formative years and was a major contributor to the defining periodical of the 1890s, *The Yellow Book*' (1971: 215). Le Gallienne's fame, however, did not survive his time, and scholars have criticized his 'anachronistic romanticism' and 'blindness' to the emerging literary developments (Stanford 1970: 205; Nelson 1971: 215).

At The Bodley Head, Le Gallienne stood out for his eccentric persona, with expensive outfits, effeminate looks and long hair. With a Francophile gesture, he had added 'Le' to the original 'Gallienne', and Whittington-Egan and Smerdon comment that 'nothing infuriated him more, intoxicated as he was with the mellifluous cadences of "Richard Le Gallienne", than to be hailed as Tom, Dick or Gallienne' (1960: 44). His biographers stress his attitude as a *poseur*, his tendency to play a role and live beyond his means (Burdett 1925: 176), and note that he was at heart a 'new hedonist' enamoured of beauty (Nelson 1971: 250). They also underline his religious enthusiasm: 'throughout his life, he defined himself as an Anglican, a deist, a Buddhist and a phallus-worshipper' (Whittington-Egan and Smerdon 1960: 56).

Le Gallienne was associated with the decadents, but his attitude towards the movement was ambivalent. In his editorial role, he supported the work of Arthur Symons, W. B. Yeats and Lionel Johnson, as well as the New Woman writer George Egerton (Mary Dume) (Brack 1987: 173). In the 1890s, however, he began to position himself among the English traditionalists. The collection *English Poems*, published in 1892, condemned the unwholesomeness of contemporary poetic production and its foreign influence, while the parody 'A Decadent to his Soul' defined decadence as a longing for strange and perverse sins (Thornton and Thain 1997: 33). In his weekly reviews, Le Gallienne built on Paul Bourget, Max Nordau and Havelock Ellis's concern with the part–whole relationship and described decadence as 'any point of view, seriously taken, which ignores the complete view'. He also noted that 'decadence [...] comes of the decadent regarding of his theme *in vacuo*, isolated from its various relation — of morality, of pity, of humour, of religion' (Le Gallienne 1896a: 25). Like his predecessors, he characterized decadence as a form of insanity through which artists lose sight of the whole and focus on isolated fragments and experiences:

> In all great vital literature, the theme, great or small, is considered in all its relations near and far, and above all in relation to the sum-total of things, to the Infinite, as we phrase it; in decadent literature the relations, the due proportions, are ignored. To notice only the picturesque effect of a beggar's rags, like Gautier; the colour-scheme of a tippler's nose, like M. Huysmans; to consider one's mother merely prismatically, like Mr. Whistler — these are examples of the decadent attitude. At bottom, decadence is merely limited thinking, often insane thinking. (Le Gallienne 1896a: 231)

These statements appeared paradoxical for an artist whose work was considered the epitome of decadence, and led Hubert Crackanthorpe to note that, in criticizing the decadents, Le Gallienne was 'hoist[ed] with his own petard' (1984: 266). In sum, while Le Gallienne sympathized with some of the decadents' accomplishments, he condemned their excesses (Burdett 1925: 190), and became increasingly opposed to the movement during the 1890s (Dowling 1978: 283; Nelson 1971: 211).

After Wilde's arrest, Le Gallienne published 'The Boom in Yellow' (1896b), an essay that attempted to dissociate *The Yellow Book* from the French literature that had inspired it. In this piece, he defended the positive association of the colour yellow and described green as the colour of 'the green carnation', 'the badge of but a small schism of aesthetes, and not worn by the great body of the more catholic lovers of beauty' (Le Gallienne 1896b: 79). For late Victorian readers, this was a reference to Wilde, as *The Green Carnation* was the title of a novel by Robert

Hichen in which the protagonist was modelled on the author of *The Picture of Dorian Gray*. Moreover, Wilde had used the subtitle 'A Study in Green' for his essay 'Pen, Pencil and Poison', in which he commented that the 'curious love of green [...] in individuals, is always the sign of a subtle artistic temperament, and in nations is said to denote a laxity, if not a decadence of morals' (Wilde 2007a: 108). Furthermore, green was the colour that Havelock Ellis and John Addington Symonds, in *Sexual Inversion* (1897), had associated with same-sex interaction (Bredbeck 1994: 48). A few years later, Le Gallienne regretted that he had not been able to support Wilde. He acknowledged 'I often wish I had made some sign to him [Wilde] in those days — but, God knows, my own hill needed climbing, and doubtless, I could have done little with him with that crew around him, and that *folie des grandeurs* in his brain' (Whittington-Egan and Smerdon 1960: 403).

Whittington-Egan and Smerdon describe Le Gallienne's *The Worshipper of the Image*, written in 1898 and published in 1899 by The Bodley Head, as 'an unwholesome little book, palely reflecting all the melodramatic stage properties of decadence'. They also underline Wilde's influence throughout the text: 'Reading it, one understands the oft-quoted criticism of Le Gallienne's work as "largely Wilde-and-water". It comes out of the Dorian Gray stable for sure' (1960: 362). Like *The Picture of Dorian Gray*, *The Worshipper of the Image* combined the gothic and the fantastic and engaged with the relationship of art and life. It described the transformation of a young man triggered by a portrait, and became increasingly dark in its development, concluding with a moral message. However, the portrait around which the story revolved was not a painting, but a mask. Moreover, the mask was not the fruit of the author's imagination, but a historical artefact, the so-called cast of the *Inconnue de la Seine*, of which Le Gallienne owned a copy (Phillips 1982: 322).

In *The Worshipper of the Image* the mask, like the portrait in Wilde's novel, captures its model's youth and beauty and is at the same time a memento of death. Antony, a poet who lives in a lonely valley with his wife Beatrice and their daughter Wonder, finds in a sculptor's shop, among Greek and Roman sculptures, the death mask of a drowned young woman that reproduces exactly the features of his wife. He brings it home, christens it Silencieux, and gradually falls in love with the image, neglecting his wife and spending his days in the company of the mask, who becomes a muse for his poetry. One day, he finds poison on Silencieux's lips. When his child, after kissing the mask, falls ill and dies, he resolves to destroy it, but he is unable to break it and buries it in the woods. A few months later, he retrieves it and descends into madness. Feeling abandoned, Beatrice commits suicide by drowning and when Antony goes back to the mask, he finds its eyes open and its peaceful features distorted into an image of death.

Throughout the story, the death mask mostly hangs on the wall like a portrait, but Antony occasionally wears it as a disguise. Like the portrait in Wilde's tale, the mask functions as a fetish in an anthropological and sexual sense. Insofar as Antony believes that it speaks to him and even promises it a sacrifice, the cast, as the title suggests, is as an object of worship and devotion. On the other hand, Antony experiences a 'strange desire' for the mask, that he defines as 'a fanciful variation of earthly love'; 'a love of beauty centring itself upon some form midway between life and death, inanimate and yet alive, human and yet removed from the accidents of humanity' (Le Gallienne 1900: 30–31). He is initially drawn to the cast because of its resemblance to his wife, and when the attraction becomes autonomous, he convinces himself that, like the Dante of *Vita Nova*, he has transformed the earthly passion for Beatrice into spiritual love. Soon, however, he admits that his desire is a form of erotic yearning.

Louise Kaplan notes that 'unlike a fully alive human being with dangerous, unpredictable desires who must be wooed and courted, fetish objects are relatively safe, easily available, and undemanding reciprocity' (2006: 7). In *The Worshipper of The Image*, the mask petrifies and deadens the features of the female character and provides an easily reachable object of desire for the male protagonist. As an imperfect human being, Beatrice demands too much attention and, once a muse, has become a distraction to Antony's dedication to poetry. 'Women, as some witty French men once put it,' notes Lord Henry in *The Picture of Dorian Gray*, 'inspire us with the desire to do masterpieces and always prevent us from carrying them out' (Wilde 2005: 236). 'To turn a muse into a wife,' reflects Antony, 'however long and faithfully loved, is to bid good-bye to the muse' (Le Gallienne 1900: 26). A few pages later we learn that 'Beatrice was beginning to bore him, not merely by her sadness, which his absorption prevented his realising except in flashes, but by her very resemblance to the Image — of which, from having been the beloved original, she was, in his eyes, becoming an indifferent materialisation' (Le Gallienne 1900: 34). Like Wilde's novel, the tale is embedded in moral physiognomy. Reflecting on the likeness with Silencieux, Beatrice wonders: '[I]f there is any truth in those who tell us that in the mould and lines of our faces and hands — yes! And in every secret marking of our bodies — our fates are written as in a parchment; would it be not reasonable to surmise, perhaps to fear, that the writing should mean the same on one face as on the other, and that the fates as well as the faces prove identical?' (Le Gallienne 1900: 20).

As in Wilde's tale, the portrait gradually begins to change and to assume human features. From the point of view of the protagonist it is treated and referred to as if it were a whole person. As early as the first description it is referred to as a 'face' and even as a 'woman':

> *The face* was smiling, a smile of great peace, and also of a strange cunning. One other characteristic it had: *the woman* looked as though at any moment she would suddenly open her eyes, and if you turned away from her and looked again, she seemed to be smiling to herself because she had opened them that moment behind your back, and just closed them again in time.
> It was a face that never changed and yet was always changing. (Le Gallienne 1900: 13, emphasis added)

In naming the portrait of Beatrice Silencieux ['the silent one'], Antony defies grammatical conventions and declines the French adjective in the masculine. Le Gallienne comments on this idiosyncrasy in a footnote, acknowledging that he is aware of the mistake, but that 'in such fanciful names [...] such licence has always been considered allowable' (Le Gallienne 1900: 11). The christening of the mask initiates transformation through which Silencieux, no longer the exclusive double of Beatrice, begins to acquire androgynous features.

As in Wilde's novel, an inverse relation develops between the model and the image. In the second chapter, we learn that the mask looks 'terribly alive' and that Beatrice is 'as white as the image'; in the same episode, it is Beatrice who is referred to as a 'created thing' (Le Gallienne 1900: 22, 21, 19). Gradually, Silencieux replaces Beatrice in Antony's affection: 'Every day new life welled into Silencieux's face, as every day life ebbed from the face of Beatrice [...]. For the love he gave to Silencieux Antony must take away from Beatrice, from whom as the days went by he grew more and more withdrawn' (Le Gallienne 1900: 32). As the story progresses, Beatrice grows more and more passive, while Silencieux, through Antony's hallucinations, begins to speak, eat, dance and drink as if it were a woman. Beatrice regains her role as a character when Antony, after losing his daughter, buries the mask in the wood, and falls again into passivity once he retrieves it. In the first chapter, Antony 'almost' addresses Beatrice as 'Silencieux,' and he becomes confused again when, in his delirium, he mistakes Beatrice for the mask. Silencieux also takes over Beatrice's role as a muse for Antony's poetry. When, addressing her as 'Sphynx of the North', he dedicates a poem to Beatrice, she rejects any association with it, claiming that it was written for the mask. Later in the story, Antony describes the poetry written under Silencieux's influence as 'barren' and 'not good' (Le Gallienne 1900: 59).

Like Dorian, Antony leads a double life and develops an interest in costumes and disguises. He also delights in playing with the cast, providing it with an imaginary body. As soon as he brings the cast home, he lays it down in a corner of the couch and covers its neck with a black cloak, as it 'has veritably been a living woman weary for sleep' (Le Gallienne 1900: 22). He repeats this game, in different poses, when he sneaks out of the house to meet Silencieux at night. Soon the mask's imaginary body merges with his own, as he lies 'in a hollow with her head upon his knee' and covers 'her' with his coat (Le Gallienne 1900: 37). As Antony's madness progresses, Silencieux entertains him with theatrical spectacles:

> ... they ran in and out among pleasures together, joined strange dances and sang strange songs. They clapped their hands to jugglers and acrobats, and animals tortured into talent. And sometimes, as the gaudy theatre resounded about them, they looked so still at each other that all the rest faded away, and they were left alone with each other's eyes (Le Gallienne 1900: 60–61)

Since a mask does not have hands to clap, the passage suggests that Antony has begun to wear Silencieux, and that the death mask has turned from a decorative item into a performative tool. Through Silencieux's conversations with Antony, in which the cast 'echo[es]' his words, often repeating exactly what he says, we learn that Silencieux has had many male and female lovers, 'far from here' and 'long ago' (Le Gallienne 1900: 46), and that all of them were poets. Silencieux's first appearance was in Mytilene, where she loved the Greek poet Sappho (Le Gallienne 1900: 47). We then learn of Silencieux's link to the French decadents, and her decision to step into the Seine because of a 'young poet of Paris' (Le Gallienne 1900: 50). Through these allusions, Silencieux's smile comes to resemble 'the unfathomable smile, always with a touch of something sinister in it' (Pater 1976: 101) of Leonardo's Gioconda as described by Walter Pater in *The Renaissance*. Moreover, the journey of the Gioconda through time and history, as described by Pater, closely resembles the adventures of Silencieux, who like the Mona Lisa is associated with water.[9] Antony's romance with Silencieux, in turn, echoes Dorian's infatuation with Sybil Vane. 'To-night she is Imogen ... and tomorrow night she will be Juliet,' Dorian enthusiastically tells Lord Henry as he describes his love for Sybil (Wilde 2005: 216). Antony similarly delights in Silencieux's roles and dresses the cast in the 'wardrobe of her past' (Le Gallienne 1900: 61):

> 'To-night, you shall go clothed as when you loved that woman in Mitylene,' Antony would say.
> Or: 'To-night you shall be a little shepherd-boy, with a leopard-skin across your shoulder and mountain berries in your hair.'
> Or again: 'To-night you shall be Pierrot — mourning for his Columbine.'
> Ah! how divine was Silencieux in all her disguises! — a divine child. (Le Gallienne 1900: 61–62)

By enabling cross-dressing, and through her accounts of same-sex romances, Silencieux increasingly blurs gender and sexual boundaries. In this light, the cast is no longer exclusively the portrait of Beatrice but begins to reflect aspects of the male protagonist. Antony is aware that Silencieux lives through his imagination, and does not find his infatuation remarkable. Echoing Lord Henry, who, in *The Picture of Dorian Gray*, argues that love is always a form of deception (Wilde 2005: 214), he reflects: 'There is in all love a component of make-believe. Every woman who is loved is partly the creation of her lover's fancy' (Le Gallienne 1900: 35).

As a mask with a masculine name that shares with Antony a sort of telepathy, and a death effigy that reflects Antony's unconscious desire to see Beatrice dead, Silencieux comes to resemble Antony as much as it resembles Beatrice. In this light, the kisses that Antony bestows on Silencieux, like the kiss Dorian gives to his own portrait, enact a 'mockery of Narcissus' (Wilde 2005: 257). As in Wilde's philosophy, the mask does not double, but multiplies. Elisa Glick uses the metaphor of a magnifying glass to emphasize how, in *The Picture of Dorian Gray*, the portrait functions for each of the protagonists as the reflection of their individual ego (2001: 135): Dorian sees in it his own guilt, Basil his love for Dorian, Lord Henry a product for the art market. As Wilde wrote in the book's preface, 'it is the spectator, and not life, that art really mirrors' (Wilde 2005: 168). In *The Worshipper of the Image*, the mask similarly functions as mirror. Antony, who is often called a 'child' and is entirely absorbed in his own poetry, sees in Silencieux a magical object; Beatrice, who takes on the role of the moralizer, perceives it as a frightful object that threatens their happiness. In Wilde's novel, Basil eventually recognizes in the portrait 'some foul parody, some infamous ignoble satire' (Wilde 2005: 298) and concludes that his friend has gone mad (Wilde 2005: 297–99). In chapter XXII, Beatrice arrives at a similar conclusion regarding Antony:

> 'O God, he is going mad,' she cried to herself.
> Antony was sitting in a big chair drawn up to the fire. Opposite to him, lying back in her cushions, was the Image draped in a large black velvet cloak. A table stood between them, and on it stood two glasses, and a decanter nearly empty of wine, Silencieux's glass stood untasted, but Antony had evidently been drinking deeply, for his cheeks were flushed and his eyes wild. (Le Gallienne 1900: 134–35)

The doctor describes Antony's illness as a disease with no name, 'a form of madness all the more malignant because the sufferer, and particularly his friends, might go for years without suspecting it' (Le Gallienne 1900: 137). If Dorian is poisoned by a French novel, Antony's insanity is triggered by a muse with a French name with poison on its lips, who inspires him to compose corrupt and 'barren' verses. The poems dictated by the muse distance him from his wife and are the indirect cause for the death of his child, thereby marking the end of the reproductive sexuality that the child represents. By encouraging sexual practices like narcissism and fetishism, Silencieux constitutes a threat to the traditional family, and by extension, to the society that relies on it.

In *The Picture of Dorian Gray*, Dorian admits that Sybil's death does not affect him, and is reconciled with the event by the thought that 'she passed again into the sphere of art' (Wilde 2005: 260). Similarly, Antony is moved by how beautiful Beatrice looks as they draw her from the pond 'with lilies in her hair', and comforted by the thought that 'she [...] live[s] for ever in Silencieux' (Le Gallienne 1900: 142). In both tales, the portrait, as a double, changes from an image of beauty and youth to one of horror, as the protagonist realizes that at the core of his desire there is death. When Antony goes back to Silencieux, we learn that her eyes 'were wide open, and from her lips hung a dark moth with the face of death between his wings' (Le Gallienne 1900: 143). This image reflects a dream of Antony's, who as a child had loved this insect with 'the passion of a Japanese artist' (Le Gallienne 1900: 11), but it is also a means through which the enigmatic smile of Silencieux-Gioconda turns into the gaze of the Medusa. As Silencieux warns Antony, all her lovers died when they saw her eyes open (Le Gallienne 1900: 46). Like Medusa, Silencieux-Gioconda is associated with art, and like Medusa's head, the cast takes on autonomous life.

In Wilde's novel, Basil warns Dorian that 'Love is a more wonderful thing than art' (Wilde 2005: 241), and Dorian learns that turning his life into a piece of art does not result in moral impunity. Similarly, Antony acknowledges that 'the immortality of art is one of those curious illusions of man's self-love which a moment's thought dispels' (Le Gallienne 1900: 117). In a letter to Shaw, Wilde regretted that the moral message in his novel was too obvious, and in the 1891 preface he commented: 'There is no such thing as a moral or an immoral book. Books are well written, or badly written. That is all' (Wilde 2005: 167). In contrast, Le Gallienne believed that it was necessary to heal English literature of the unwholesomeness of foreign influences. For Max Nordau, as for Le Gallienne, the first symptom of degeneration was ego-mania, the egotism that Oscar Wilde, in 'The Critic as Artist' describes as 'delightful' (Wilde 2007b: 124), and that in *The Worshipper of the Image* leads Antony to fall in love with a mask that echoes his words. The second symptom

FIG. 3.1. Left: Anonymous, *Inconnue de la Seine*. Deutsches Literaturarchiv, Marbach, photo by Chris Korner, by kind permission of DLA Marbach; right: Caravaggio, *Medusa*, 1595–96, oil on canvas mounted on wood, diameter 55 cm, Uffizi gallery, Florence.

was the excessive concentration on fragments and isolated experiences, 'the limited thinking, often insane thinking' (Le Gallienne 1900: 231) that blurs Antony's perception, leading him to substitute a fetish for a real woman and to confuse the artificial with the natural.

Le Gallienne's biographers interpreted the story as a fantasy based on his nostalgia for his first wife, Mildred, and his incompatibility with his second wife, Julie Nørregaard: 'It cannot have been a comforting bit of bedside reading for Julie, and one does not have to be a psychiatrist to discern in it the feelings of guilt, inadequacy, frustration and despair which the writer put on the page for the whole world to see' (Whittington-Egan and Smerdon 1960: 363). As support for this thesis, they note that Le Gallienne often referred to Julie as 'The Sphynx' — the subject of the poem that Antony writes for Silencieux. However, they also reproduce a letter in which Le Gallienne, writing to Julie, regrets that so many copies of *The Worshipper* remain unsold, and in which he notes that Julie was very fond of this piece (1960: 399).[10] Just like Wilde's *Picture of Dorian Gray*, the novella cannot be reduced to biographical interpretations, and contains parodic elements that must be read in connection with Le Gallienne's ambivalent stance about decadence, his admiration for Wilde, and the shaping of new ideas about sexuality in late Victorian culture.

Conclusions

At a time in which *The Picture of Dorian Gray* had become inseparable from the association with Wilde's homosexuality, Beerbohm and Le Gallienne borrowed the structure and theme of Wilde's novel and rewrote it by deploying inversion, one of

Wilde's favourite rhetorical devices. Both tales focused on the relation between art and life, and featured protagonists affected by what Wilde called 'new hedonism' — the cultivation of experience for its own sake — and Nordau 'ego mania' — a form of narcissism that leads to a split in the self and the cult of disguises. In taking over the role of the portrait as a magical tool and object of erotic yearning, both engaged with the mask as a fetish.

By getting rid of the homosocial context and substituting a heterosexual romance, Beerbohm and Le Gallienne 'corrected' Wilde's novel, bringing the plot into line with dominant values in Victorian culture. However, the works also involved subtexts that sabotaged the explicit moral message. References to *The Happy Hypocrite* in Beerbohm's essays and letters challenged the conservative function of the mask as tool of transformation from criminal to bourgeois, and redirected attention to hypocrisy. Le Gallienne's tale featured a heterosexual romance based on the adoration of a man for his wife, but also experimented with the mask's potential to disrupt gender and sexual norms. In both cases, while the mask functioned as an expression of the non-normative, it only did so in relation to male characters. In contrast, the masks forced upon female characters did not encourage fluidity, but marked their status as 'dear little creatures', 'wonderful little beings' (Beerbohm 1896: 7) confined to the domestic sphere. As Rita Felski has argued, the rejection of traditional masculinity, in late Victorian culture, did not necessarily entail a rejection of patriarchy and often involved a misogynistic strain (Felski 1995: 93).

Both *The Happy Hypocrite* and *The Worshipper of the Image* are self-reflective pieces and didactic allegories that, in engaging with *The Picture of Dorian Gray*, reflected the authors' ambivalent stance towards the movement with which Wilde had become associated. By condemning the protagonist's extravagant way of life, his dandyism and the display of wealth, and redirecting him to a way of life in which objects are directly linked to their context of use, *The Happy Hypocrite* took distance from decadence. At the same time, the tale extolled the cult of artifice, disguise and self-fashioning that Beerbohm identified as the core of decadent poetics. *The Worshipper of the Image* illustrated the danger inherent in a French-inspired style, as well as the nefarious consequences of focusing on the detail, the fragment, the isolated experience, at the expense of the whole. However, just as in Wilde's novel the aphorisms subvert the moral of the story, by reproducing the poems issued by the 'insane' artist, Le Gallienne implicitly invited late Victorian readers to enjoy the same 'barren' and 'corrupt' style that he was denouncing.

Notes to Chapter 3

1. In defining these texts as parodies, I am referring to Hutcheon's definition of parody as a major form of modern self-reflexivity. Hutcheon distinguishes parodies from pastiche and satire (see Hutcheon 2000: 10).
2. Unless otherwise stated, I refer to the 1891 edition of *The Picture of Dorian Gray* reproduced in *The Complete Works of Oscar Wilde* (Oxford University Press, 2005).
3. Like Wainewright, Dorian aspires to be a dandy, sees life as a form of art, and leads a secret life of crime. Just as Wainewright's crimes give 'strong personality to his style' (Wilde 2007a: 120), Dorian's sins guide his aesthetic taste, and bring about a form of regression, a penchant for the

primitive exemplified by his interest for 'the few savage tribes that have survived contact with Western civilization' (Wilde 2005: 85). Like Wainewright, Dorian wears many masks and, after committing a murder, feels 'the terrible pleasure of a double life' (Wilde 2005: 314). Both works question the permanence of personality as a metaphysical problem, and reflect on the relation between hidden and public life. Ultimately, both associate writing with poison: Wainewright is both an art critic and a murderer; Dorian is poisoned by a book that has a determining influence on his path of moral corruption.

4. In Huysmans' À Rebours, the protagonist similarly sees in the portraits of his ancestors 'the defects of a debilitated constitution and the excess of lymph in the blood' (Huysmans 1998: 3).
5. Before serving as a model for the portrait, Dorian poses as Narcissus for Basil; later, 'in boyish mockery of Narcissus' (Wilde 2005: 257), he kisses the lips of the figure in the painting. When the portrait begins to age, he grows 'more and more enamoured of his own beauty' (Wilde 2005: 277).
6. We also learn — curiously, in a footnote — that despite his delight in costumes, Lord George 'never disguised his face' (Beerbohm 1914: 17).
7. 'I hear that ass Oscar is under surveillance', Beerbohm wrote to Turner. 'I suppose he is playing the giddy goat. Can't someone warn him to be careful?' (Beerbohm 1964: 120).
8. '... Oscar has been quite superb. His speech about the Love that dares not tell his name was simply wonderful, and carried the whole court right away, quite a tremendous burst of applause' (Beerbohm 1964: 102).
9. 'Like the vampire, she has been dead many times, and learned the secrets of the grave; and has been a diver in deep seas, and keeps their fallen day about her...' (Pater 1976: 102).
10. 'O my sad little *Worshipper* — so lonely and dark in the dank cellars of Lane, how my heart bleeds for you my forgotten beauty! I hear you crying to yourself in the dark ... for you too there shall be a day of glory and modish new editions' (Whittington-Egan and Smerdon 1960: 399).

CHAPTER 4

Fragments: Gabriele D'Annunzio and Medusa's Head

> La maschera alzata nell'infinito, con la bocca e gli occhi pieni di cielo, non sembra dal silenzio e dalla luce ricommista alla natura come quando nelle origini era fatta di fresco fogliame?
>
> [Doesn't the mask raised to the infinite, with its mouth and eyes full of the sky, seem unified with nature by silence and light, as when, originally, it was made out of fresh leaves?] (D'Annunzio 1924b: 30)

Throughout the 1880s, fetishism became a prominent topic of discussion in medico-psychiatric research, as well as in anthropological and sociological investigations. In 1887, the French psychologist Alfred Binet published 'Le Fétichisme dans l'amour' [Fetishism in love] in which he drew, among others, on Cesare Lombroso to define fetishism and its relation to other perversions, applying the concept, which Charles de Brosses had used to address the worship of images in primitive societies, to the sexual sphere for the first time. In stressing that the fetish is born out of 'ideas associated by resemblance of contiguity' and that, in fetishism, 'the part substitutes the whole' (2011: 49), Binet suggested that it followed the logic of metonymy and synecdoche, thereby participating in the *fin-de-siècle* concern with the part–whole relationship. Among typologies of fetishism, he distinguished the preference for one part of the body of a loved person, which, in his view, was a feature of all sexual love, and attraction to inanimate objects, that he considered pathological. For Binet, fetishism originated in childhood experiences, and its function was to procure sexual excitement through means contrary to reproductive sexuality; in doing so, it functioned as an umbrella term for a variety of perversions that challenged heteronormativity. Fetishism and narcissism, he contended, were closely related, since in some cases, fetishism could have the self as an object. Sexual inversion, as a particular type of narcissism, was, in turn, a development of fetishism (2011: 72–75). Drawing on Binet, Freud built his own theory of the fetish, which relied on the male child's interpretation of the female genitalia as castrated (Freud 1978b: 88). As Charles Bernheimer has stressed, this premise lacked any scientific evidence, and functioned on the one hand as a 'decadent fantasy', and on the other as a 'master trope' that underpins Freud's theorizing on the unconscious (Bernheimer 2002: 170). In Freud's theory, Medusa's head, at once an embodiment of the fear of castration and a figuration of the phallic mother, maintains intact the fetishist's original belief in sexual undifferentiation (Freud 2003: 85). As a fetish, it allows the male child to overcome horror for the woman's body, 'saving' him from homosexuality, and has therefore a normative function (Freud 1978b: 88).

Binet's article appeared at a time in which Gabriele D'Annunzio had set out to work on *Il Fuoco* [The Flame], and to develop his own vision of modern tragedy. As Barbara Spackman and Mary Ann Frese Witt have noted, D'Annunzio engaged with fetishism in his own fictional and dramatic writing, where the fetish is articulated through the Greek myth of Perseus and Medusa (Spackman 1989; Witt 2001). Building on this scholarship, this chapter examines references to masks and fragments in the novel *Il fuoco* (1900) and in the dramas *La città morta* (1898), *La Gioconda* (1899), *La Gloria* (1899) in connection to D'Annunzio's belief in the autonomy of art and to his poetics of the fragment. It argues that D'Annunzio's conception of the fetish parallels Binet's and, to a certain extent, prefigures Freud's as he portrays the mask as a fragment originating or inspired by Ancient Greek or Renaissance art; in engaging with *pars-pro-toto* debate, he establishes a metonymic link between masks, broken sculpture, and severed heads. Imposed on female figures, the mask becomes a tool to draw attention to the poet's narcissism but also enables the indirect articulation of gender and sexual identities that challenge the texts' explicit emphasis on hyper-masculinity.

Tragic Masks and Severed Heads: Fragments in *Il fuoco*

D'Annunzio's activity as a journalist contributed to the construction of his image a dandy, poet and politician. Born into a landowning family in Abruzzo, he moved to Rome, married a noblewoman and developed an aristocratic aesthetic. At the age of seventeen, after issuing his first collection of poems, he courted publicity by publishing his own obituary describing a tragic riding accident. Through love affairs with Italian and foreign divas, adventures as an aviator, and interventions in Italian politics — which culminated in the occupation of the city of Fiume in 1919 — he shaped a larger-than-life persona that dominated the Italian cultural scene for many years.[1] D'Annunzio's work introduced Italian literature to the international circuits of decadence through references to French and English authors. Aestheticism, archaic vocabulary and a complex syntax evidence the extent to which his writing was embedded in the cultural landscape of the *fin-de-siècle*; on the other hand, his understanding of the power of mass media and experiments on the integration of different art forms qualify him as a modernist (Mirabile 2014: 16).

D'Annunzio's emphasis on self-fashioning was in line with his fascination with masks, and must be considered in connection to his cult of beauty and the thought of Friedrich Nietzsche, with which he had become acquainted in the 1890s. Although his knowledge was limited to texts available in French translations, he was the first to introduce Nietzsche's philosophy to Italian audiences (Schnapp 1988). In 'La bestia elettiva' [The Elective Beast], published in 1892 (see D'Annunzio 2003b), he condemned democracy and welcomed Nietzsche's philosophy as a guide towards the rise of a new aristocracy. Critical of the increasing commodification of culture, he argued that the poet should act as the defender of beauty. This did not prevent him from engaging in politics, since he saw no separation between the aesthetic and the political and envisioned the poet as a spokesperson for the nation. In 'The Case of Wagner' (1893) and 'La rinascenza della tragedia' [The Rebirth of Tragedy] (1897), he drew on Nietzsche's *Birth of Tragedy* to outline his vision of a modern tragic theatre (see D'Annunzio 2003a; 2003d). Inspired by the cycle of spectacles organized by the *Félibres* at the Roman theatre at Orange, he embraced the cause of a 'Latin Renaissance' and juxtaposed the 'Mediterranean soul' to the Nordic spirit of Wagner's dramas. In addition, he described the leading role that poets would play in restoring drama to its ancient dignity by infusing it with a religious spirit. In the same years in which he outlined his conception of modern tragedy, he became involved in Italian politics, took up a seat in the Italian parliament as 'deputy of beauty' and experienced the excitement of speaking to the masses (Schnapp 1988: 260). Echoing Nietzsche, he defined his stance as 'beyond left and right as well as beyond good and evil' and argued for the union of aestheticism and nationalism; conversely, his conception of drama took on political connotations (Chomel 1997: 36; Witt 2007: 75).

D'Annunzio began to work on *Il fuoco* in 1894, interrupted the work to write for the theatre, and then finished the manuscript in 1900. Since the first part constitutes a meditation on the *Gesamtkunstwerk*, which D'Annunzio endeavoured to demonstrate was invented in Baroque Italy, and the second part outlines the poet's vision of a modern tragic theatre, the book can be considered a treatise on modern drama (Andreoli 2001: 56). On another level, it offers a fictionalized account of the relationship between D'Annunzio and Eleonora Duse, who in the fiction inform the characters of the poet Stelio Effrena and the actress Foscarina.[2]

D'Annunzio's speech on the occasion of Venice's first International Art Exhibition, which took place 1895 and attracted crowds of listeners, is transcribed almost *verbatim* in the first part of novel. At the time in which the speech took place, Duse was thirty-six years old, five years older than D'Annunzio. The novel contrasts the youth and energy of the hero with the frailty and vulnerability of the actress, portraying Foscarina as an older woman haunted by thoughts of decay and prone to hysterical attacks. It also underlines the hero's repugnance for the woman's ageing body, his sadistic joy in observing her panic, and his indifference to her suffering. Throughout the novel, Foscarina, the actress no longer in her prime and tired of life, blends in with Venice, the decadent city *par excellence*. When *Il fuoco* was published, it encouraged an interpretation of the relationship between the two celebrities as an abusive bond between a sadist and his victim. Duse's friends advised her to request the book's withdrawal from publication; the actress, however, announced that she was willing to sacrifice herself for the sake of art. Recent scholarship has underlined that, in reality, the relationship between the poet and the actress was primarily a commercial alliance, and that both benefitted from it. If D'Annunzio exploited Duse's popularity to draw attention to his own work, Duse knew that the novel would raise expectations about the Italian premiere of

La città morta, in which she was to play the lead (Re 2004: 95; Andreoli 2013: 22). Moreover, the hysterical attacks that Foscarina suffers in *Il fuoco* and the attention that D'Annunzio draws to her age must be seen in conjunction with the myth that Duse had crafted around her acting. As the actress Adelaide Ristori noted, Duse had been able to use limitations and idiosyncrasies, including the signs of aging and her chronic anxiety, to her advantage, and had introduced in her repertoire 'a complete collection of abnormal types with all their weaknesses, reveries, twitches, and languors', thereby constructing an archetype of 'the quintessential modern woman with all her neuroses and weaknesses' (Guerreri 1962; see also Re 2004: 102 and Andreoli 2013: 37).

While Ristori saw in Duse's neurosis the trademark of modernity, D'Annunzio recognized in it the exaltation of the Dionysian. For his fictional alter ego Stelio, the actress Foscarina embodies multiplicity and becoming; he claims to be able to discern on her features the 'hundred masks' that she has worn on stage (D'Annunzio 2016: 41, 83). As the poet's instrument, Foscarina is 'la vivente materia atta a ricevere i ritmi dell'arte, a essere foggiata secondo i ritmi della poesia ... innumerevole come le onde del mare' [living material ready to receive the rhythms of art, to be shaped according to the laws of poetry ... as varied as the waves of the sea] (D'Annunzio 2016: 196). On and off stage, she is compared to a Maenad, a woman possessed and driven mad by Dionysus, and described as 'l'attrice ardente che passava dalla frenesia della folla alla forza del maschio, la creatura dionisiaca che con l'atto di vita coronava il rito misterioso come nell'orgia' [the radiant actress who used to pass from the frenzy of the masses to the power exerted by the male, the Dionysian being who crowned the mystic rite with the act of life as though in an orgy] (D'Annunzio 2016: 124).

In contrast, the masks that Stelio, as a poet and playwright, designs for Foscarina are rigid and motionless. At the beginning of the novel, Stelio gazes, fascinated by the red velvet lace that Foscarina wears around her neck. He then compares her features to those of Persephone, the queen of the dead, at the moment when she is about to return to the underworld and her features are transformed into a dark tragic mask:

> Vi ricordate la scena in cui Persefone è sul punto di sprofondarsi nell'erebo, mentre il coro delle oceanidi geme? Il suo volto somiglia al vostro quando s'oscura. Rigida nel suo peplo tinto di croco ella abbandona indietro il capo coronato, e sembra che la notte fluisca nella sua carne divenuta esangue e s'addensi sotto il mento, nel cavo degli occhi, intorno alle nari, trasformandola in una cupa maschera tragica. È la vostra maschera ...

> [Do you recall the scene where Persephone is about to throw herself into Erebus while the chorus of Oceanides are lamenting? Her face is just like yours when shadows pass over it. She stands stiffly in her saffron robe, her crowned head thrown back, and it is as though night itself were flowing through her bloodless flesh, gathering there beneath her chin, in the hollows of her eyes, around her nostrils, transforming her into a darkly tragic mask. That is your mask ...] (D'Annunzio 2016: 20)

Since Persephone is about to return to the realm of death, the mask that Stelio perceives on Foscarina is also a death mask. Indeed, Stelio often fantasizes about Foscarina's death. As he starts working on his new tragedy, he has a vision of the actress's features transformed into marble and, after making love to her, closes her eyes 'come si chiudevano gli occhi degli estinti' [as one closes the eyes of a corpse] (D'Annunzio 2016: 161). In keeping with this fantasy, the dramatic persona that Stelio designs for Foscarina in his new play is a blind woman, a liminal figure whom he describes as inhabiting the threshold of life and death (D'Annunzio 2016: 306). Stelio acknowledges the contrast between the mobility of Foscarina's features and the mask that he is shaping for her: 'gli parve inerte la maschera cieca ch'egli voleva porle sul volto, angusta la favola tragica per ove ella doveva passare dolorando' [the blind mask that he wanted to put over her face seemed too stiff, the tragic tale through which she was to move and suffer seemed too confined] (D'Annunzio 2016: 196). While mutability is connected to life, Stelio's tragic mask is designed for a 'semiviva' [half-dead woman] (D'Annunzio 2016: 279). Foscarina, terrified by Stelio's ability to decipher her emotions, recognizes that the mask encapsulates her own grief. As a stage persona, she perceives the mask as limiting her actions, constraining her creativity: 'Egli leggerà nella mia anima le mute parole che porrà in bocca alla sua creatura, e io non potrò pronunziarle se non su la scena, di sotto la maschera!' [He will read silent words in my soul that he will put into the mouth of his creation, and I shall only be able to speak them on a stage, behind a mask!] (D'Annunzio 2016: 294).

Throughout the novel, references to tragic masks are intertwined with allusions to severed heads and contribute to the ongoing comparison between Foscarina and Medusa. By marking her reduction to a tragic mask, the red velvet lace that Foscarina wears around her neck also symbolizes decapitation. At the beginning of the novel, Foscarina recognizes the features of Medusa in her own reflection in a well (D'Annunzio 2016: 22). In his public speech, Stelio compares his situation to that of a lover who suddenly hears hissing serpents in the hair of his beloved (D'Annunzio 2016: 68). Moreover, the fountain where the sacrifice takes place in the drama in which Foscarina will play the lead is named after Perseus (D'Annunzio 2016: 188).

When Stelio describes his play to his friend Daniele Glauro, he re-enacts the Gorgon's decapitation. The allegory is the first of three parables through which he deploys an imagery of fragmentation and dismemberment to outline his artistic vision:

> Hai mai veduto, in qualche istante, l'universo intero dinanzi a te come una testa umana? Io sì, mille volte. Ah, reciderla come colui che recise d'un colpo la testa di medusa, e tenerla sospesa dinanzi alla folla, da un palco, perché essa non la dimentichi mai più! Non hai tu mai pensato che una grande tragedia potrebbe somigliare al gesto di Perseo? Io ti dico che vorrei togliere dalla Loggia dell'Orcagna e trasportare nell'atrio del nuovo teatro il bronzo di Benvenuto, per ammonimento.
>
> [Have you ever seen the whole universe before you, just for a second, like a human head? I have, thousands of times. If I could only cut it off, like the man

who cut off the head of the Medusa, and hold it up from the scaffold to the crowd, so that they would never ever forget it! Haven't you ever thought that a great tragedy might be like that deed which Perseus performed? I tell you I would like to take Benvenuto's bronze away from the Orcagna loggia and put it in the entrance hall of my new theatre as a warning.] (D'Annunzio 2016: 188)

In retelling the slaying of Medusa, Stelio compares artistic creation (his new tragic theatre) to a violent act perpetrated on the body of a woman. In her analysis of *Le Vergini delle Rocce* [*The Virgins of the Rocks*], Barbara Spackman has suggested that D'Annunzio may have been familiar with a passage in Plato's *Symposium* in which Medusa's head is associated with the power of rhetoric to control the audience (Spackman 1996: 26). Building on Spackman, Witt has argued that Stelio's allegory 'encompasses both mastery over a female threat and the "petrifying" power of speech. [...] Both women and the audience could, potentially, petrify and emasculate the poet-hero-orator; to defy this threat he must "possess" them, silencing their speech by himself controlling the Gorgon's head, which he holds back from them' (Witt 2001: 42).[3] However, the slaying of Medusa, in Stelio's parable, is mediated by Cellini's *Perseus*.[4] In this sixteenth-century work of art, Perseus's androgynous facial features contrast with his hyper-masculine body, evoking sexual ambiguity. Moreover, the Gorgon's features resemble those of the hero, challenging the distinction between masculinity and femininity. As Tobin Siebers noted:

> When the statue is seen from behind, Perseus and Medusa resemble each other; the hero's tangled locks mimic the coils of the serpents that entwine his victim's head [...]. Viewed from Perseus' right side, the statue reveals another Janus figure; the hero and the monster displaying identical profiles. The aquiline noses, delicate cheekbones, and lowered eyes twin each other, presenting a baffling spectacle for those in need of clear distinctions between the heroic and the monstrous. Standing in front of the statue, the beholder is mortified to discover that the faces of the slayer and victim are doubled. (Siebers 2003: 197)

Since the statue portrays the Gorgon's face as a replication of that of the hero, Stelio's use of Cellini's statue as a term of comparison for artistic creation establishes a relation between the fetish (the Gorgon's head) and the particular strand of fetishism that Binet defined as an obsession with a part of the self. Furthermore, by identifying with Benvenuto Cellini, Stelio compares himself to a Renaissance artist who, for *fin-de-siècle* aesthetes like John Addington Symonds, embodied the cult of beauty but whose life also offered a pretext to explore same-sex desire. The parable thus brings together Greek myth and Renaissance art, fetishism, narcissism and same-sex passion.

In his second tale, Stelio explains his conception of the modern tragic theatre to Foscarina, and uses the ending of Plutarch's *Life of Crassus* as a comparison for the manifestation of fate in his own drama. In Plutarch's narrative, a soldier brings Crassus's bleeding head to a banquet, where it becomes a prop that participants use to enact Euripides' *Bacchae* — a play that revolves around the cult of Dionysus, the 'suffering God' associated with inebriation and fragmentation. Stelio, in his interpretation, underlines that the play turns into a ritual when Pomaxoethres, the soldier who beheaded Crassus, suddenly jumps into the performance and takes

FIG. 4.1. Benvenuto Cellini, *Perseus with the Head of Medusa*, c. 1554, bronze, Loggia dei Lanzi, Piazza della Signoria, Florence, photo by Marie-Lan Nguyen / Wikimedia Commons / CC-BY 2.5 <https://commons.wikimedia.org/wiki/File:Perseus_by_Cellini_Loggia_dei_Lanzi_n06.jpg>

over the role of Agave, mother of King Pentheus, who, in the frenzy of Dionysian rituals, has mistaken her son for a lion and has torn him to pieces:

> Il Coro salta di gioia. E, come Agave dice d'aver preso senza rete quel leoncello, il Coro chiede chi l'abbia colpito prima. E Agave risponde:
> 'Mio è il vanto...'
> Ma balza in piedi Pomassetre, che stava cenando tuttavia, e strappa di mano il teschio all'attore furioso e grida che a lui spetta più che a Giasone il dir quelle parole, egli essendo l'uccisore del Romano. Senti tu la bellezza portentosa della scena? Il volto feroce della Vita lampeggia a un tratto accanto alla maschera di metallo e di cera; l'odore del sangue umano eccita la frenesia ritmica del Coro; un braccio datore di morte lacera i veli della finzione tragica.
>
> [And the Chorus leaps with joy, and when Agave says she has caught the lion cub without a net, the Chorus asks who wounded it first, and Agave answers:
> 'Mine is the honour...'

> But Pomaxoethres who had still not finished dining, leaped to his feet and tore the head from the frenzied actor, shouting that he was more worthy than Jason to say those words, since he was the man who killed the Roman. Can't you feel the portentous beauty of such a scene? The fierce face of Life suddenly flashing beside the Mask of wax and metal, the scent of human blood arousing the rhythmic frenzy of the Chorus, an arm that has inflicted death tearing the veil of tragic fiction.] (D'Annunzio 2016: 300)

Following a metonymic logic, the head of Medusa here turns into that of Crassus. Unlike Perseus, Pomaxoethres does not celebrate his victory over a female threat, but impersonates the Maenad who is responsible for the death of her own son. It is the fragmented male body that here functions as a fetish, exciting and inspiring the actors. While the beheader (Pomaxoethres) and the beheaded (Crassus) are both male, Pomaxoethres' victory can only be enacted through a cross-gendered performance.

A male head plays a central role in the tale of the glass-master Dardi and his hydraulic organ, a fable he invents for Foscarina as they are sailing in the lagoon. Dardi, a skilful Venetian artisan, endeavours to build an organ of glass that will use the water and winds of the lagoon as a power source. When he announces that the instrument will compete in splendour with the Doge's palace, the Venetian council decides to support his enterprise, but reminds him that, in case of failure, he will lose his head. As a warning, Dardi must wear a red thread around his neck, a decoration that becomes a source of fear and attraction. For months, Dardi dedicates his energies to the construction of the organ, neglecting the courtesan Perdilanza, who grows more and more distressed as the construction of the work progresses. When the organ is completed, the sound is so astonishing that the Doge stops his boat to listen, but the mechanism suddenly jams and the music stops. Perdilanza, Stelio explains, has drowned herself out of grief, and her long hair, in the depths of the sea, has clogged the pipes of the organ. As a consequence, Dardi loses his head:

> Un burchiello si spicca dal Buncinturo, portando l'uomo rosso col ceppo e con la scure. Il colpo ha per segno il filo scarlatto, ed è preciso. La testa cade; è scagliata su l'acqua ove galleggia come quella d'Orfeo…
>
> [A small boat left the galley, bearing the red-headed man with his axe and his block. The blow aimed at the scarlet thread and did not miss. The head fell, and was thrown into the water where it floated like the head of Orpheus…] (D'Annunzio 2016: 317)

While unable to decipher the tale's meaning, Foscarina interprets it as an allegory, and fears that she must somehow be involved in it. In fact, the name of the heroine, *Perdilanza*, resembles the nickname that Stelio has given to Foscarina, *Perdita*. Moreover, the red thread that Dardi wears around his neck recalls the velvet lace worn by Foscarina. However, the victim of decapitation is not Foscarina/Medusa, but Dardi, whose severed head is compared to that of Orpheus. A poet-musician, Orpheus is known for descending into hell to retrieve his spouse Eurydice, and for affecting Hades and his wife Persephone — to whom Foscarina is compared — with the beauty of his song. D'Annunzio, however, alludes to another aspect of the myth,

FIG. 4.2. Gustave Moreau, *Orpheus*, 1865, oil on wood panel, 154 × 99.5 cm, Musée d'Orsay, Paris

the death of the poet, described in Book XI of Ovid's *Metamorphoses*. Here Ovid recalls how Orpheus, inconsolable after the loss of Eurydice, refused the approaches of the Thracian women and 'was the first of the Thracian people to transfer his affection to young boys' (Ovid 2000: 83). Offended by Orpheus's rejection, the Thracian maenads tore him to pieces during a Bacchic orgy and threw his head into a river. The artist Gustave Moreau, whose art had a great influence on the French decadents — who in turn influenced D'Annunzio — illustrated the aftermath of the episode in a painting that portrays a Thracian maiden who, having retrieved Orpheus's head, carries it on the poet's lyre. An implicit reference in Stelio's tale, Moreau's painting shares a connection with Cellini's *Perseus* in displaying the features of the severed head and those of the maiden as identical. Since the girl gazes lovingly at the severed head, as looking at a mirror image, the painting functions as another visual representation of the connection between fetishism, explained by Binet as an attraction to a component of the self, and narcissism, the particular type of fetishism that Binet saw as closely connected to attraction to the same sex.[5]

After telling the story of the hydraulic organ, Stelio reflects on the similarities between Dardi's endeavour and his own artistic mission: 'Ahimè, sì, v'è forse qualche somiglianza tra la mia audacia e quella del muranese. Credo che anch'io dovrei portare intorno al collo un filo di scarlatto, per ammonimento' [Good heavens, yes, maybe there is some resemblance between my daring and that of the man from Murano! I think perhaps I should wear a scarlet thread around my neck too, as a warning] (D'Annunzio 2016: 318). By identifying with Dardi, he implicitly recalls his affinity to Orpheus, which is reinforced by several allusions throughout the novel.[6]

Foscarina interprets Stelio's last fable as an admonishment not to interfere with his work. At the end of the novel, she leaves for a tour of North America with the aim of providing funding for Stelio's open-air theatre. Portrayed as sterile — a degenerative feature that in decadent narratives goes hand in hand with non-normative sexuality (Spackman 1989: 20)[7] — she nevertheless contributes to the birth of a creative project. She also facilitates Stelio's relationship with the younger Donatella Arvale, the singer whom Stelio compares to a Greek winged victory, and in whom he sees another instrument for his own tragic theatre. While Stelio, as D'Annunzio's alter ego, continues to represent heterosexuality and hyper-masculinity, the three parables function as a subtext that subverts this narrative, connecting the fetish to a wider range of phenomena that, in nineteenth century sexology, were seen as 'perversions', from necrophilia to narcissism to gender and sexual inversion.

Death Masks in *La città morta*

Inspired by a journey to Greece, during which he had visited the excavations at Mycenae, D'Annunzio began *La città morta* in 1896, while he was still working on *Il fuoco*. In this play, the five gold funeral masks that Schliemann believed belonged to Agamemnon's family become the objective correlative of the spirit of tragedy that he was trying to reconstruct in his theatre. *La città morta* was D'Annunzio's first tragedy and attempted to put into practice his vision of drama as a form of ritual, as outlined in *Il fuoco* and 'La rinascenza della tragedia'. While his objective was to restore the ceremonial spirit of drama, he did not intend to reconstruct ancient Greek tragedy, but to draw on it to create a new form that would represent the 'spirit of the race' (D'Annunzio 2016: 197). This objective made his theatre a political project. Although open to all social classes, it nevertheless reflected an aristocratic aesthetic as the aim was not to educate the masses but to impress them with the words of the poet/leader. The piece had been written for Duse, but she encountered difficulties finding enough actors for the Italian production, and the play premiered in Paris starring Sarah Bernhardt in 1897. The Italian text was published the following year, while the production with Duse did not take place until 1901.

In *Il fuoco*, the playwright Stelio stresses the importance of the mask as a stage prop, and specifies that the masks featuring in his play will be made of fine material (D'Annunzio 2016: 338). For the Italian production of *La città morta*, D'Annunzio ordered accurate reproductions of Greek masks, entrusting their realization to Alessandro Morani, son-in-law of the archaeologist Helbig, who worked under the supervision of the German Institute. He also commissioned copies of statues and bas-reliefs from the Pantheon. The attention to stage props was unusual in the Italian context, where theatre companies were still itinerant and used to improvising. By considering these details, D'Annunzio was moving away from the type of theatre that relied exclusively on the star performer, and taking on a directorial role (Bisicchia 1991: 53). In line with this ambition, he followed all rehearsals. As the critic Leporello noted in an article published in *L'illustrazione Italiana* in 1901, he was, however, more interested in the arrangement of masks and sculptures than in the actors' performances:

> Tutte le raffinatezze sue, di artista e di archeologo, volle soddisfare il poeta senza risparmio nell'allestimento scenico. A una delle ultime prove, a cui mi fu dato di assistere, egli si gloriava più di questa perfezione che della efficacia drammatica dell'opera sua; e conducendomi in giro per la scena mi mostrava i tesori raccolti per ornare la sala del primo atto [...]. Ma più ancora egli esaltava di gioia nel mirare l'effetto nella sala degli ori, al secondo atto: colle lucenti armature e le maschere, e i diademi e le coppe, e le else decalcati con scrupolosa esattezza sugli originali che si trovano al museo nazionale di Atene. E indulgente nella recitazione, fu alle prove scrupoloso per gli effetti di luce, per la posizione degli accessori ...

> [The poet wanted to satisfy all his artistic and archaeological ambitions, sparing no expense in the choreography. During one of the last rehearsals I attended, he boasted more about the perfection of the staging than about the dramatic strength of his play. Accompanying me on stage, he showed me the treasures he had gathered to decorate the setting of the first act [...]. He was even more excited when he admired the effects of the Room of Gold in the second act, which was adorned with shiny armours, masks, diadems, goblets, and sword hilts modelled with meticulous attention after the originals exhibited in the National Museum in Athens. During rehearsals he was indulgent with acting but scrupulous about light effects and about the position of accessories...]
> (Angioletti 2010: 110)

Fig. 4.3. Death-mask known as 'Agamemnon Mask', 1550–1500 BC, gold, found in Tomb V in Mycenae by Heinrich Schliemann (1876), National Archeological Museum, Athens

In the lodge overlooking the Acropolis that provided the setting for the first, third and fourth acts, sculptural fragments, according to D'Annunzio's directions, filled the walls as 'testimonianze d'una vita remota, vestige d'una bellezza scomparsa' [evidence of distant life, vestiges of vanished beauty] (D'Annunzio 2013a: 93). The golden masks, instead, dominated the setting of the second act.

While the Greek background apparently distanced the play from socio-political concerns, the male characters represented aspects of the poet/leader who, for D'Annunzio, was to become the spokesperson for the nation. The archaeologist Leonardo, in whom Witt sees an avatar of the 'warrior-imperialist' (2001: 47), aims to take possession of Mycenae's treasures; the poet Alessandro hopes to be inspired by the ancient spirit of the Greeks to compose powerful new poetry. Both are convinced of their intellectual and moral superiority, and focused on the appropriation of the past for their own purposes. Leonardo is accompanied by his sister Bianca Maria, Alessandro by his blind wife Anna. After lifting up the golden masks of Agamemnon and his family and looting their graves, Leonardo incurs the Greek curse and develops a mysterious illness, a 'condition of the nerves' that has all the symptoms of degeneration described by Cesare Lombroso and Max Nordau.

As Alessandro notes, 'I suoi nervi sono affranti da una tensione troppo lunga a troppo fiera. ... non impunemente un uomo scoperchia i sepolcri e guarda il viso dei morti' [His nerves are strained by too long and too fierce a tension. [...] A man cannot uncover the sepulchres and look at the faces of the dead with impunity] (D'Annunzio 2013a: 147). The immersion in the past leads to a deviation from the sexual norm, which manifests itself in an incestuous passion for his sister Bianca Maria, and eventually leads him to a criminal act. Spreading like an infection, the illness contaminates Alessandro, leading him astray from his poetic mission and distancing him from his blind wife, as he too develops a passion for Bianca Maria and uses the power of rhetoric to seduce her. When Leonardo becomes aware of this, he sacrifices his sister by drowning her at Perseus's fountain.

Through references to the myth of Iphigenia, Antigone and Electra, Bianca Maria draws attention to her role as sacrificial victim and faithful sister. Frequently present on stage but excluded from the main action, Anna, whom D'Annunzio modelled from the outset thinking of Duse, introduces the rest of the characters to the audience, thereby fulfilling a function of the Greek chorus (Nikopoulos 2010: 155). In the Italian production, Duse signalled her liminal position by avoiding the front of stage, emphasizing pauses and silences, and speaking in a soft voice that suggested aloofness (Angioletti 2010: 95). Anna's closeness to death was strengthened by the comparison of her features to those of a death mask:

> E quante volte anche mi comprimo il viso con le palme — così, come ora — per coglierne l'impronta nella sensibilità delle mie mani. Ah, qualche volta mi sembra veramente di portare impressa nelle mie mani la mia maschera fedele come quella che si ricava col gesso dai cadaveri; ma è una maschera inerte.
>
> [I often press my face with the palm of my hands — like this — to leave its imprint in the softness of my hands. Ah, at times I think I have truly imprinted on my hands my faithful mask, like those copied in plaster from the dead; but it is a mask without life.] (D'Annunzio 2013a: 97)

In the second-act scene that D'Annunzio considered the pivotal moment of the play, Anna holds the death mask of the prophetess Cassandra, who like herself has the gift of seeing the future, and stresses her closeness to the Greek heroine: 'Com'è grande la sua bocca! Il travaglio orribile della divinazione l'aveva dilatata' [How large her mouth is. The terrible work of divination dilated it] (D'Annunzio 2013a: 152).

In the Italian production, such passages invited the audience to contemplate the mobility of Duse's features in contrast to the rigidity of the mask. They also provided a pretext to admire Duse's famous gaze. While D'Annunzio's attention to masks as stage props was in line with a modern conception of theatre in which scene sets, lighting and recitation all contributed to the final effect, the frequent mask-metaphors embedded in the text thus underlined the virtuosity of the main actress. Since D'Annunzio saw in Duse's acting the absolute effacement of subjectivity in favour of the poetic text, they also drew attention to the words of the playwright.

Towards the end of *Il fuoco*, Foscarina recalls her childhood, the poverty she experienced in her youth. Her silences and poses are here attributed to the inspiration that, like many of her contemporaries, she found in classical statues:

> Le statue [...] mi sembravano bellissime, e io mi provavo a imitare i loro gesti. [...] La folla s'impazientiva per quelle pause troppo lunghe... certe volte, quando dovevo aspettare che finisse la gran tirata dell'interlocutore, prendevo l'attitudine di qualcuna che m'era più familiare e rimanevo immobile come se fossi di pietra. Incominciavo già a scolpirmi...
>
> [The statues [...] seemed quite beautiful to me, and I would try to imitate their gestures. [...] The crowd used to lose patience with those over-long pauses of mine... Sometimes, when I had to wait for the end of an actor's big speech, I would take up the position of one of the most familiar statues and stay motionless as if I too had been made of stone. I was already starting to shape myself...] (D'Annunzio 2016: 276)

Similarly, in *La città morta*, Anna is described as a statue, and her pauses and silences invite the audience to see her as such.[8] In turn, Bianca Maria is compared to *Nike*, the Greek statue of victory that features wings in most statues and paintings (D'Annunzio 2013a: 110). However, she is also associated with Medusa, thereby oscillating from 'petrified' to the role of 'petrifier'. At the beginning of the play, she recalls how Alessandro, when they were on their way to Perseus's fountain, once jokingly placed a snake's skin 'like a ribbon' on her head (D'Annunzio 2013a: 99). The same scene is evoked at the end of the play, when the two walk towards the spring for the last time (D'Annunzio 2013a: 203). At Perseus's fountain, Leonardo drowns Bianca Maria and, by involving Alessandro in the crime, renews his close bond to him. A few pages earlier, Anna had wondered: 'Non pensate, Bianca Maria, che debbano essere felici le statue delle fontane? [...] Io vorrei essere una di loro, poiché ho in comune con loro la cecità [Do you not think, Bianca Maria, that the statues at the fountains must be happy? [...] I would like to be one of them, since I have blindness in common with them] (D'Annunzio 2013a: 109). At the end of the play, it is Bianca Maria/Medusa who is compared to an inanimate artefact, as her body becomes an object of devotion, an item among many in her brother's collection: 'Ora ella è perfetta. Ora ella può essere adorata come una creatura divina... Nel più profondo dei miei sepolcri io l'adagerò e le metterò intorno tutti i miei tesori...' [Now she is perfect. Now she will be adored as a divine creature... I will place her in the deepest of my sepulchres and I will surround her with all my treasures...] (D'Annunzio 2013a: 203). If the straining of the nerves had resulted in the transformation of the man of genius into the criminal, this fantasy signals his conversion into a fetishist and a necrophile.

As Witt notes, Alessandro's concern with hiding the body and protecting the murderer similarly mirrors the thinking of the born criminal (Witt 2001: 48). Moreover, his passion for Bianca Maria is also marked by narcissism. Shortly before her murder, Bianca Maria warns him that his desire is nothing but a mask, a projection of self-love: 'Voi siete ebro di voi medesimo. Quel che voi vedete in me è nelle vostre pupille. La vostra parola crea dal nulla l'imagine che voi volete amare' [You are intoxicated with your own emotions. What you see in me, is in your own eyes. Your words create out of nothing the image you wish to love] (D'Annunzio 2013a: 144). However, she also acknowledges that the same obsession confers upon Alessandro a creative power (D'Annunzio 2013a: 144).

The sociologist Mario Morasso, who like D'Annunzio abhorred democracy and dreamed of a system of 'pure individualism' (Adamson 2015: 174), saw in Leonardo the hero of imperialism, but found the ending of the play puzzling and nonsensical (D'Annunzio 1992a: 82). Leonardo's fall into madness, however, was in keeping with Cesare Lombroso's theories, in which genius was interpreted as kind of insanity. Moreover, it reflected the association of fetishism with narcissism and other perversions. In *La città morta*, narcissism and fetishism also featured as the source of artistic imagination and creative power.

Medusa and the Body in Pieces: *La Gioconda* and *La Gloria*

In a note from 5 October 1898, D'Annunzio wrote addressing the genesis of *La Gloria*: 'Sempre qualcosa di carnale, qualcosa che somiglia a una violenza carnale, un misto di atrocità e di ebrietà, accompagna l'atto generativo nel mio cervello' [The creative process in my brain is always accompanied by a carnal act, something resembling carnal violence, a mixture of atrocity and intoxication] (D'Annunzio 1924a: 10). By tracing the origin of creativity to a violent sexual act, the note recalls the parable of Perseus and Medusa manipulated by D'Annunzio in *Il Fuoco*, in which the act of creation is compared to an injury to a woman's body. On another level, it implicitly draws on Nietzsche's conception of the Dionysian, a state of intoxication and inebriation linked to the loosening of the *principium individuationis*. In *La Gloria* and its 'sister play' *La Gioconda*, both written and performed in 1899, the two aspects merge as the Gorgon's gaze is brought into connection with broken statues, the Dionysian and the body in pieces.

La Gioconda, dedicated to 'Eleonora Duse dalle belle mani' [Eleonora Duse of the beautiful hands] (D'Annunzio 2013b: v), was written for Duse and designed to highlight her virtuosity. Silvia, the main character, appears in ten out of the eleven scenes of the four acts; her movements, mimicry and changes of mood all emphasized Duse's strengths (Perria 1992: 53). Ermete Zacconi, who specialized in interpreting 'pathologically over-excited beings with exaggeratedly contorted movements and facial expressions' (Re 2004: 102), played the role of Lucio, the male protagonist.[9] In reproducing a bourgeois setting and revolving around a love triangle, the play did not challenge the conventions of nineteenth-century Italian theatre. However, the numerous, albeit implicit references to Walter Pater demonstrate D'Annunzio's interest in English aestheticism and testify to his attempt to modernize and internationalize Italian drama (Evangelista 2018: 276). Moreover, the main theme was not adultery, but mutilation. While the fetish here shifts metonymically from the mask/bust/severed head to the actress's hands, the mutilation takes place under Medusa's gaze and is juxtaposed to a symbolic decapitation. The text is peppered with references to Medusa's power to turn people into stone, and the Gorgon's severed head is literally placed on stage through a replica of the Medusa Ludovisi, a Roman reproduction of a Greek larger-than-life head.

In the play, the sculptor Lucio Settala, another 'man of genius' and artist of Nietzschean sensibility, is torn between his role as Silvia's husband and his attraction to the model Gioconda Dianti, who has inspired a sculpture that he considers his masterpiece. The two women are respectively associated with the Apollonian and the Dionysian,[10] with Leonardo's *Mona Lisa* and the Gorgon's gaze, but contrasts are ultimately undone as Gioconda/Medusa appears as a two-faced herm.[11] The encounter of the Apollonian and the Dionysian, of Ancient Greece and the Renaissance, facilitates the creation of the 'perfect' work of art, although at the cost of the mutilation of the female body.

The first act takes place in Silvia's house, located on the Florentine hills, where she is nursing her husband after he has attempted suicide. Silvia's windows look onto a Renaissance landscape, the Basilica and cloister of San Miniato. In the opening dialogue, the sculptor Lorenzo Gaddi draws attention to Silvia's hands, and compares them to those of a Renaissance bust, Andrea del Verrocchio's '*dama col mazzolino*' [Lady with a bouquet], celebrated by Pater in his essay on Leonardo da Vinci.[12] Silvia's sister, Francesca, and Gaddi then compare her to a winged Nike. Struck by her sister's strength and energy, Francesca notes that Silvia seems about to spread her wings; Gaddi similarly comments 'Esce dal suo martirio alata' [She comes winged out of her martyrdom] (D'Annunzio 2013b: 238). These allusions underline the resemblance between Silvia and Lucio's masterpiece, a Sphynx which Lucio's friend Cosimo describes as featuring 'ali imprigionate vive negli omeri' [wings imprisoned alive in the shoulders] (D'Annunzio 2013b: 244) and already suggest the conflation between Renaissance and Ancient Greek art that culminates in the ending of the play.

The sculpture has, however, been inspired by Gioconda, a model who, like the *Mona Lisa* described by Pater in *The Renaissance*, has a dark, vampiric, mysterious look. The thick veil that hides her features 'come una maschera fosca' [like a dark mask] (D'Annunzio 2013b: 303) contrasts with the stress Lucio places on her changeability: 'Mille statue, non una! Ella è sempre diversa' [A thousand statues, not one! She is always diverse] (D'Annunzio 2013b: 267). From Lucio's conversations with his friend Cosimo, we learn that his obsession revolves around Gioconda's gaze:

> La vita degli occhi è lo sguardo, questa cosa indicibile, più espressiva di ogni parola, d'ogni suono, infinitamente profonda e pure istantanea come il baleno, più rapida ancora del baleno, innumerevole, onnipossente: insomma *lo sguardo*. Ora imagina diffusa su tutto il suo corpo di lei la vita dello sguardo. Comprendi? [...] Potrai tu scolpire lo sguardo? Gli Antichi accecarono le statue. Ora — imagina — tutto il corpo di lei è come lo sguardo.
>
> [The life of the eyes is the gaze, that indefinable thing, more expressive than any words, than any sound, infinitely deep and yet instantaneous as a breath, swifter than a flash, innumerable, omnipotent: in a word, *the gaze*. Now imagine the life of the gaze spread out over all her body. Do you understand? [...] Can one chisel a gaze? The ancients made their statues blind. Now, imagine, her whole body is like the gaze.] (D'Annunzio 2013b: 267)

Like the Gorgon's gaze, Gioconda's look inspires the creation of statues, and is both a source of fascination and a threat. Like Medusa, she cannot be directly confronted. As Cosimo stresses: 'Ella è terribile. Non si lotta contro di lei se non di lontano' [She is terrible. One cannot fight against her save at a distance] (D'Annunzio 2013b: 259).

Fig. 4.4. Head of Erinni Ludovisi, known as Medusa Ludovisi, National Roman Museum, Palazzo Altemps, Rome, by kind permission of the Ministry of Cultural Heritage and Tourism

A weak Perseus, Lucio, the artist on the verge of a nervous breakdown who describes his perception as 'life under narcotics', does not have the energy to fight her. The challenge is taken up by Silvia, who, as a wife and mother, represents strength, health and fertility, features that characterize her as the opposite of her rival.

The stage directions for the fourth act contrast the 'carnal, victorious and creative' energy of Lucio's studio and the domestic, withdrawn ambience of Silvia's house (D'Annunzio 2013b: 298). In the tall, spacious studio, a bas-relief of Demeter is arranged next to a vase of ears of wheat, the head of the Medusa Ludovisi next to a small Pegasus. The door leading to the model's studio, where Lucio keeps his Sphynx, is decorated by two statues, the *Nike* by Poenius and *Nike* of Samothrace, and by an architrave featuring reproductions from the Phidian frieze of the Parthenon. As Spackman has noted, all the objects in the room are either fragments, or thematically linked to the notion of the fragmentary: 'the Nike of Samothrace is armless and headless; the Nike of Paionios handless, faceless, and wingless; the Panathenaic fragments are fragments of fragments; the bas-relief, a fragment; the Medusa, beheaded [...] The trait shared by all is mutilation' (1989: 197).[13]

When Silvia tells Gioconda that Lucio has sent her to ban her from the studio, the two women step into the door decorated with Greek fragments and a confrontation takes place off stage. Gioconda, in a fit of rage, attempts to destroy the statue she has inspired by pushing it to the floor. Silvia rushes forward to save it, and her hands are crushed by the weight. The sculpture is likewise mutilated, but its charm increases through the loss of the arms. In the fourth act, which is set in Silvia's house next to the sea, Verrocchio's Renaissance bust, placed on a shelf, stands directly behind Silvia and, by displaying its intact hands, underlines her mutilation. In her interpretation, Duse wore a white high-necked, long-sleeved robe that gave her the look of a statue.

Katia Laura Angioletti sees Silvia's comparison to the mutilated statue as symbolic of her fall; for her, Silvia will never be able to match the masterpiece; she is neither a muse nor a wife, and the mutilation also changes her role as a mother (2010: 119). Duse's biographer Helen Sheehy similarly notes that the ending conveys a powerful image of women 'literally and figuratively crushed by the demands of masculine art' (2003: 184). Spackman argues that the drama functions as 'a mise en scène of the fetishist's *Verleugnung*' [denial]. Silvia's hands, she contends, become a fetish through the oscillation between acknowledgement and disavowal, and her mutilation is a symbolic castration (1989: 202). This reading finds endorsement in the way in which Silvia's sister refers to the mutilation, which she addresses as 'cosa orrenda' [horrible thing] (D'Annunzio 2013b: 326). Duse's elegant impersonation, however, suggested that the device was first and foremost a homage to her acting, as well as a way to underline a poetics of the fragment inspired by Classical art. In *Il fuoco*, Duse's alter ego Foscarina recalls how she learned to act by imitating the poses of statues, and acknowledges that she preferred broken statues to whole ones:

> Alcune [statue] mi sembravano bellissime, e io mi provavo a imitare i loro gesti. Ma rimanevo più lungamente in compagnia con le mutilate, quasi per istinto di consolarle. [...] Amai teneramente una che non aveva più le braccia, con cui un tempo reggeva su la testa un canestro di frutti. Ma le mani erano rimaste attaccate al canestro, e mi facevano pena....
>
> [Some [statues] seemed quite beautiful to me, and I would try to imitate their gestures. But I always stayed longest with the mutilated ones, as though I were instinctively trying to comfort them. [...] I really loved one statue that had lost the arms that used to support a basket of fruit on its head. But its hands were still fastened to the basket, and I used to feel such pity.] (D'Annunzio 2016: 276)

After seeing the play performed by Eleonora Duse in Vienna, Rainer Maria Rilke emphasized the beauty of the female body as a fragment, and compared Silvia's handless body to a 'real' work of art, the armless and knee-less statue by Rodin, *La Meditation*:

> One recalls the Duse; how, in one of d'Annunzio's dramas, when painfully abandoned she attempted to embrace without her arms and to clasp without

hands. This scene, in which her body learned a caress that passed far beyond it, belongs to the unforgettable moments of her acting. She conveyed the impression that arms were an excess, an adornment, something for the rich and the profligate, which one could cast aside in order to be truly poor. In that moment she didn't seem to have given up anything important; she was more like someone who had given away her goblet to drink from a brook, like a person who is naked and still a little helpless in the depths of his exposure. It is the same with the armless statues of Rodin: nothing is necessarily missing. One stands before them as before something whole, perfected, which allows no augmentation. (Rilke 1979: 35)

For Rilke, the handless body is in itself a fragment, and the fragment is perfect, as it already contains in itself a totality.[14]

At the beginning of the play, Silvia and Gioconda share a connection to the Renaissance: Gioconda is named after Leonardo's painting, but it is Silvia who, in the first act, faces the viewers as if in a *tableau vivant*, her figure framed by the window against the Renaissance landscape (D'Annunzio 2013b: 229; see also Angioletti 2010: 117; Syrimis 2017: 382). Both Silvia and Gioconda represent the ideal of art as celebrated by Pater 'a beauty wrought out from within upon the flesh, the deposit [...] of strange thoughts and fantastic reveries and exquisite passions' (Pater 1976: 102). By end of the play, they are both associated with Ancient Greece. Gioconda, standing next to Medusa's head, calls the fragments as witnesses to the bond between her and Lucio. Through the mutilation, Silvia literally becomes a fragment and resembles the Sphynx created in Lucio's studio.

In *La Gloria*, masks are brought into connection with decapitation. Set against the background of Rome, the play portrays the death of a dictator, Cesare Bronte, and the ascent of a charismatic leader, Ruggero Flamma, who promises to Italians the 'ricostituzione della città, della patria, della forza Latina' [the regeneration of the city, the homeland, the Latin strength] (D'Annunzio 2013c: 348). Between them stands Elena Comnèna, the decadent *femme fatale* in whom D'Annunzio saw the real protagonist. Although married to Cesare Bronte, Comnèna realizes that Flamma has the support of the people, so she poisons her husband and incites Flamma to become a ruthless tyrant. When she sees that he no longer has the confidence to confront and dominate the crowd, she kills him too and shifts her support to another emerging political figure.

Written and produced in 1899, *La Gloria*, like *La Gioconda*, was designed for Duse and Zacconi. Since the tragedy had two main male roles, and Duse could not think of an additional actor who would be able to sustain the part, D'Annunzio assigned to Zacconi the roles of both Flamma and Bronte, justifying the strategy as an attempt to revive the spirit of Greek tragedy at the time of Aeschylus (D'Annunzio 1992b: 148–49). In keeping with this aim, he presented a multitude of characters on stage as a way to reawaken the spirit of the chorus. As Valentina Valentini has emphasized, the representation of the masses constituted a novelty in Italian dramaturgy, and resonated with *fin-de-siècle* anxieties about the rise of democracy and the increasing power of the working classes (Valentini 1992: 92). In the drama, the crowd played a pivotal role and was listed among the *dramatis personae*. Onstage, it manifested itself through emphasis on shouting and crescendos.

La Gloria shared numerous similarities with *La Gioconda*. Both plays revolve around a masked, mysterious woman who is on the one hand associated with Leonardo da Vinci's masterpiece, and on the other with the Gorgon, and who, like the *Mona Lisa* described by Pater, continues to assume different shapes.[15] Unlike Lucio, Ruggero Flamma is not an artist but a revolutionary; however, not unlike D'Annunzio, he envisions his political mission as a work of art. In a note that described the essential features of each character, D'Annunzio highlighted how the themes of masks and the gaze were pivotal in the play:

> Cesare Bronte pareva s'ingrandisse d'attimo in attimo, ingigantisse, tutto rilievi e cavità, tutto cicatrici e scabrezze, tutto nocchi e punte, ora tronco e ora macigno. Lo sguardo di Ruggero Flamma talvolta era inquieto e incerto, era come una mano che palpi una muraglia buia per trovare gli interstizi d'una porta; si perdeva talvolta, cessava, come se l'occhio si votasse interamente, simile al buco che rimane nell'orbita delle teste di bronzo, ond'è balzato via lo smalto. Elena Comnena, la seduttrice e la devastatrice, non era abbastanza bella. Le cambiavo la maschera, e non aveva ella ancora la sua vera e propria bellezza. Ma già la sua bocca rosseggiava della sua parola mortale e immortale: 'La Gloria mi somiglia'.

> [Cesare Bronte seemed to become larger and larger, like a giant, with bumps and cavities, scars and roughness, knots and lumps; now a trunk, now a rock. Ruggero Flamma's gaze was often restless and unsteady, like a hand that that feels a dark wall to find the outline of a doorway. Sometimes his gaze was lost, it stopped, as if his eyes were completely empty, similar to the hollow orbits of bronze heads where the varnish has come off. Elena Comnena, the seducer and the destroyer, was not beautiful enough. I changed the mask on her, and she did not have yet her own, true beauty. But her mouth became redder because of her mortal and immortal Word: 'Glory resembles me'. (D'Annunzio 1924a: 12)

Flamma's weakness is associated with blindness, and his hesitant gaze is compared to the hollow eyes of a decaying statue, an image that suggests immobility and belatedness. Elena Comnèna, the 'seducer-destroyer', is instead a powerful figure, connected to masks and becoming.

In *La Gioconda*, Lucio's friend Cosimo recalls a young girl, an androgynous creature whom he 'purchased' during his trip to Egypt:

> Nell'isola d'Elefantina avevo un'amica di quattordici anni: una fanciulla dorata come un dattero, magra, svelta, arida, con le reni forti e arcate, legambe diritte e potenti, i ginocchi perfetti [...] dava imagine d'un'arme da lancio precisa e fine [...] Avrei voluto portartela con le statuette, con gli scarabei, con le stoffe, col tabacco, con i profumi, con le armi. Ma t'ho portato un bell'arco, che ho comperato ad Assouan e che le somiglia un poco.

> [On the island of Elephantina I had a little friend of fourteen; a girl golden as a date, thin, lithe, firm, with strong, arched loins, straight, strong legs, perfect knees [...] which gave one the impression of a javelin, sharp and precise [...]. I should like to have taken her away with the statuettes, the scarabs, the cloths, the tobacco, the scents, the weapons. I have brought you a beautiful bow that I bought at Assouan, and that is a little like her.] (D'Annunzio 2013b: 247)

Like Cosimo's nameless friend, Comnèna, a Byzantine princess, comes from the East. Like her, she is described as a weapon, 'Un'arme formidabile e lucente, che chiede di essere brandita da un pugno invitto' [a formidable, shining weapon, that asks to be brandished by an unconquered fist] (D'Annunzio 2013c: 362). Both women are perceived as merchandise, goods to be sold and exchanged. Cosimo sees the Egyptian girl as an item in his collection; Cesare Bronte addresses Elena as 'la merce infetta, la cosa da guadagno, l'ordigno di froda e di morte' [infected goods, an object to be won, a device of fraud and death] (D'Annunzio 2013c: 384). These shared traits underline that the imperialistic vision sustained by Flamma in *La Gloria* is not very different from Lucio's vision as an artist.

Since the cult of Dionysus was believed to have come to Greece from the East, Comnèna's origins strengthen her connection to the Dionysian. Born in Trebizond, the last city of the Byzantine Empire, Comnèna is the last offspring of a corrupted family. Described as sterile, she is at once a decadent *femme fatale* and a female version of the typical decadent hero. Like Gioconda, Comnèna makes her appearance on stage with her features covered by a thick veil; in addition, she wears a 'strange' metallic head cover that, as the stage directions indicate, resembles a winged helmet, and her only jewellery is a Medusa's head that shines on her breast 'as though on an armour' (D'Annunzio 2013c: 400). Her guise recalls the look of Athena, goddess of war and patron of Perseus's endeavours, who in the myth places Medusa's head on her shield (see Trebbi 1996: 115; Witt 2007: 84). As an incarnation of Athena, Comnèna protects Flamma's mission, providing him with strategic advice. When she removes her veil, she does not quite reveal her true self, but another disguise, as her features are described as 'immobile as a mask' (D'Annunzio 2013c: 381). In other scenes, she stands motionless beside a door or under a ledge 'quasi marmorea, immobile come una caryatide' [almost marmoreal, motionless like a caryatid] (D'Annunzio 2013c: 387).

By the third act, Comnèna, with a metonymic shift, turns from Athena into the Gorgon, from Flamma's protector into a threat. In the fourth act, Flamma, unsettled by his lover's lust for destruction, compares his feelings towards Comnèna to 'l'orrore di sentirti impietrito a poco a poco dalla faccia della Gorgone' [the horror of feeling turned to stone little by little by the face of the Gorgon] (D'Annunzio 2013c: 428). Like Lucio, Flamma is too weak to confront the Gorgon. Even at the apex of his power, he suffers from nervous attacks — an affliction that for *fin-de-siècle* sexologists was typical of women — and is unable to overcome 'l'orrore fisico della folla, il raccapriccio istintivo che gli dà il contatto col mostro' [the physical horror generated by the crowd, the instinctive disgust that contact with the monster provokes] (D'Annunzio 2013c: 350). As he confesses to Comnèna, he is not afraid of death, but he cannot stand the idea that the crowd may gouge out his eyes, disfigure his body and tear it to pieces. What he fears most of all is the devastation of the body through mutilation, referred in *Gioconda* as a 'cosa orrenda' (D'Annunzio 2013b: 326).

When he first sees her, Flamma dreams of capturing Comnèna 'come una preda di guerra' [as spoils of war] (D'Annunzio 2013c: 369). Witnessing Flamma's popularity among the masses, Comnèna calls upon him. However, when Flamma shows signs of weakness, he becomes unable to appease her. Comnèna's desire, as he acknowledges, is insatiable: 'se io tendessi il mio arco fino a spezzarlo, non coglierei il segno a cui tu aspiri. Il tuo desiderio va sempre più lontano, di là da tutti i termini...' [even if I stretched my bow to the point breaking it, I wouldn't hit the target you are aiming at. Your desire always goes farther, beyond all boundaries] (D'Annunzio 2013c: 411). In the course of the play, an inverse relationship develops between the two characters: as Flamma becomes weaker, and assumes feminine traits, Comnèna increasingly acquires virile features. In the fourth act, after a young man has tried to assassinate Flamma, she plays with the weapon intended for the murder and suggests that Flamma should give it to her as a gift. She then asserts her control over him: 'si avvicina all'uomo, lo avviluppa, lo serra, se ne impadronisce' [she approaches the man, envelops him, holds him tight, and possesses him] (D'Annunzio 2013c: 434). When Flamma resolves to use the knife to kill her, his hands tremble, and Comnèna takes it from him. Initially compared to a weapon, she now flaunts the knife, ready to penetrate her lover. In the fifth act, when Flamma loses control and the crowd demands his death, she embraces him and stabs him. In the end of the play, Comnèna shows herself to the masses and announces Flamma's death. The crowd responds by asking for his head, repeating the words 'la testa! La Sua testa! Gettateci la testa!' [his head! His head! Throw us his head!] with increasing intensity.

D'Annunzio's inversion of Medusa's myth reflects the reversal of gender roles: by the time the decapitation has taken place, Flamma has been feminized, while Comnèna has appropriated masculine traits. Witt goes as far as suggesting that 'Freud could have used *La Gloria* to illustrate his theory of castration anxiety based on the sight of Medusa' (2001: 76). However, for Freud, Athena represents the unapproachable mother, whereas Comnèna, as Flamma repeats incessantly, is sterile. Moreover, rather than being horrified by the feminine, Flamma increasingly identifies with it.

During the premiere at Bellini's theatre in Palermo (15 April 1899), *La Gioconda* was whistled at by an outraged audience.[16] Nevertheless, Duse's talent ensured its success in the subsequent national and international tour, where it was acclaimed by critics of the stature of Rainer Maria Rilke and Hugo von Hofmannsthal. *La Gloria* premiered shortly after *La Gioconda*, on 27 April 1899 at the *Mercadante* theatre in Naples. Duse and Zacconi had only one week to put together the production, and the result was a fiasco: the audience whistled, booed and went so far as to demand the author's death. The scandal put an end to productions of the play. While Duse successfully toured Europe with *La Gioconda*, *La Gloria* was not staged again until 1928, when it acquired a very different meaning as an allegory of fascism.[17]

FIG. 4.5. Anonymous, Head of Medusa, Flemish School, 16th or 17th century, oil on panel, 49 x 74 cm, Uffizi gallery, Florence

Conclusions

D'Annunzio blamed the actors for the flop of *La Gloria*, accusing Duse's company of being stuck in the Italian tradition and unable to look beyond it and take on modern roles. Since another production was not sustainable, he defended the play as an essay-text, an 'opera d'arte e di pensiero' [a work of art and thought] designed to be read, rather than staged (D'Annunzio 2003c: 374). Moreover, in an article for *L'illustrazione italiana*, he translated excerpts of a review published in French by Enrico Belanger and argued that *La Gloria*, despite the negative reception in Italy, was highly praised abroad. Belanger's review began with a description of the painting of Medusa held in the Uffizi gallery, which, at that time, was attributed to Leonardo da Vinci and, like the *Mona Lisa*, had come to symbolize the Renaissance:[18]

> V'è in una piccola sala della Galleria degli Uffici una testa di medusa di Leonardo da Vinci, figura a un tempo reale e chimerica, di cui ogni particolare è minuziosamente vero, e che tuttavia si perde in quel sogno infinito dove la morte e la vita si agguagliano. Ho sentito lo stesso fremito d'arte leggendo *La Gloria* di Gabriele d'Annunzio.
>
> [In a small room of the Uffizi Gallery there is a head of Medusa by Leonardo Da Vinci, a figure that is at the same time real and chimerical, realistic in every detail and yet lost in that infinite dream where death and life are alike. I experienced the same artistic shiver reading *The Glory* by Gabriele D'Annunzio.] (D'Annunzio 2003c: 375)

In establishing an association between D'Annunzio's drama and the beheading of Medusa, Belanger was developing an artistic topos already rooted in D'Annunzio's works. Like the author of the painting, D'Annunzio portrayed Medusa as a woman, rather than a monster, and focused on the moment after decapitation, when the head, already severed from the body, acquired an apotropaic function. However, whereas the painting held at the Uffizi portrayed a head in isolation, D'Annunzio concentrated on the bond between hero and monster. Cut off from the Gorgon's body, the severed head enters into a dynamic relationship with the beheader. In reflecting aspects of the hero's subjectivity, it also functions as a mask.

In *Il fuoco*, Stelio admires Foscarina as, rehearsing for his new tragedy, she pretends to hold Cassandra's mask: 'Ah, io t'ho creata, t'ho creata!' [Ah, I have created you! I have created you!] (D'Annunzio 2016: 295) he cries, concluding that 'ella era anche una volta quale egli voleva foggiarla...' [She was once more what he wanted to make of her] (D'Annunzio 2016: 213). Since the actress is Stelio's creation, his astonishment at her acting is a form of self-admiration, and mask-imagery involves elements of self-referentiality. Writing under the influence of Nietzsche, D'Annunzio created heroes convinced of the superiority of their artistic and political missions. Most of them, however, suffer from a nervous condition, are effeminate, and display an excessive focus on the self — symptoms that for Lombroso and Nordau were typical of degeneration.[19] The protagonist of *Il fuoco*, apparently 'healthier' than his dramatic alter egos, shares with them the urge 'to be noticed, to occupy the attention of the world with himself, to get talked about' (Nordau 1993: 317) that Nordau called *ego-mania*. Tellingly, he argues that 'per ottenere la vittoria sugli uomini e sulle cose, nulla vale quanto la costanza nell'esaltare sé medesimo nel magnificare il suo proprio sogno di bellezza o di dominazione' [in order to conquer both men and circumstances, it is essential to assert one's Self and to magnify one's dreams of beauty and of power] (D'Annunzio 2016: 43).

While the parables of Medusa and Orpheus trace the source of the work of art in fetishism, Stelio's words establish a connection between artistic endeavours, political missions, and narcissism. As for Binet, for D'Annunzio fetishism and narcissism were closely connected. In D'Annunzio's works, fetishism revolves around a preference for a part of the body, such as the face or the hands, and acquires a pathological connotation as the fetishist shifts his attention to an inanimate object, the mask, or to a human fragment, the severed head. Moreover, fetishism features as a master-narrative that encompasses other perversions. Following nineteenth-century socio-anthropological inquiries, it crosses the boundaries of the psychological to intrude into the social and political spheres.

Through the close link to images of gender undifferentiation, the fetish provides a suitable reading for Freud's fear of castration. However, the mutilated female body is characterized as beautiful. Moreover, the interchangeability between the slaying of Medusa and the death of Orpheus complicates a reading in which the fetish, as in Freud, has a normative function. D'Annunzio manipulates Medusa's myth and plays with narrative inversion to draw attention to sexual inversion. The substitution of Medusa with Orpheus, and the progressive feminization of male characters and virilization of female figures, indicate not so much the triumph of the *femme fatale* or the aversion for the feminine but a fascination with the interchangeability of sexual and gender roles. The insistence on masks, images of decapitation and severed heads, rather than redirecting the hero to reproductive sexuality, is associated to a web of non-normative sexual practices, most prominently narcissism and same-sex desire.

Notes to Chapter 4

1. For recent biographies of D'Annunzio, see Andreoli's *Il vivere inimitabile* (2001); Woodhouse's *Gabriele D'Annunzio: Defiant Archangel* (2008); Hughes-Hallett's *The Pike: Gabriele D'Annunzio, Poet, Seducer and Preacher of War* (2013).
2. As a dandy-aesthete and actress-diva, D'Annunzio and Duse shared the cult of masks and poses. On the similarities between the dandy and the diva in *fin-de-siècle* culture, see Felski, *The Gender of Modernity* 1995: 110–11.
3. Witt also notes that Stelio's fantasy recalls the passage of *The Birth of Tragedy* in which Apollo is portrayed fighting against Dionysian forces by holding against them the Gorgon's head (2001: 42): 'For some time [...] the Greeks were apparently perfectly insulated and guarded against the feverish excitements of these festivals, though knowledge of them must have come to Greece on all the routes of land and sea; for the figure of Apollo, visiting with pride, held out the Gorgon's head to this grotesquely uncouth Dionysian power — and really could not have countered any more dangerous force' (Nietzsche 1967: 39).
4. Benvenuto Cellini, for D'Annunzio, was the Italian artist who, anticipating Wagner, invented the concept of the total work of art that Stelio aims to recreate in his tragic theatre.
5. In displaying the standing figure and the severed head in the same pose as in Moreau's painting of Salomé holding the head of John the Baptist — which had become an archetype for the decadents — it also suggests a link to the decadent *femme fatale* and evokes the theme of decapitation.
6. 'Non so più rivolgermi indietro, Fosca' [I cannot go back now, Foscarina] (D'Annunzio 2016: 158), Stelio comments for instance alluding to the action that Hades forbids to the poet as he searches for his spouse.
7. References to sterility also highlight D'Annunzio's manipulation of Duse's biography, who already had a daughter.
8. 'Tu sei bianca come quelle statue. Nessuna donna è bianca come tu sei...' [You are as white as these statues. No woman is as white as you are], says Anna's nurse. 'Ah perciò sono diventata cieca, come le statue! Guardami negli occhi, nutrice. Non sono come due pietre opache?' [Ah! That is why I became blind, like the statues! [...] Look at my eyes, Nurse, are they not like two opaque stones?], answers Anna (D'Annunzio 2013: 106).
9. On 5 March 1899, D'Annunzio wrote to Zacconi offering him both *La Gioconda* and *La Gloria*, and stressed that only his talent would be able to render these 'maschere viventi terribili' [terrible living masks] (D'Annunzio 1992b: 142).
10. See Witt 2001 and Symiris 2017.
11. The dyad Gioconda/Medusa reflects the dyad life-death that Mario Praz identifies as a core feature of Romanticism inherited by the decadents (Praz 1970: 27–31).
12. A fifteenth-century sculpture that exemplifies the Renaissance tradition of the bust-portrait inspired by devotional wax effigies, the bust is itself a fragment (Spackman 1989: 198). Pater's essay on Leonardo da Vinci (1869), which contributed to the popularization of the sculpture, was subsequently reprinted in *The Renaissance*.
13. The vase of ears of wheat, which apparently interrupted the pattern, is a symbol of fertility linked to the Eleusinian mysteries and underlines the connection between Lucio's art and the Dionysian.
14. A similar impression, for Rilke, was conjured by the headless and armless torso of Apollo held at the Louvre, to which he dedicates a poem in the *Neue Gedichte*.
15. Flamma evokes Walter Pater's description of the *Mona Lisa* as, contemplating the young Comnèna, he remarks: 'La tua anima è antica quanto il mondo! Tutta la vecchiezza del mondo

posa nei tuoi pensieri' [Your soul is as old as the world! The world's ancientness weights on your thoughts] (D'Annunzio 2013c: 416), a comment reminiscent of Pater's 'All the thoughts and experience of the world have etched and moulded there [...] She is older than the rocks among which she sits' (Pater 1976: 102). Gioconda has the power to create statues; Comnèna is compared to one. In threatening and defying the male protagonist, they both share a connection to the Dionysian.

16. The manipulation of the myth had a political dimension, as the hero's decapitation corresponded to a sudden change in a political landscape. As Witt notes, 'Perseus encounters the Medusa but is undone — in effect castrated — by her. In historical terms, an Italy dominated by bourgeois ideals and a bourgeois government is itself mutilated, not yet ready to emerge victorious in the pursuit of its historical destiny' (Witt 2001: 77). For Andrea Bisicchia, Flamma's downfall symbolized the crisis of Western culture, in which Bronte and Flamma represent the West, and Elena Comnèna the irrational, corrupt East. In Flamma's decapitation, Bisicchia sees an aesthetic topos, a fetish that was literally realized in the production, when D'Annunzio's play was effectively 'mutilated' in the disastrous mise en scène (1991: 70).
17. Coming across the play in 1924, Mussolini was so enthusiastic that he adopted the slogan of Elena Comnèna, 'chi s'arresta è perduto' [he who stops is lost]. In the 1928 production, the character of Flamma became a prototype of the fascist hero.
18. For a comment on the importance that this painting acquired for the Romantics, and subsequently for the decadents, see Praz 1970: 27–31.
19. As early as 1906, the psychologist Scipio Sighele, whose work was influenced by Lombroso, analysed D'Annunzio's characters, including the protagonist of *Il fuoco*, as Lombrosian types, and elaborated on D'Annunzio's representations of the mob in conjunction with his own theory of the crowd (Sighele 1906: 3–94). More recently, Barbara Spackman (1989) and Jonathan Hiller (2013) have investigated the extent to which Lombroso's idea of delinquency found fertile ground in D'Annunzio's fiction. Derek Duncan has argued that, since Lombroso identified similarities between criminality and sexual inversion, in resembling the criminal type, some of D'Annunzio's characters also recall the prototype of the homosexual as constructed in the late nineteenth century (Duncan 2006: 19).

CHAPTER 5

Masks-Phobia: Jean Lorrain

Avez-vous remarqué que le masque, faux visage, terrifie les jeunes enfants, même quand ses traits rient? C'est sans doute qu'avec lui s'insinue un décollement intrinsèque.

[Have you noticed how a mask, a false face, terrifies young children, even when its features are laughing? No doubt that's because decapitation is intrinsically implied.] (Kristeva 2012: 117)

In his seminal study on *fin-de-siècle* literature, originally published in 1930, Mario Praz described Jean Lorrain (1855–1906) as 'a *fumiste* of deplorable taste', 'a case of virility complex in a being of feminine sensitivity', and 'a hysteric, with homosexual tendencies' (1970: 352). In Praz's eyes Lorrain, despite his efforts to resemble the criminal type, was simply a 'chronic invalid [...] disguised as a werewolf' (1970: 353). While these comments debunk the coupling between homosexuality and criminality, they still echo the association of masking and perversion that was rooted in nineteenth-century sexology. This chapter examines Jean Lorrain's *Histoires de masques* (1900) and the novel *Monsieur de Phocas* (1901) in relation to a literary and pictorial tradition of artists concerned with masks and against the background of *fin-de-siècle* medical discourses and the emerging theories of psychoanalysis. It argues that, in Lorrain's fiction, masks appear at the crossroads between the teaching of E. T. A. Hoffmann, Marcel Schwob and James Ensor, the non-normative sexual practices classified by sexologists, and the societal and historical decline that Lorrain and his contemporaries perceived was affecting France and Europe.

Born into a middle-class family from Normandy, Paul Duval, as Lorrain was originally called, cultivated the pose of the dandy-aesthete but was obliged to work as a journalist, and became one of the most powerful cultural critics of the *belle époque*. From the beginning of his career, he signed his articles with female and male aliases, moulding public personae inseparable from his role as a writer (Koos 1999: 199; Ziegler 1994: 31). 'Jean Lorrain', which became his artistic signature, was invented by his mother, who feared that her son would discredit the family by writing in his own name (Kyria 1973: 13–22). Openly homosexual, Lorrain challenged societal norms by dyeing his hair, wearing make-up, sporting female jewellery, and bragging about sexual encounters with men. His biographers emphasize how, from childhood, he delighted in disguising himself and performing in public (Kyria 1973: 32; Jullian 1974: 72). As a friend of the writer Rachilde, who since the 1880s had worn male clothes, he shared with her a fascination with drag and appeared at official receptions, dinners and masked balls in outfits that ranged from wrestling tights to butcher's uniforms to pink swim suits (Cima 2009: 72; Ziegler 2008: 29). The cult of disguises was in keeping with his obsession for mask as props and artefacts, and both were tinged with fetishism and necrophilia. Dressed as a Turk or Arab, Lorrain often exhibited himself in exotic dances that concluded with a mimicry of ritual suicide. Moreover, he displayed in his living room a female plaster head that he had torn down from a statue and decorated with blood clots (Jullian 1974: 146).[1]

Lorrain was familiar with the theories of Ambroise Tardieu, who in his *Études médico-légale sur les attentats aux mœurs* [Forensic study on offenses against morals] (1857) had described attraction for the same-sex as an inborn — albeit despicable — feature, as well as with the work of Cesare Lombroso, who associated sexual inversion with criminality (Winn 1997: 78). Like the young Freud, he attended Jean-Martin Charcot's lectures on hysteria at the *Salpêtrière* in the late 1880s and developed an interest in 'obsessional neurosis', a term that he used to define the protagonist's illness in *Monsieur de Phocas* (Noir 2004: 13). He was also acquainted with the work of Paul Moreau de Tours, who belonged to the same psychological school as Valentin Magnan and Alfred Binet. Krafft-Ebing's *Psychopathia Sexualis*, *the* European textbook on sexology, was translated into French in 1895 (Foucault 2003: 195), and it is not far-fetched to assume that Lorrain had come across it.

Like these psychologists, Lorrain established a connection between masks, cross-dressing, and sexual perversions, and characterized the sexual deviant as a degenerate. Moreover, he traced the origin of the obsession with masks in childhood experiences, thereby prefiguring aspects of Freud's theory of the uncanny. As *fin-de-siècle* intellectuals, Freud and Lorrain shared a similar cultural background: both were familiar with Charcot's work, explored the notion of hysteria, and shared an appreciation for E. T. A. Hoffmann (1776–1822). Both were particularly struck by Hoffmann's short story 'The Sandman,' which played an important role in prompting Freud's reflections on the uncanny and features as a crucial intertext in *Histoires de masques* and in *Monsieur de Phocas*. Freud's concept of the uncanny shared with his theory of homosexuality an origin in childhood experiences and in primitive stages of society (Freud 1953: 145).[2] Moreover, homosexuality, and the related concept of fetishism, were in Freud's thought both consequences of the castration complex, to which the uncanny, as a manifestation of the return of repressed childhood experiences, was closely related.

In Lorrain's fiction, masks disrupt gender markers, challenging sex and gender as binary categories. However, they do not convey playfulness and the delight of adopting multiple personas, but are associated with crime, perversion, drug addiction, illness and decay. As fetish objects linked to the return of the repressed, they acquire uncanny connotations and become expressions of queerness, understood as all that fails to comply with the heteronormative (Edelman 2004: 17). How do Lorrain's texts reconcile the embrace of gender as performative and the association of masks and degeneration? Does Lorrain, as scholars have argued (Winn 1997; Cima 2009), condemn same-sex desire in the same way as most nineteenth-century sexologists, or does his use of scientific categories contribute to the formation of counter-discourse, in the sense intended by Foucault (1978: 101), which enables homosexuality to speak in its own right (1978: 101)? By exploring the links between fetishism and narcissism in relation to masks, portraits and severed heads, this chapter sets out to answer these questions.

The Empty Signifier: *Histoires de masques*

Masks function as a privileged motif and as an organizing principle in *Histoires de masques*, the collection issued by Paul Ollendorf in 1900, which gathered the short stories published by Lorrain in the 1880s. In the first story of the collection, 'L'Un de d'Eux' [One of Them], Lorrain gives his first definition of the mask: 'Le masque, c'est la face trouble et troublante de l'inconnu, c'est le sourire du mensonge, c'est l'âme même de la perversité qui sait corrompre en terrifiant; c'est la luxure pimentée de la peur' [The mask is the disturbed and disturbing face of the unknown; the smile of mendacity; the very soul of that terrifying perversity which understands depravity; it is lust spiced with fear] (2006: 16). In 'Trio de masques' [Three Masks], he repeats with variations: 'le masque; c'est le rire du mystère, c'est le visage du mensonge fait avec la déformation du vrai, c'est la laideur voulu de la réalité exagérée pour cacher l'inconnu' [the mask is the laugh of mystery; the face of mendacity made by deforming the truth; the intended ugliness of the real, exaggerated to hide the unknown] (2006: 79). These definitions, however, characterize not so much the mask, or the shapes and configurations masks assume in the tales, but rather the perception of the onlooker, who is always 'unmasked'. Moreover, the structure of the 'story within a story' allows the narrator, who introduces himself as an expert on masks, to distance himself from the mask-wearers. Throughout the collection, three 'great deformers' provide him with an inspiration for his tales: the Romantic writer E. T. A. Hoffmann (1776–1822), the symbolist Marcel Schwob (1867–1905), and the painter James Ensor (1860–1949). Lorrain's relationship to these artists sheds light on aspects of the mask that he chooses to emphasize.

Hoffmann's tales had become particularly popular in France through the operatic version by Jacques Offenbach. In 'Lanterne magique' [The Magic Lantern], which is set at the opera, Hoffmann becomes a pretext to denounce the corruption of contemporary Parisian society as the members of the audience are matched with the characters of 'The Sandman', a story that revolves around fearful childhood memories, a fixation with the eyes, and a mechanical doll named Olympia. The narrator accuses his companion, an electrician, of being worse than Coppelius, the wicked protagonist of Hoffmann's tale, for having killed the fantastic imagination. The electrician, in turn, defends himself by suggesting that the fantastic is very much with them, and that the Opera has turned into a setting worthy of Hoffmann's tales. Through the sober point of view of a working-class man, he comments on the opera's audience, identifying an enamelled beauty as the doll

Olympia, and introducing another spectator as a devotee of executions who shivers with pleasure at the sight of severed heads. The women of the new aristocracy, the electrician stresses, are 'médicamentées, anémiées, androgynes, hystériques et poitrinaires' [medicated, anaemic, androgynous, hysterical and consumptive] (2006: 52). Through layers of make-up, they have been transformed into masks, 'cadavres échappés du cimetière et vomis par la tombe à travers les vivants' [cadavers spewed from the tomb and escaped from the cemetery into the world of the living] (2006: 52).

As a master of the fantastic, and as 'first of *déformateurs*' (2006: 80), Hoffmann is mentioned again in 'Trio de masques' [Trio of Masks], which begins by rooting the fascination and fear of masks in the experiences of childhood.[3] Here the encounter with the mask takes place at a Carnival ball, the type of venue that, in *fin-de-siècle* Paris, offered opportunities for same-sex encounters. In search of distraction, the protagonist wanders up to the top floor and, in an empty ballroom, observes a couple dancing accompanied by the guitar-playing of a female dwarf in a Japanese costume. The narrator lingers on the description of the couple, which he first interprets as two women, a squat creature and a slender beauty. As he looks more carefully, however, he discovers that the first is a man in women's clothes, and that his companion's fan hides a magnificent beard. Travesty triggers the 'sensation of falling into an abyss, into the absurd, into the impossible' (2006: 85) that introduces the fantastic in Hoffmann's tales. The story also establishes a connection between the gendered performance of the two dancers and the ethnic masquerade of the musician as all three appear to the narrator, who positions himself as a 'healthy' bourgeois, as an aberration. In 'L'Homme au complet mauve' [The Man in the Mauve Suit], a man dressed as a woman is instead referred to as a 'sexual deviant' (2006: 137). Positioned between Hoffmann's fantastic and the theories of contemporary sexology, Lorrain's cross-dressers, like those of Krafft-Ebing, Magnan and Charcot, make a point of stressing the independence of gender behaviour and sexual preferences and come close to today's conception of transgender.[4]

Like Hoffmann's 'The Sandman', Lorrain's collection foregrounds the motif of bodily fragmentation. As a type of fragmentary portrait, the mask shares a connection with the severed head, and in Lorrain's tales assumes similar undertones. The association between masks, portraits and severed heads becomes evident in 'La Dame aux portraits' [The Lady with the Portraits], in which an aristocrat only allows herself to be painted with a high-necked pearl collar that hides a hideous scar. Other stories stress the connection between disembodied heads, fetishism and sexual inversion. In 'L'Homme au bracelet' [The Man with the Bracelet], the face of a prostitute becomes alluring because it appears isolated in a lighted window, a 'tête sans corps' [a head without a body], 'tel un masque' [like a mask] (2006: 98). In 'Le Coup de grâce' [The Mortal Blow], masks explicitly feature as fetishes, while the connection to severed heads takes place at a subtextual level. Here a high-class prostitute suspected of having killed a decrepit millionaire recalls how the 'maniac' had the habit of making her wear a mask and would address her as a historical character. The famous dandy Beau Brummell; Antinoüs, the Bithynian Greek loved by the Emperor Hadrian; the Princesse de Lamballe, rumoured to be the lover of Marie Antoinette, and Mme Dubarry, official lover of Louis XV, feature among her impersonations. The list establishes a relationship between dandyism and gender inversion, and, since the Princesse de Lamballe and Mme Dubarry were decapitated during the revolutionary terror, also underlines the connection between masks, severed heads, revolutionary impetus and the savage instincts of the crowd. Just like Krafft-Ebing, Magnan and Charcot, Lorrain is far from defending his characters, whom he characterizes as degenerate.

In other tales, the focus shifts from cross-dressing to gender undecidability. The author of the collection *Le Roi au masque d'or* (1892), Marcel Schwob, who attended the seminar of Ferdinand de Saussure and Michel Bréal at the *École pratique des hautes études* (Viegnes and Granger 2009: 270), introduced Lorrain to the idea that the mask functions as a sign.[5] In his own fiction, Schwob used masks to reflect on the sign's arbitrary nature, underlining that masks and roles do not share a natural connection; moreover, he noted that the mask, like the linguistic sign, has no intrinsic value and assumes a meaning in relation to the signs that surround it.[6] In *Histoires de masques*, Schwob is mentioned as the inspiration for several tales of the collection. In the first, 'Chez l'une d'elles' [At her place], the narrator, after attending a masked ball, meets a masquerader standing by the Seine. He infers from the fur, shoes and stockings that he must be a young man, but as he gently pushes him away from the river, he revises his interpretation: 'C'était une fille. Au bout de dix minutes, je n'avais plus un doute' [It was a girl. After ten minutes, I no longer had any doubt] (2006: 29). Intrigued, he invites the masquerader to spend the night with him, but he is puzzled when he discovers that his companion's voice is coarse and husky. The masked youth leads him to a scruffy hotel, and, perceiving the narrator's hesitation to enter, reassures him that he works there as a bellboy. Throughout the story, there is no unmasking: we only learn of the shame and horror of the narrator, not the sex of his masked companion.

While Schwob is not explicitly mentioned in 'L'Un d'eux' [One of them], the tale follows the same logic. Here the narrator lingers on in Paris during a carnival night and notices a figure in a green costume with a frog embroidered on the chest. He meets the same person on his way to the railway station, and wonders whether he has not deliberately followed him. It is then that he notices the hybrid nature of the costume: whereas the face is hidden by the hood, the costume divides the figure into a male and a female part 'si bien qu'il était double, ce masque, et joignait au charme terrifiant de sa face de goule le trouble équivoque d'un sexe incertain' [so well that it was double, this mask, and it joined to the terrifying charm of its ghoulish face the ambiguous confusion of an uncertain sex] (2006: 20). Fear and anguish follow: the costume evokes leprosy, plague, lust, the Orient. The narrator swears that he would rather spend the night in Paris than travel with this creature, but cannot resist the temptation to take the same train as them. He finds the masquerader seated, intent on contemplating their reflection in a small mirror that can only reflect the costume's hood. As in 'Chez l'une d'elles', the signifier bears no connection to the signified, the costume no connection to sex and gender.

The frog that the masquerader displays on their chest is a recurrent motif throughout Lorrain's stories, and in 'Le Masque' [The Mask] it is associated with a traumatic childhood event.[7] Philippe Jullian remarks that Lorrain, who had a fascination with frogs and collected frog-shaped statuettes, identified with the animal, in which he recognized 'the opprobrium in which his family held his sexual tastes' (1974: 167). Moreover, all the masqueraders in Lorrain's stories are dressed in green, a colour that Havelock Ellis, in *Sexual Inversion* (1897), associated with attraction to the same sex. While homosexuality fits into the masks' field of signification, it does not, however, exhaust it. As Renée Kingcaid noted, Lorrain's masks are uncanny not only because they challenge sexual and gender conventions, but also because they refuse to signify (1992: 87). In uncovering the gap between signifier and signified, they also push the limits of the Symbolic and disrupt the connection between 'the symbol and the thing that it symbolizes' (Freud 1955a: 244). This is exemplified by 'Les Trous du masque' [The Holes in the Mask], which Lorrain dedicates to Schwob. In this tale, an ether addict attends the masked ball of a secret society in which participants, dressed in green, hooded robes, stroll up and down in front of a wall of mirrors. For the narrator, these costumes evoke images of leprosy and contagious illnesses. When he tears off one of the hoods, however, he discovers that the costume hides nothing but air, exposing the mask as an empty signifier. In the grip of panic, he unmasks in front of the mirror and is confronted with the same void, or with the inconsistency of the subject. Eventually, he wakes up from an ether nightmare.

Although Lorrain's narrators establish a distance between themselves and the masqueraders, mask-wearers and mask-perceivers share a bond. In keeping with Freud's theory of the uncanny, what is first perceived as strange and foreign is gradually revealed to be familiar. Drawing on Schwob, Lorrain emphasizes the instability of the mask as a sign, the shortcomings of a semiotic system that links sexuality and gender. When the connection between the signified and the signifier becomes loose, the mask turns into a sign unable to produce signification. If law and the social order rely on the construction of the Symbolic, the empty signifier, as Lorrain suggests in 'L'Un d'eux', is positioned 'outside the law' (2006: 16) and beyond the heterosexual matrix.

The 1900 edition of *Histoires de masques* opened with a preface by the art critic Gustave Coquiot, who was also a friend of Lorrain. Coquiot argued that James Ensor, the third expert on masks to influence Lorrain's poetics, had achieved in the visual arts what Lorrain had accomplished in his fiction. Known as 'the painter of masks', Ensor lived surrounded by masks as artefacts and, like Lorrain, practised self-fashioning, masking and travesty. Ensor's paintings, Coquiot maintained, perfectly illustrated Lorrain's tales — conversely, he hoped that Ensor would be inspired by *Histoires de masques* to produce new masterpieces. In *Histoires de masques*, Ensor is described as the clear-sighted, discerning expert on masks, but also a 'great deformer' and a mask maker: 'Il connaît, ce clairvoyant, toutes les ressources des masques, ce qu'ils ajoutent de hideux ou de grotesque à la face humaine' [He knows, this clairvoyant, all the resources of masks; what hideousness or grotesqueness they add to the human face] (Coquiot 2006: 13). Just like Ensor, in his self-portraits, portrays himself surrounded by masks, the narrator of Lorrain's tales features as the only unmasked in a world of mask-men.

In both Lorrain's stories and Ensor's painting, there is no dichotomy between the face and the mask: the face is itself a mask, shaped by indulgence in vice. In the work of Ensor, the results are 'masklike humans and humanlike masks, creatures that are neither masks nor humans but a third species without definite qualities' (Jonsson 2001: 11). Similar creatures populate Lorrain's fiction, where this 'third species' becomes associated with a third gender. For both Ensor and Lorrain, the mask is a tool to reveal, rather than to hide. Both follow the principle of caricature and magnify human features to expose moral traits, often unearthing a resemblance with animals that suggests a subhuman status. In addition, masks are never too far from skulls as they bear a close connection to death and the death drive; often, they appear detached from the body.

Both Ensor and Lorrain used the mask at the nexus of a personal and a socio-historical narrative. For both, the mask functioned as an allegory that addressed their marginalized position in society, as well as a tool of political denunciation. Like Ensor's most famous paintings, Lorrain's tales were originally published in the 1880s, a decade marked by the centennial of the French Revolution and the foundation of the Second International. These were also the years in which mass psychology, especially through the work of Gustave Le Bon, established a connection between madness and the masses. Ensor and Lorrain's fascination with carnival and with the celebrations of the anniversary of the storming of the Bastille reflects the importance that crowds had on the *fin-de-siècle* imagination. In his introduction, Coquiot underlined that, in the work of both Ensor and Lorrain, masks mark the relapse that occurs when the individual is caught in a crowd and overcome by animal instincts. Behind the mask, he stressed, lurks the criminal, the anarchist, the madman, the prostitute — subjects that, in nineteenth-century thought, were seen as embodying regression. Beyond Coquiot's interpretation, there are, however, important differences between Lorrain and Ensor's use of masks in relation to the crowd. Unlike Ensor, Lorrain was affiliated with right-wing circles and was appalled by socialism: Pierre Kyria describes him as 'right wing, *anti-dreyfusard* and anti-Semitic' (1973: 112). While Ensor's crowd is mixed, encompassing elements of all social classes, Lorrain associated the crowd, the 'foule guenilleuse aux yeux caves' [ragged mob with hollow eyes] that emerges over and over in his tales, primarily with the working classes (Lorrain 2006: 96). Descriptions such as these betray Lorrain's antidemocratic stance and anxiety about revolutionary fervour.

In the introduction, Coquiot mentions an etching by Ensor, 'La Luxure' [Lust] (1888), which plays an important role in *Monsieur de Phocas*. The teachings of E. T. A. Hoffmann, Marcel Schwob and James Ensor are in fact evoked, implicitly or explicitly, in the masks that feature in this novel.

Masks and the Gaze: *Monsieur de Phocas*

Published by instalments in *Le Journal* as *Astarté* (1899 to 1900) and by Paul Ollendorff as *Monsieur de Phocas* (1901), Lorrain's fourth novel was advertised as 'the novel of neurosis' (Anthonay 2005: 771). The story draws on Huysmans' *À Rebours* (1884) and Wilde's *The Picture of Dorian Gray* (1891) and features a protagonist, the Duke of Fréneuse (alias Monsieur de Phocas), who adopts the lifestyle of a decadent dandy. Lorrain, who like Fréneuse 'avait une légende qu'il avait créée inconsciemment d'abord et qu'il s'était pris depuis à aimer et à entretenir' [had a legend that he had created unconsciously at first, and that he had since come to enjoy and to maintain] (Lorrain 2001: 51), must have been aware that his readers would identify the protagonist as a portrait of the author himself. By 1902, however, he complained that the association had gone too far. 'Que de maladies, que de curieux, que de fantaisies malsaines je traine après moi... Quand cesserai-je d'être pour toutes ces folles et ces fous le triste M. de Phocas?' [The maladies, curious things, and morbid fantasies I drag with me... When will I cease to represent, for these madwomen and madmen, the sad M. de Phocas?], he wrote to his friend J. F. Merlet in 1902 (Jullian 1974: 276). In an article published the following year in *Le Journal*, he reported a conversation held in Venice with a 'fan of D'Annunzio', and underlined that his reputation had travelled so far that even international readerships were unable to distinguish facts from fiction: 'Elle me parle de m. de Phocas; j'eus quelque peine à la convaincre que ce n'était pas une autobiographie, que je n'avais tué personne et ne possédais, hélas! aucun million' [She spoke to me of M. de Phocas; I had some difficulty convincing her that it was not an autobiography, that I had not killed anyone and did not have, alas! any millions] (Lorrain 2005b: 819).

Similarly to *Histoires de masques*, the novel establishes a connection between masks, regression and degeneration. The Duke of Fréneuse, the last scion of an aristocratic race, suffers from a nervous condition, a mysterious illness that leads him to see the faces around him change into hideous masks. In addition, he is obsessed by masks as artefacts, as well as by the faces of statues. In all these items, he discerns a fleeting blue and green gaze that he associates with the Semitic goddess Astarté. He initially pursues this look in the eyes of the mime Willi Stephenson and of the dancer Izé Kranile. Both disappoint him, and he concludes that Astarté's look is an illusion; however, he continues to glimpse its fleeting manifestations. One day, he meets Ethal, an English artist who claims to be able to cure him. Therapy unveils the connection between Astarté's gaze and death and exacerbates Fréneuse's illness. His vexation reaches a peak at an opium party during which he experiences frightening hallucinations. Thomas Welcôme, a handsome Irish millionaire, claims to be familiar with his condition. In the last part of the novel Fréneuse oscillates between the influence of Ethal and Welcôme. Eventually, he kills Ethal by making him swallow poison contained in his own eye-shaped ring; he then changes his name to Phocas and departs for Asia.

The story is told through a series of journal entries and letters, a device that enabled Lorrain to rework previously published material and to incorporate the art chronicles that he was writing for the *Pall-mall Semaine*. Descriptions of artefacts and works of art often interrupt the plot and inscribe the fascination with masks in a wide pictorial universe that extends from Goya to Hogarth to James Ensor, from Toorop to Whistler, from Gustave Moreau to Félicien Rops to Jeanne Jacquemine. In addition, the book features a large number of citations, from references to E. T. A. Hoffmann to Paul Valéry's verses on Narcissus to entire passages from Gide's *Les Nourritures terrestres* (Zinck 2001a: 303–14). Overall, the text presents two points of view: that of the journalist/jewellery expert to whom Phocas entrusts his memoires, and that of Fréneuse, the author of the journal. Lorrain unveils the ending before introducing the beginning, introducing readers to Monsieur de Phocas before presenting Fréneuse's manuscript. In doing so, he contrasts the point of view of the aristocrat (Phocas) with that of the bourgeois (the journalist), underscoring how Fréneuse's story can come to light only through the censorship of the latter.

Fréneuse's illness recalls many pathologies, and it coincides with none. The novel can be read as a catalogue of symptoms. At the beginning of the journal, Fréneuse confesses: 'Un démon me torture et me hante, et cela depuis mon adolescence. Qui sait? Peut-être était-il déjà en moi quand je n'étais qu'un enfant' [A demon tortures and haunts me, and has done so since my adolescence. Who knows? Perhaps it was already in me when I was but a child] (Lorrain 2001: 55). A few pages later, he links the obsession with the blue and green gaze to innate cruelty and remembers that, as a child, he liked torturing animals (2001: 64). His neurosis, he maintains, lies dormant, but it can manifest itself again if triggered by external sources (2001: 67). In line with the teaching of Charcot and Magnan, some of his acquaintances trace the roots of the illness to cerebral lesions and anaemia. Others point out that the duke's symptoms are very similar to those of syphilis, and argue that premature aging is the result of his opium addiction (2001: 58). Still others see the duke as an unnatural being, 'Un malade [...] un personnage de conte d'Hoffmann. Cette pâleur pourrissante, la crispation de ces mains effilées, plus japonaises de formes que des chrysanthèmes, ce profil d'arabesque et cette maigreur de vampire, tout cela ne vous a jamais donné à réfléchir?' [an invalid [...] a character from the tales of Hoffmann! Have you ever taken the trouble to look at him carefully? That pallor of decay; the twitching of his bony hands, more Japanese than chrysanthemums; the arabesque profile; the vampiric emaciation — has all that never given you cause to reflect?] (2001: 58). Fréneuse is adamant: the illness is innate. It follows that he does not hold himself responsible for his actions. On the contrary, he maintains that it is his neurosis that pushes him towards a life of vice. Frequently compared to an automaton, or to the doll Olympia in Hoffmann's 'The Sandman', he describes the feeling of acting like a puppet manoeuvred by a demon. As the narrative progresses, he identifies the demon with the legacy of heredity and, in line with the theories of Cesare Lombroso, defines his murderous instincts as a configuration of atavism (2001: 84). On the other hand, the masks that he perceives in the people who surround him suggest that his affliction is not an anomaly, but a condition that has infected the whole of Paris, France and Europe.

Fréneuse initially considers the mask an attribute of the lower classes who, oppressed by harsh living conditions and by the inhuman rhythms of the modern metropolis, are caught in a Darwinian struggle for survival:

> La vie moderne, luxueuse, impitoyable et sceptique a fait à ces hommes comme à ces femmes des âmes de garde-chiourme ou de bandit: têtes aplaties et venimeuses de vipères, museaux retors et aiguisés de rongeurs, mâchoires de requins et groins de pourceaux, ce sont l'envie, le désespoir et la haine, et c'est aussi l'égoïsme et c'est aussi l'avarice, qui font de l'humanité un bestiaire où chaque bas instinct s'imprime en trait d'animal.
>
> [Modern life — luxurious, pitiless and sceptical — has formed the souls of these men, and their women likewise, into those of prison guards or bandits. It has given them the flattened heads of venomous snakes, the pointed and twisted muzzles of rodents, the jaws of sharks and the snouts of pigs. Envy, desperation, hatred, egoism and avarice have re-created humanity as bestiary in which every low instinct is imprinted with animal traits...] (Lorrain 2001: 95)

By emphasizing facial features to expose moral behaviour, Fréneuse's hallucinations follow the principle of caricature[8] and have the function to reveal, rather than to hide: 'Mon hallucination n'est qu'un sens de plus, c'est l'innommable de l'âme humaine remontée à fleur de peau qui prête à tous ces visages les apparences de masques' [My hallucination is nothing but a sixth sense: it is the unnameable of the human soul which is brought forth to bloom upon the skin, and which lends to every face the semblance of a mask] (2001: 68). His visions also exemplify the prominence that social Darwinism, the application of the principle of the 'struggle for life' to social bodies, had in the late nineteenth century, and call to mind the 'disease of the nerves' that Nordau believed was caused by overstimulation and multitasking required in modern Western society.

Soon Fréneuse realizes that masks are not limited to the working classes. He first catches a glimpse of distortion in the features of his lover, the acrobat Willie Stevenson; he later begins to see masks everywhere, including the venues frequented by the high Parisian society: 'Je vois des masques dans la rue, j'en vois sur la scène au théâtre, j'en retrouve dans les loges. Il y en a au balcon, il y en a à l'orchestre, partout des masques autour de moi' [I see masks in the street, I see them on stage in the theatre, I find yet more of them in the boxes. They are on the balcony and in the orchestra-pit. Everywhere I go I am surrounded by masks] (2001: 91). In line with Baudelaire's 'Eloge du maquillage' (1863) and Max Beerbohm's 'Defence of Cosmetics' (1890) he emphasises the link between cosmetics and the mask. 'Le maquillage! C'est là d'où vient mon mal' [Cosmetics: there is the root cause of my illness!] (2001: 91). Another form of caricature, the cosmetic mask is limited to women and acquires a misogynistic undertone; its function is allegedly to expose moral corruption, however, it becomes the pretext to underline Fréneuse's discomfort with women.

Fréneuse experiences 'les côtés de spectre et de poupée des êtres' [the spectral and the doll-side of human beings] (2001: 99) for the first time in a dream in which, walking randomly in a deserted city devastated by an epidemic, he finds himself lost in a street of prostitutes:

> On eût dit de grandes marionnettes, de longues poupées mannequinées oubliées là dans la panique, car je devinais qu'une peste, quelque effroyable épidémie rapportée d'Orient par les navires avait balayé cette ville et l'avait

faite vide d'habitants; et j'étais seul avec ces simulacres d'amour abandonnés par les hommes au seuil des maisons de joie et déjà, depuis des heures, j'errais sans pouvoir sortir de ce quartier morne, obsédé par les yeux vernissés et fixes de tous ces automates, quand une soudaine idée me venait que toutes ces filles étaient des mortes, des pestiférées ou des colériques pourrissant là, dans la solitude, sous des masques de plâtre et de carmin, et mes entrailles se liquéfiaient de froid. Et malgré le froid, m'étant approché d'une fille immobile, je voyais en effet qu'elle avait un masque; et l'autre fille, debout à la porte voisine, était aussi masquée, et toutes étaient horriblement pareilles sous l'identique coloriage brutal.

[They might have been huge marionettes, or tall mannequin dolls left behind in panic — for I divined that some plague, some frightful epidemic brought from the Orient by sailors, had swept through the town and emptied it of its inhabitants. I had already been wandering for hours without being able to find a way out of that miserable quarter, obsessed by the fixed and painted eyes of those automata, when I was seized by the sudden thought that all these girls were dead, plague-stricken and putrefied by cholera where they stood, in the solitude, beneath their carmine plaster masks... and my entrails were liquefied by cold. In spite of that harrowing chill, I was drawn closer to a motionless girl. I saw that she was indeed wearing a mask... and the girl in the next doorway was also masked... and all of them were horribly alike under their identical crude colouring...] (Lorrain 2001: 90)

The illness is first identified as 'plague', then as 'cholera', but its association with sexuality as an epidemic 'brought back from the Orient by sailors', characterizes it rather as syphilis, or more generally as a venereal disease. The mask worn by the prostitutes becomes the objective correlative of the illness. Like the protagonist of Huysmans' *À Rebours*, Fréneuse sees prostitutes as identical automata, a motif that Rita Felski reads as emphasizing the 'superficiality, interchangeability of women', the 'mechanical, depersonalized, ultimately soulless quality of femininity', but also the standardization of modern life, the logic of mass production dreaded by the dandy (1995: 107).

In the dream, Fréneuse wanders for hours in the neighbourhood without being able to find a way out. The episode bears a curious resemblance to the memory that Freud described in his essay on the uncanny, when he recalled the experience of getting lost in a city and finding himself over and over '... in a quarter of whose character I could not long remain in doubt. Nothing but painted women were to be seen at the windows of the small houses' (Freud 1955a: 237). Freud quoted this anecdote to illustrate the principle of involuntary repetition, according to which human beings feel compelled to re-enact painful experiences despite the trauma they originally suffered — an idea that he developed further in *Beyond the Pleasure Principle*, when he articulated the theory of the death drive.

In *Monsieur de Phocas*, Fréneuse recognizes the mask of the dream in another Hoffmannesque character, the singer performing at the *Théâtre des funambules*: 'je n'écoutais pas chanter une femme vivante, mais un automate aux pièces disparates et montées de bric et de broc. Peut-être pis encore, une morte hâtivement reconstituée avec des déchets d'hôpital' [I did not hear the singing of a living woman, but of some automaton pieced together from disparate odds and ends — or perhaps even worse, some dead woman hastily reconstructed from hospital remains] (2001: 92). The show reinforces the link between Fréneuse's fear of masks and his repulsion for women. 'Heureux suis-je, maintenant, quand ce ne sont que des masques!' he concludes, 'Parfois, je devine le cadavre dessous, et ce sont souvent plus que des masques, puisque ce sont des spectres que je vois' [I am happy, now, when there are only masks! Sometimes, I detect the cadavers beneath, and remember that beneath the masks there is a host of spectres] (Lorrain 2001: 91).

Through his journal entries, Fréneuse identifies in the mask the unnameable, the corrupt, the frightening. During a carnival night, he comes across two masqueraders, a girl dressed as a male student and young man wearing a priest's gown. The couple conjures in his mind 'dangerous and uncanny feelings' and 'abominable and sacrilegious ideas' (2001: 89). Yet he is attracted just as much as he is repelled by the sight: after the encounter, he begins to attend masked balls and the performances of actresses specializing in cross-dressing, which become a pretext to describe the masks worn by 'tout le Lesbos des premières' [all the lesbos of the premieres] (2001: 199). He also becomes fascinated with the mask as an artefact: 'J'ai la fascination du masque,' he writes in his journal. 'L'énigme du visage que je ne vois pas m'attire, c'est le vertige au bord du gouffre' [Masks fascinate me. The enigma of the face that I cannot see attracts me strongly; it is the vertigo of the brink of the abyss] (2001: 89). The note exemplifies the relation between the gaze of the mask and the pleasure of looking. In blocking the onlooker's view, the mask triggers the compulsion to look — a drive that nineteenth-century sexologists were defining as scopophilia.

Following the logic of the fetish, the lure of the mask extends to fragmentary objects that bear a resemblance to it. Fréneuse spends entire days at the Louvre Museum, pursuing the gaze of the bust *Antinoüs Mandragone*, a fragment that formed part of a colossal statue and that, like a mask, features void sockets. During a trip to Naples, he recognizes the same gaze in statues of Venus 'dont les yeux fulguraient, splendidement vides, dans leur masque de métal noir' [whose eyes glittered, splendidly empty, behind their masks of black metal] (2001: 77). The faces of statues fill him with enthusiasm: 'Leur immobilité est autrement vivante que les grimaces de nos physionomies. Comme un souffle divin les anime, et puis quelle intensité de regard dans leurs yeux vides!' [Their immobility is a kind of existence very different from the grimaces of our features. A divine breath animates them — and then, how intense is the gaze of their empty eyes!] (2001: 61). By quoting a line by Charles Vellay ('Se mirer dans les yeux, s'y noyer comme Narcisse à la fontaine!' [to admire oneself in the eyes, to drown oneself like Narcissus at the spring!]) he associates the fixation with eyes with narcissism (2001: 72). While the eyes of statues continue to charm him, the gaze that he pursues in living beings disappoints him: 'Il n'y a rien dans les yeux, et c'est là leur terrifiante et douloureuse énigme, leur charme hallucinant et abominable. Il n'y a rien que ce que nous y mettons nous-mêmes' [there is nothing to be found in the eyes, and that is their terrifying and dolorous enigma, their hallucinatory and abominable charm. There is nothing but that which we put there ourselves] (2001: 74).

Lorrain followed nineteenth-century sexologists in establishing a relation between fetishism and narcissism, and anticipated Freud in stressing the link between narcissism and homosexuality. The connection between these forms of 'inversion' emerges most clearly when, after quoting Paul Valéry's 'Fragment du narcisse', Fréneuse compares the fascination with Narcissus to the obsession with Antinoüs, and brings the latter into relation with the fear of masks:

> Et les beaux vers de Paul Valery! Quel calme leur mélancolie nostalgique et sublime apportait en moi! à mon horrible mal ils substituaient, ces vers, la brulure de Narcisse; et cette brulure était encore la fraicheur auprès de l'âme de soufre et de phosphore qu'ont allumée en mon être les yeux dolents de l'Antinoüs... Les saphirs ne m'apaisent plus depuis que je suis hanté par les masques.
>
> [And those beautiful lines by Paul Valery! What calmness their sublime nostalgic melancholy brought me! Those lines substituted for my terrible sickness the plight of Narcissus; and thereby cooled that suffering and phosphorescent soul which the plaintive eyes of Antinous has lighted in my being. But sapphires no longer appease me, now that I am haunted by the masks.] (Lorrain 2001: 93)

When Ethal approaches the duke as a fellow visionary, Fréneuse is immensely relieved to be no longer alone. He soon discovers that Ethal's visionary quality is even greater than his own; not only can he perceive the animal masks on people's faces, but, like a sorcerer, he is able to evoke, to materialize the masks and to lead other people to recognize them.[9] Ethal prescribes to Fréneuse a cure that resembles a homeopathic treatment. He encourages the duke to handle masks as much as possible, arguing that becoming familiar with the artefacts will help him to endure the masks he encounters in his daily life, and then introduces Fréneuse to his own personal collection, which includes a wide range of masks:

> Des masques de Deburau, faces pâles de Pierrot aux narines pincées, aux sourires minces; masques japonais, les uns de bronze, les autres de bois laqué; masques de la comédie italienne, ceux-là de soie et de cire peinte, quelques-uns même de gaze noire tendue sur des fils de laiton, des masques de Venise énigmatiques et légèrement horribles comme ceux des personnages de Longhi; c'était toute une guirlande grimaçante posée autour de l'eau dormante du miroir.
>
> [There were Deburau masks: the pale faces of Pierrots with pinched nostrils and tight smiles. There were Japanese masks, some in bronze and others in lacquered wood. There were masks from the Italian *commedia*, made of silk and painted wax, and a few of black gauze stretched over brass wire. There were enigmatic and cleverly horrid Venetian masks, like those of the characters of de Longhi. An entire garland of grimaces had been posed around the sleeping pool of the mirror.] (Lorrain 2001: 99)

Divested of their original function, the masks have turned from theatrical props into decorative objects; placed around a mirror, they do not reveal a gaze, but reflect to infinity the emptiness of their sockets. Ethal declares that he has been able to overcome the fear of masks by living among them, and leads Fréneuse to a reclining bed in which 'charming and terrible' masks have been arranged among the pillows. He praises the Japanese masks, eager to display his knowledge from years spent in that country, and is equally enthusiastic about the Venetian masks, which remind him of the characters of Hoffmann's tales and of the animal traits that he is able to divine in people's features. As part of the cure, he suggests that Fréneuse familiarize himself with the work of artists knowledgeable about masks: Rowlandsom, Hogarth, Goya, Félicen Rops and Ensor. He considers the latter a fellow visionary, who, like him, has been marginalized and ostracized from society: 'sa vision est d'une probité parfaite, d'une précision géométrique presque; il est même un des seuls qui voient. Il a l'obsession des masques comme nous, c'est un voyant comme vous et moi; les bourgeois le traitent de fou' [his vision is perfectly accurate, of an almost geometric precision. He is one of the few who really can see. Like you, he has an obsession with masks; he is a seer as you and I are. The bourgeois, of course, thinks he is mad] (2001: 117). In the course of the therapy, Ethal sends to Fréneuse a number of paintings by Ensor and by other artists, and encourages him to visit museums to observe their works. In all the paintings, Fréneuse recognizes alternatively the fight for life or the lure of the green-blue eyes under whose charm he suffers.

After introducing Fréneuse to his collection of masks, Ethal presents him with a series of wax heads. Fréneuse stares astonished at 'les yeux vitreux et les lèvres fanées de plus de vingt bustes de mortes' [the vitreous eyes and faded lips of more than twenty busts of dead women] (Lorrain 2001: 125–26). Among the waxworks, he recognizes renowned pieces exhibited in the French museums: a sculpture known as *Tête de cire du temps de Raphael*; a reproduction of the *Inconnue de la Seine*, and several historical profiles, among which that of Marguerite de Valois (1553–1615), the queen of France who allegedly practised incest and nymphomania, Agnes Sorel (1422–1450), the lover of Charles VII, and Mary Stuart (1542–1587), Queen of Scots. The waxes exemplify the cult that artists associated with decadence and aestheticism, following Walter Pater, had for the Renaissance, and by portraying figures condemned to violent death or decapitation, also underscore the link between masks, busts and severed heads.

A head that Ethal hands over to Fréneuse with particular care apparently interrupts the series: it portrays a sickly-looking adolescent, and it is Ethal's own work. Ethal recalls that he modelled the bust on Angelotto, a Neapolitan child he had found shivering in front of his atelier. He recounts how, fascinated by the child's thinness and by the signs of consumption, he strove to capture his soul and worked passionately on the sculpture until the model died of exhaustion. His power over the boy is exemplified by the way in which his hand, heavy with jewels, rests on Angelotto's head 'comme une serre, en vérité, une serre d'oiseau de proie' [like a grip, like the talon of some bird of prey] (2001: 129). Although Ethal, who later in the journal is called a '*Barbe bleue*', a 'sorcerer' (2001: 264), claims that, in sculpting this youth on the threshold between life and death, he was able to mould his soul, the sculpture rather captures his fascination with androgyny, fetishism and necrophilia. Fréneuse recognizes in the bust the same suffering gaze which he perceived through the eyes-holes of the masks. Ethal's story fills him with rage; he regrets not having met the child, and imagines that he would have saved him from

Ethal's murderous influence. Shortly afterwards, however, he acknowledges that his feelings are not entirely disinterested: 'J'en voulais moins à ce monstre de l'avoir tué que de l'avoir connu... c'était comme de la jalousie!' [I resented the monster not so much for having killed him but for having come to know him... it was like jealousy!] (2001: 134).

As fragmentary portraits, and as death masks, the wax heads function as intermediaries between masks and severed heads. The latter are the personal obsession of Sir Thomas Welcôme, the handsome Irishman who proposes to Fréneuse an alternative therapy. Welcôme shares with Fréneuse a supernatural perception, but in a slightly different form. He explains: 'les masques qui vous hallucinent se précisaient en moi dans une tête coupée. Cela m'était devenu une maladie, une déséquilibrante obsession; oh! J'ai souffert. J'en voyais partout; partout des rictus de décapités me raillaient, me sollicitaient' [The hallucinatory masks which haunt you took the specific form in me of a severed head. Oh, how I suffered from that malady, that unbalancing obsession! I saw them everywhere; on every side that rictus of decapitation was railing at me, taunting me] (2001: 178).

In an effort to subtract Fréneuse from Ethal's influence, Welcôme claims that the painter is exacerbating, rather than curing his illness. He confesses that he himself had once fallen into Ethal's hands and had spent more than ten years searching for the blue and green look in the Orient. Only once, he argues, did he recognize Astarté's gaze. The look manifested itself as, sailing down the Nile with Ethal, he noticed a mysterious figure leaning on a Sphinx:

> C'était *une forme jeune et svelte*, vêtue, comme les âniers fellahs, d'une mince gandoura bleue, avec des anneaux d'or aux chevilles, *la forme adolescente ou d'un Prince ou d'un esclave*, car l'attitude de ce sommeil offert était à la fois royale et servile: royale de confiance, servile de complaisante et abandon.
> La gandoura s'ouvrait sur une poitrine plate, d'une blancheur d'ivoire; mais au cou saignait, comme une large entaille, une cicatrice ou une plaie!
>
> [It was a slender figure, dressed like a donkey driver, in a thin blue robe, with rings of gold at the ankles. It was the profile of an adolescent, but I could not tell whether a prince or a slave, for the attitude of the sleeper seemed both royal and servile, embodying royal confidence, servile complaisance and conscious abandon.
> The robe was open at the neck, exposing a flat chest, as white as ivory — but there was a gaping bloody gash across the neck: a huge scar or an open wound!]
> (Lorrain 2001: 175, my italics)

As an artist, Ethal gained a reputation for women's portraits. By portraying decapitated women and turning their heads into masks, like a modern Perseus, he symbolically slays Medusa and appropriates her petrifying gaze for his own purposes. The severed male head calls instead to mind the myth of Salomé, the biblical figure that in the *Belle Époque* embodies both the *femme fatale* and the castrating woman (Kristeva 1998: 127). Fréneuse repeatedly invokes Salomé as he is watching the performance of the dancer of Izé Kranile, and is later sent by both Ethal and Welcôme to the *Gustave Moreau* museum, where he stops to admire the Salomé paintings described by Huysmans in *À Rebours*. 'Modern incarnations of

Salomé' (Lorrain 2002: 96)[10] are also found at Ethal's opium party, where the artist has invited to perform two Javanese dancers. The Salomé figures (Izé Kranile, the Javanese dancers) and the victims of (symbolic or real) decapitation (Angelotto, the Egyptian figure) are separated in Lorrain's narrative, but are all characterized by androgynous features.[11]

After meeting Welcôme, Fréneuse has a vision in which he is transported in front of the guillotine and sees a severed head raised by the crowd toward the sky, 'une tête exsangue aux yeux éteints et fixes, le masque de décapitée qui hantait les nuits de Welcôme' [a head drained of blood, with fixed and extinguished eyes; the mask of decapitation which haunted Thomas Welcome's nights] (2001: 212). The head belongs to the Princesse of Lamballe (1749–1792), lady in waiting and alleged lover of Marie Antoinette, who was beheaded during the revolution. In the dream, Fréneuse witnesses how a crowd of ugly men parades the human fragment, passing it around and kissing it in mockery, and describes one of the men exhibiting 'une équivoque moustache blonde, on dirait des poils de sexe' [an equivocal blond moustache, looking like pubic hair] above his lips (2001: 212). Ambiguous sexual markers are also found in the 'androgynous deity' (2001: 207) worshipped by Welcôme, a statuette of the Goddess Astarté which features a skull in the place of the sex.

The androgynous statue and Fréneuse's nightmare call to mind both gender-blurring and the interchangeability of heads and genitals, prefiguring Freud's use of castration as a master trope for perversion (Bernheimer 2002: 120). But the sexual threat, in this context, turns into a political threat and embodies the disruption of the old regime. Fréneuse often fantasises about the French Revolution. At the beginning of the journal, he elaborates on the similarity between the 'sensual and murderous' crowd of the working classes and the revolutionaries who brought the aristocrats to the scaffolds (2001: 61). During the celebration of the storming of the Bastille, he recognizes among the crowd icons of homosexuality and debauchery, 'masques d'affranchis bithyniens et de courtisanes de la décadence' [masks of liberated Bithynians and courtesans of the Roman decadence] (2001: 62). Degeneration features in the text both as an individual and a socio-historical phenomenon, and anxieties about sexual deviancy are closely bound to preoccupations about the vigour of the nation. Like other perversions in the novel, the fixation with severed heads assumes a socio-historical connotation as it signals Fréneuse's and Welcôme's distance from the democratic, bourgeois values of the Third Republic and from the increasing appeal of revolutionary fervour.

Fréneuse's Masks

Throughout the novel, Fréneuse describes his feelings of vulnerability at being the only person without a mask in a crowd of masqueraders: 'C'est une chose vraiment par trop effroyable que de se sentir seul, à la merci de toutes ces faces d'énigme et de mensonge, seul au milieu de tous ces ricanements et de ces menaces immobilisées dans des masques' [It is truly frightening to feel alone and at the mercy of those enigmatic and deceptive faces, alone amid all the mocking laughters and threats frozen in the masks] (2001: 91). Gradually, however, he begins to suspect that he may be wearing a mask himself. His violent drives bring him close to strangling a prostitute, and he savagely beats a dog in front of an astonished crowd. Reluctant to acknowledge these instincts as his own, he attributes them to a double self: 'Y aurait-il en moi un être double?' [Might there be a second self lurking within me?] (2001: 64). 'Un autre homme est installé en moi ... et quel homme!' [Another man has taken hold inside me ... and what a man!] (85).

With his deformed, dwarfish features, Ethal embodies the inadmissible, the 'monstrous' impulses of Fréneuse's psyche, and functions as a catalyst through which he becomes aware of his unconscious desires: 'Ce sont mes pensées, même les plus lointaines, les pas encore nées, celles que je ne soupçonnais pas, que sa parole évoque et fait naître. Ce mystérieux causeur me raconte à moi-même, donne un corps à mes rêves, il me parle tout haut, je m'éveille en lui comme dans un autre moi plus précis et plus subtil...' [His words evoke and bring into being thoughts which are my very own, although not yet fully formulated: thoughts still distant from my consciousness; ideas of which I had as yet no suspicion. This mysterious provocateur is telling me about myself, putting flesh on my dreams. He speaks to me so distinctively that something like him is awakening in me. It is as if another self — more precise and more subtle, born out of his conversations, has taken root within me] (2001: 109). Although homosexuality remains unnamed in the novel, Ethal explicitly addresses Fréneuse's attraction to other men (2001: 112). Fréneuse blames the painter for these thoughts, and maintains that he is suffering from his corrupting influence. At the same time, he cannot stop thinking of him, and misses him terribly when he is away.[12]

Welcôme is initially introduced as the opposite of Ethal: if the former is a monstrous dwarf, the latter is a handsome tall man, who contrasts Ethal's fascination with death with a passion for life and travel. Nevertheless, Fréneuse guesses that the two share a bond: 'Je sens bien qu'il existe comme une complicité, quelque chose d'irréparable et d'obscur entre ces deux hommes!' [I have a definite feeling that there is some kind of complicity, some obscure and unbreakable bond between the two men] (2001: 171). At his opium party, Ethal speaks of Welcôme as a close friend and frets at his late arrival. Welcôme radiates strength and rigour, but his hands, like those of Ethal, are covered with rings. During the hashish *fumerie*, the narrator deliberately confuses whose hand is holding that of Fréneuse. Both men rely on a fortune that enables them to avoid work so as to dedicate themselves entirely to the cultivation of sensations. Both share a criminal past: Ethal is accused of poisoning his models; Welcôme of murdering a man with whom he had a homosexual relationship. They both have travelled to the Orient and are keen admirers of Asian art. Welcôme exalts India as the realm of liveliness, youth, virility and health, and contrasts it to the 'existences artificielles, surchauffées et nerveuses des Paris et des Londres' [artificial, overheated and hysterical existence of Paris and London] (2001: 176). By prescribing the 'Orient' as a destination for Fréneuse's journey, he also maps its boundaries. The Orient, in *Monsieur de Phocas*, begins on the coast of Italy, includes Spain and the islands, and extends to the Far East. It comprises all the places that, according to Welcôme, have been left out of the tourist guides of Baedeker and Thomas Cook (2001: 176).[13] As Phillip Winn has noted, these regions correspond to the territories that Sir Richard Burton, in his 'Terminal essay' (1885), associated with a 'Satanic Zone' in which homosexuality was practised and widespread (Winn 1997: 87). Ethal, who has spent just as much time in the Far East, warns Fréneuse: 'Allez en Sicile, à Venise et même à Smyrne, ah! ... Malade que vous êtes, vous emporterez votre mal avec vous' [Go to Sicily, or to Venice, or even to Smyrna ... sick as you are, you will carry your illness with you] (2001: 137). He advises Fréneuse to search for corners of the Orient within European cities, and thus reinforces Welcôme's innuendo that the 'Orient', more than just a physical location, stands for the inadmissible in European society.

In the exchange of letters that Fréneuse reproduces in his journal, both Ethal and Welcôme encourage Fréneuse to visit the Moreau museum. Here, Fréneuse recognizes the gaze that obsesses him in Moreau's *Massacre des prétendants* (1859), and particularly in two agonizing male figures. Finally, if Ethal's appearance is remarkably similar to the dwarf painted by Antonio Moro in the Louvre, to the point that Fréneuse refers to him as 'l'effarant sosie du gnome encapuchonné du maître flamand' [the frightful double of the Flemish master's hooded gnome] (2001: 107), Fréneuse identifies Welcôme's double in Jean Destreux, a handsome farmer whom he adored as a child and who was killed in an accident, run over by a cart. 'Comme Thomas Welcôme lui ressemble!' [How he resembles Thomas Welcome!] (2001: 227) he cries as he revisits his childhood trauma. As in Hoffmann's 'The Sandman', each character thus functions as the double of another who has, in turn, his own double. Like Wilde's *Picture of Dorian Gray*, the novel tells the story of the 'invisible et forte chaîne' [invisible and strong chain] (Lorrain 2001: 240) that unites three men who exert an influence upon one another. On another level, Ethal, Welcôme and Fréneuse are aspects of the same person.[14] Fréneuse never explicitly acknowledges the link that binds him to Ethal and Welcôme, but becomes aware that Ethal's features have spread to his own face when a gipsy proposes to him a deal that he considers worthy of the Orient: 'En être venu là, porter imprimé sur mes traits un tel masque qu'on arrive à me chuchoter, en plein Grenelle et Vaugirard, les propositions murmurées dans les rues du Caire et sur les quais de Naples!' (261) [To carry imprinted on my features such a mask that they come forth to whisper to me, in Grenelle and in Vaugirard, the kind of propositions that are murmured in the streets of Cairo and in the quays of Naples!] (2001: 238). He also recognizes his own portrait in a painting by James Ensor titled 'La Luxure', part of a series on the capital vices, which he imagines retouched by Ethal.

After murdering Ethal, Fréneuse writes of the impression of being split: 'J'étais comme dédoublé et il me semblait assister en spectateur à un drame judiciaire dont je dirigeais moi-même l'intrigue, les jeux de scène et jusqu'aux gestes d'acteurs' [It was as if I was split in two. I seemed to be a helpful witness in a judicial drama whose intrigue — all the scenes and gestures of the actors — I was also directing] (2001: 279). If Fréneuse's self is divided, Ethal and Welcôme reflect opposite possibilities of his destiny. Following the model set by Oscar Wilde in *The Picture of Dorian Gray*, *Monsieur de Phocas* camouflages homoeroticism behind the gothic theme of the double. In doing so, the text also articulates same-sex desire as an extension of self-love.

Conclusions

The critic Olympe Gilbart, who reviewed *Monsieur de Phocas* in 1901, described Fréneuse as 'le type extrême et définitif de la race qui se meurt' [the extreme and definitive type of the dying race] (2001: 333). In the change of name of the protagonist from *Fréneuse* to *Phocas*, scholars have identified a symbolic rebirth, a replacement of 'decadent femininity' with 'vigorous masculinity' (Ponnau 1991: 89).[15] But 'Phocas' is, first of all, the name of the Byzantine emperor under whose reign the frontiers of the Roman Empire began to collapse. Following Max Nordau and Krafft-Ebing, Lorrain's novel associates sexual and gender ambiguity with the decline of birth rates that nineteenth centuries sociologies saw as typical of exhausted civilizations. Like Magnan, Lorrain blamed heredity for the manifestations of perversions, but like Krafft-Ebing and Nordau, he also stressed environmental causes, first and foremost the abuse of drugs like opium and ether, among the factors that weakened and corrupted the population. Whereas Nordau believed that the working classes were fundamentally healthy, and that degeneration was a bourgeois phenomenon, Lorrain conceived of degeneration as a force that engulfed the whole of the population. In *Monsieur de Phocas*, the working classes are portrayed as savage, sensual masses still living in pre-history, the bourgeoisie are identified with their commercial values, the new aristocracy pictured on its way to extinction. Similarly, narcissism features in the texts as an individual pathology and as socio-historical condition, symptomatic of the decline of a civilization 'locked into colonialist enterprise and mass-market capitalism' (Birkett 2000: 29).

By linking masks to crime, illness and drug use, Lorrain echoed *fin-de-siècle* medical, anthropological and legal discourses and represented 'sexual inversion' as an illness, even a form of crime. In several ways, Lorrain's narratives parallel and even anticipate the theories of the emerging science of psychoanalysis by foregrounding the role of masks as catalysts for the return of the repressed. In establishing a link between masks, the fixation with the eyes, and severed heads, and in presenting heads and genitals as interchangeable, Lorrain's texts, just like Freud's, go as far as suggesting a metaphorical equivalence of decapitation and castration. Samuel Weber has observed that 'the distinctive character of the uncanny ... involves the recurrence and repetition of castration, which however, is itself ... a form of repetition and not to be confused with a unique, visible event' (1973: 1123). In Lorrain's texts, masks similarly become uncanny through a pattern of repetition by which theatrical props, wax busts and severed heads continue to evoke the same experience. Overall, Lorrain's texts pile up objects linked to the mask by a shared function or a relation of resemblance — on the one hand, busts and statues with empty eyes and severed heads, and, on the other, life-like automatons, death-like beings and projections of the self — extending them into the narrative segment. This strategy creates a redundancy, a piling-up of signifieds (the manifold embodiment of the mask) that in turn take on the role of signifiers for an ever-shifting object of desire. The substitution of the signifier by a series of signifieds, combined with their accumulation throughout the narrative, leads to a point in which metaphorical meaning becomes autonomous from the literal sense, just like, for Freud, events become uncanny when 'a symbol that takes over the full functions of the thing it symbolizes' (Freud 1955b: 244). While, in many ways, Lorrain's texts reflect contemporary medico-legal discourse, it is precisely in this aspect that we can identify a subversive potential.

Queerness, as Lee Edelman has stressed, cannot reproduce the politics of signification, and defies a Symbolic order in which there is no place for what does not comply with the heteronormative (2004: 27). The association of same-sex desire with the attraction for death, which permeates especially *Monsieur de Phocas* (see Praz 1970: 361–62; Bernheimer 2002: 120–21), appears troubling to contemporary readers (Du Plessis 2002: 86). On the other hand, for Edelman, who draws on Lacan, the death drive unveils 'the excess embedded within the Symbolic', uncovering the order of the law and the stability of the subject as a social fantasy (2004: 9). Queerness, Edelman notes, exposes the link between sexuality and the death drive through the 'instance of repetition', the 'resistance to determinations of meaning' and the 'rejection of spiritualization through marriage to reproductive futurism' (2004: 27) — features that can all be found in Lorrain's texts. By avoiding the term homosexuality, Lorrain refused to essentialize identities that challenged the order of patriarchy. In disrupting sexual and gender markers through travesty and cross-dressing, and in undoing the coupling of gender and sexual preference, Lorrain's masks and costumes challenge notions of 'natural' sexuality and foregrounded gender and sexuality as individual performances. By widening the gap between signifier and signified and refusing to signify, they also underline the instability of the mask as a sign and participate in a discourse of resistance that defies the construction of the Symbolic on which order and law rely.

Notes to Chapter 5

1. Oscar Wilde recognized in the sculpture the head of Salomé when he visited Lorrain in Paris in 1881 and was allegedly inspired by the sculpture to work on his own *Salomé* (1883), which he wrote originally in French (Lorrain 2005a: 444).
2. In his three essays on homosexuality, Freud argued that the homosexual is unable to overcome the narcissistic stage that characterizes childhood. In a footnote, he added that homosexuals display 'archaic constitution and primitive physical mechanisms' (1953: 145).
3. 'Qui n'a pas dans son enfance écouté, durant des heures et des jours, sangloter dans les peupliers d'un jardin de province les tristes et monotones averses, qui n'a pas senti peser sur ses jeunes années l'oppriment ennui des veilles rues solitaires et le vide affreux des semaines et des mois toujours pareils dans l'humanité fade d'un éternel ile gris, celui- là ne peut savoir quelles grimaçantes faces peuvent surgir à la brune d'une souche de saule, quelles étranges vielles femmes apparaissent accroupies sur les marches disjointes d'un perron de villa sans jardin, le soir, celui-là pourra, seul, sans émotion, traverser plus tard dans la vie l'hallucinante et lumineuse atmosphère des fêtes, celle des bals masqués où le faciès humain se complique d'inconnu sous le

satin des loups, comme des femmes émaillés et fardés arrivent à ressembler à des masques.' [Those who in their childhood have not listened, for hours and days, to the sad, monotonous sobbing of poplars in a provincial garden; those who have not felt weigh upon their young years the oppressive boredom of lonely, old roads and the awful emptiness of weeks and months, always the same among the dull humanity of an eternal grey isle — these people cannot know what grimacing faces may suddenly appear in a brownish willow stump, what strange old women appear crouching on the disjointed steps of a gardenless villa in the evening. Those alone may, later in life, experience without emotion the hallucinatory and luminous atmosphere of parties, those masked balls where the human face becomes complicated with the unknown under the satin of dominos, as women, enamelled and painted, come to resemble masks.] (Lorrain 2006: 78–79).
4. At the beginning of the nineteenth century, this notion was included under 'sexual inversion', but it disappeared as 'inversion' was substituted by homosexuality, intended as attraction for the same sex (Hekma 1996: 213).
5. Schwob introduced Lorrain to Wilde on the occasion of Wilde's visit to Paris. Lorrain attentively followed Oscar Wilde's trial in 1895, as well as the debates that ensued, but refrained from expressing an opinion on his incarceration.
6. Set in the space of myth, Schwob's 'Le Roi au masque d'or' (1892), a well-known piece in symbolist circles, tells the story of the last king of a noble race whose members have been wearing golden masks for generations. When he publicly unmasks, he exposes the face of a leper, a revelation that challenges not only the role given to him at birth but the power system upon which the court is based. Alone in the gallery with the portraits of his ancestors, the king attempts to discover his family history by tearing the painted masks from the canvases. The bare wall that emerges behind the masks exemplifies the gap between signifier and signified, or, in Freud's words, the disruption of the connection between 'the symbol and the thing that it symbolizes' and exposes the mask as an empty signifier. Lorrain elaborated on this idea and compared the laws of the social and political order to those that regulate sex and gender.
7. Vous savez? L'histoire du crapaud, la soudaine apparition dans une source, où vous veniez de boire, d'un flasque et monstrueux batracien! Circonstance aggravante, l'ignoble bête avait les yeux crevés, e l'eau, que vous veniez de puiser, en prit dans votre bouche un effroyable goût de sang... Eh bien, moi aussi l'ai un crapaud dans ma vie, et ce crapaud est une histoire de masques. [Do you remember? The story of the frog, its sudden appearance by a spring, where you have just drunk, a spineless, monstrous amphibian! Aggravating circumstance, the vile beast's eye sockets were empty, and the water, which you had just drawn, acquired in your mouth the horrifying flavour of blood... Well, I too have had a frog in my life, and this frog is a story of masks.] (Lorrain 2006: 38).
8. As a form of caricature, the animal-masks are reminiscent of the work of J. J. Grandville, the nineteenth-century French artist who drew animal faces on his characters to mock their behaviour (Rapetti 2009: 134).
9. Many of the figures from English and French high society that Ethal introduces to Fréneuse are unknown today, but would have been immediately recognizable to Lorrain's contemporaries. Count Aimery de Muzarrett is a veiled caricature of Robert de Montesquiou (who also appears in the novel under his real name); the Princesse de Seiryman-Frileuse is modelled on the American Winnaretta Singer, heir to the Singer fortune, who had several female lovers. The actress Maud White and her brother Reginald are inspired by the incestuous protagonists of *Zo'har*, an 1886 novel by Catulle Mendès. Ethal shares several traits with the American artist James Abbott McNeill Whistler (1834–1903) (Zinck 2001b: 315–26). Like Whistler, he poses as an aesthete, is arrogant, witty, confident, the talk of the town and famous for his piercing gaze. Moreover, he takes pride in his knowledge of Asian art, and just as Whistler publicly accused Wilde after the 1895 trials, Ethal does not refrain from mocking Fréneuse for his homosexuality.
10. The Javanese had performed at the Universal Exhibition in 1899 and 1900. In an opium-dream, Fréneuse sees the bodies of the dancers disappear, their faces float in isolation swollen and inflated, and perceives sharp fingernails threatening his eyes — a fantasy that prefigures Freud's association between images of blinding and decapitation and the fear of castration:

'Je voyais ricaner les faces singulièrement gonflées de deux Javanaises. Elles flottaient sans corps comme deux vessies transparentes et vernies; diadèmes de longs vers blancs, leurs yeux mi-clos laissaient filtrer, comme par deux fentes, un regard huileux et mort. Les deux vessies riaient, tandis qu'approchées de mon visage, leurs quatre mains sans bras, quatre mains molles et exsangues menaçaient mes yeux de leurs ongles aigus' [I saw the singularly bloated faces of the two Javanese servants, laughing mockingly. They floated in mid-air, disembodied, like two transparent varnished bladders, whitely diademed. Percolating from their half-closed eyes, as if shining through two slots, was a dead and greasy gaze. The two bladders laughed, while four hands without arms came towards my face: four soft and cadaverous hands, menacing my eyes with their sharp fingernails] (Lorrain 2001: 167).

11. Under different names, Angelotto's bust and the Egyptian figure already feature in short stories previously published by Lorrain ('L'Homme aux têtes de cire' and 'Un Démoniaque'). In these texts, Lorrain emphasizes gender ambiguity by describing the bust as 'tête de femme ou de jeune garçon' [head of a woman or of a young boy] (2001: 131) and the Egyptian vision as 'la forme adolescente ou d'un Prince ou d'un *une* esclave' [the adolescent profile of a prince or of a female slave] (my emphasis).
12. 'Quelle place il a prise dans ma vie, comme il manque! Sa présence m'est devenue tellement nécessaire que, depuis son absence, comme une faim me creuse et me tenaille l'être' [What a vital role he has assumed in my life! How I miss him! His presence has become so necessary to me that since he has gone it is as if a kind of hunger were tearing at me and hollowing me out] (2001: 112).
13. Fréneuse, who defines himself as an 'oriental', notes that 'En France, l'admiration seule des statues est permise, les pays du soleil n'ont pas ces préjugés' [In France, it is only permissible to admire statues but tropical countries have no such prejudices] (2001: 57).
14. In the short story 'Un Démoniaque' (1895), which contains the main themes of the novel, the three are in fact merged into one figure.
15. José Santos points out that the name *Fréneuse* features a feminine suffix, which contrasts with the masculine ending of the names *Phocas* and *Destreux* (1995: 50). Winn draws attention to the assonance between Fréneuse–*Névrose* [neurosis] and Phocas–*Faux case* [fake case] (1997: 155).

CHAPTER 6

Masquerades:
The Child, the Criminal and
the 'Savage' in Hofmannsthal and Bely

Hugo von Hofmannsthal's *Andreas* (1907–32) and Andrei Bely's *Petersburg* (1916), two novels that are considered milestones of modernism, are both concerned with masks and disguises as devices for anonymity and exposure, effacement and transformation. These works have never been compared before, as the plots elicit limited similarities. Surprising connections emerge, however, if one examines the way in which masks, as symbolic leitmotifs, function within the narratives in relation to period's preoccupation with degeneration.

Hugo von Hofmannsthal (1874–1929) and Andrei Bely (1880–1934) never met but shared a similar cultural background. Hofmannsthal was raised in a cosmopolitan environment in Italy and Vienna; his family was part of the minor Austrian nobility and was loyal to the Hapsburg monarchy. Boris Nikolaevich Bugaev grew up among Moscow's intellectual elite, and adopted the pseudonym 'Andrei Bely' to protect the reputation of his father, an internationally renowned mathematician and Dean of the University of Moscow. At the time when Hofmannsthal and Bely set out to work on their novels, Austria-Hungary and Russia were experiencing financial instability and social changes, as the lower classes challenged the privileges of aristocrats and bourgeois, and women entered the social sphere. Moreover, both Austria-Hungary and Russia were involved in military conflicts and experiencing internal tensions. In 1907, when Hofmannsthal conceived the first plan for *Andreas*, the Hapsburg Monarchy was struggling to keep protests in Hungary under control, and tensions between Germans and Czechs in Bohemia were increasing. In 1912–13, when he wrote the main fragment of the novel, the growing political role of Serbia challenged the Monarchy's domains in the Balkans. Around the same time, in 1911, Bely started working on *Petersburg*. Imperial Russia, which had suffered a humiliating defeat in the Russo-Japanese War (1904–05), was striving to extend its domains to Manchuria, facing uprisings in the Far East, and social revolts, strikes and terrorism in St Petersburg and Moscow.

As members of the intellectual elite, Hofmannsthal and Bely were aware that their generation was facing deep social and political transformations that would have an impact upon the privileges they enjoyed. Hofmannsthal was a conservative and identified with the aristocratic order. Convinced that the war would strengthen Austria-Hungary, he supported its entry into the First World War; after 1914, he continued to pay homage to the Hapsburgs' legacy.[1] In contrast, Bely welcomed social change. After the 1905 Revolution, he embraced Marxism, religious anarchy and radical politics, and planned to join a group of Socialist revolutionaries (Ljunggren 2005; Langen 2010: 191). In 1914, he saw in the First World War the opportunity for Russia's rebirth, and in 1917 he hailed the February and the October revolutions.

Despite the different political outlook, Hofmannsthal and Bely shared the same cultural references. Through the writing of Hermann Bahr, they became acquainted with the philosophy of Ernst Mach, whose *Analyse der Empfindungen* [*The Analysis of Sensations*], first published in 1886, challenged materialism and proposed a new view of the Self in relation to the world. They were both avid readers of Schopenhauer and Nietzsche, whose philosophy influenced their conception of the mask. Neither was fond of Max Nordau, and they thought positively about decadence as a creative principle (Kitzinger 2013: 406; Wermuth-Atkinson 2012: 35). However, like Nordau, they believed that their generation had inherited weak nerves and a sense of exhaustion, that Europe was undergoing a cultural crisis, and that mental and moral decline would affect individuals as well as the body of society. Both were familiar with Bahr's essay 'Überwindung des Naturalismus' [The Overcoming of Naturalism] (1891), in which the experience of modernity was characterized as dominated by the nerves and decadence as a masquerade,[2] as well as with Paul Bourget's definition of decadence as a proliferation of fragments (Bourget 1883: 25). Moreover, both had a profound and lasting interest in psychology and psychoanalysis. Hofmannsthal studied thoroughly Freud's *Traumdeutung* [*The Interpretation of Dreams*] (1899), with which Bely was also familiar (Wermuth-Atkinson 2012: 8). In this book, besides theorizing dreams as expressions of unconscious desires, Freud established a parallel between dreams and neurosis, in which he saw a regression to an infantile stage of libidinal development. In *Three Essays on the Theory of Sexuality*, published in 1905, he argued that the child was naturally perverse, and that narcissism and bisexuality were natural in children and primitive stages of societies, but indicated an arrested stage of sexual development, as well as 'archaic constitution' in the Western male adult (Freud 1953: 146). In 1913, when Hofmannsthal and Bely were working on their projects, Freud published *Totem and Taboo*, in which he drew an explicit connection between the operating mode of the unconscious, the psyche of primitive man, and contemporary aboriginal people. Before Freud, Lombroso had advanced the theory that criminals and anarchists were atavistic beings, and thus shared the same mental life and sexual drives as primitive man.

Drawing on Hofmannsthal's and Bely's shared cultural framework, this chapter argues that masking and doubling, in *Andreas* and *Petersburg*, reflect anthropological and psychoanalytical associations between the child, the criminal and the 'savage', and investigates the process through which masks, in these texts, function as psychological tropes that address the protagonists' sexual crisis, as well as political tropes that reflect the impasse of an expansionist power.

'Masks are the distinguishing factor': Hofmannsthal's *Andreas*

Hofmannsthal started working on *Andreas* in Venice in 1907; he wrote the main fragment, about 100 pages long, between 1912 and 1913, resumed writing in 1917, and continued working on the project until 1927, leaving about 400 pages of notes in which he described the characters and the development of events. From this material, we know that the novel was to be about 300 pages long and would comprise four books, only the first of which was completed. As Hofmannsthal wrote in a 1927 essay, the novel's fragmentary form was not a limitation but a way to address the context in which he was writing: '... Je großartiger, fragmentarischer er sich gibt, um so großartiger wird er verlangen, als ein Ganzes, als das einzige Ganze dieser zerrissenen Welt genommen zu werden...' [... The greater, the more fragmentary [the work of art] becomes, the more greatly it demands, as a whole, to be taken as the only whole of this fragmented world ...] (1980: 33). Moreover, the engagement with the fragment found a correspondence in the novel's themes, the fragmented self and social dissolution (Aurnhammer 1995: 296; Schnitzler 2011: 448).[3]

The book involves several autobiographical elements. Set in 1778, it tells the story of Andreas von Ferschengelder, a young man of the minor Austrian nobility who is sent by his parents on a journey from Vienna to Italy to complete his education, broaden his knowledge of other cultures and refine his manners. Andreas has not quite found his place in the world, has a nervous disposition, often loses himself in daydreaming, and is tormented by the memories of his childhood. His sense of self, as Hofmannsthal underlines, is fluid: he is extremely receptive to external influences, empathizes with strangers and imagines himself in other people's roles. On his way to Venice, Andreas is tricked into hiring Gotthelf, a servant who turns out to be a criminal in disguise. In Carinthia, the two are hosted by the Finazzer family. Andreas is struck by the Finazzers' daughter, Romana, with whom he spends an idyllic day in the countryside. The harmony is broken by Gotthelf, who poisons the Finazzers' dog, abuses their maid, sets the stable on fire, and runs away with Andreas's horse and the money sewn into the saddle. Three days and several adventures later, Andreas reaches Venice. Here he is greeted by a masked figure who introduces him to an impoverished family of the Venetian nobility. During his first day in the city, he meets the characters who will have a main role in the novel, among whom are Count Prampero's daughters, the actress/courtesan Nina and her sister Zustina, Sacramozo, the 'Knight of Malta', a mysterious man with connections to the Orient, and a Spanish woman, Maria, who suffers from a personality disorder. In Hofmannsthal's plan the climax of the novel was to take place at a masked ball in which Andreas, Sacramozo and Maria all participated. Andreas was eventually to return to Austria and marry Romana. Some of the notes, however, cast doubts on this conclusion and conjure a darker scenario.

The novel evokes the *Bildungsroman* and the adventure novel, but destabilizes these models by fragmenting the narrative into letters, journal entries, memories and dreams (Miles 1972: 106–09; Schnitzler 2011: 449). The main fragment begins with Andreas's arrival at Venice, and the three days in Carinthia emerge as a recollection as he sets out to write a letter to his parents. Andreas never actually writes the letter; he only plans what he would like to write but is distracted by daydreaming. Through this device, which is used twice in the main fragment, the author introduces readers to the difficult relationship Andreas has with his father, as well as with his tormented childhood. Moreover, the narrative voice frequently recalls Andreas's experiences by resorting to impersonal structures such as 'Ihm war als ob...' [It seemed to him that], followed by the subjunctive, and thereby creating a sense of ambiguity as to whether events occurred in reality or in Andreas's imagination.

When Hofmannsthal began working on the novel, he had just read Morton Prince's *The Dissociation of a Personality* (1906), a psychological study of a woman suffering from severe schizophrenia, and Philippe Monnier's *Venise au dix-huitième siècle* (1907), a historical account that emphasized Venice's licentious atmosphere and explained moral dissolution as a consequence of political and economic decline (Alewyn 1958: 105–41). Both had a profound impact on Hofmannsthal. Monnier's book stresses that, in the last years of the Venetian Republic, carnival was at its height. Citizens were allowed to wear masks for three months, and masked balls were popular with Venetian high society. Setting Andreas's adventures in this context offered an opportunity to reflect on the split psyche — the subject of Prince's treatise — as well as to render the sense of surveillance to which a visitor would be subjected in a city 'where even walls had ears' and spies hid behind every corner (Monnier 1907: 5). As in Monnier's book, Venice is in Hofmannsthal's novel a city where 'die Leute fast immer maskiert gehen' [people almost always wear masks] (1982a: 13).

Masks are embedded in the novel on a thematic, stylistic and symbolic level. With the exception of Andreas — interestingly, we know nothing about his features — grotesque traits dominate the faces of each of the characters and metonymically represent them. In the tradition of physiognomy, faces acquire mask-like features and become maps for moral qualities. Moreover, the Venetian characters display acrobatic, pantomimic movements that call to mind the *commedia dell'arte*, and communicate by gesticulating, rather than by using words (Frye 1992: 155). Count Prampero's house, where Andreas rents a room, faces the *Teatro San Samuele*, the celebrated theatre in which Carlo Goldoni worked as a director and Giacomo Casanova as a musician. All the members of Prampero's family are somehow involved with the theatre; his oldest daughter used to be an actress. On meeting Andreas, Count Prampero declaims a theatrical speech, but we learn that the effect of this performance relies not so much on the words as on his 'inimitable gestures' (Hofmannsthal 1982a: 79). Andreas often reflects on the meaningless of words, and comes to the conclusion that tones and looks have a deeper impact (Hofmannsthal 1982a: 61; 1982b: 259). Traditional disguises, mask-like beings, pantomimic gestures all fit into the same symbolic network. Overall, the figures whom Andreas encounters on his journey are all masked or affected by a dissociation of the self; they are independent characters, but they also reflect aspects of the protagonist (Hederer 1960: 179).

Features of Venice, in this light, are already present in Austria. In the city of Villach, during the first break on his way to Venice, Andreas meets as an unpleasant-looking man who insists on offering his services as a lackey. The servant, who introduces himself as Gotthelf ['God help'], stands in contraposition to Andreas. He is as confident and determined as Andreas is insecure and hesitant, as greedy for money as Andreas is heedless of it. Mysteriously well informed about Andreas, he uses his weaknesses to manipulate him into accepting him into his service. He brags of having served the nobility whom Andreas admires but has never had occasion to meet and is particularly loquacious about his sexual conquests, while Andreas is self-conscious about his lack of experience. As they travel together, Gotthelf's boastful stories alarm and disgust Andreas, but also excite him and arouse his imagination. In the 1912–13 version, as Gotthelf recalls a sexual adventure with a countess, he imagines himself as the protagonist of the story, is overwhelmed by the thought of and sees in it 'nichts Galantes u. Ehrbares mehr und nicht Schönes sondern ein wildes Tun, ein Morden im Dunkeln' [nothing romantic or honourable, nothing beautiful but a wild action, a murder in the dark] (Hofmannsthal 1982a: 51). In a fragment from 1921, Gotthelf licks his lips as he tells the story, and drives his horse close to Andreas to touch his master's knees (Hofmannsthal 1982a: 194). Andreas's disgust is such that he distances himself from the present by imagining he has witnessed the scene, rather than taking part in it. He finds relief picturing himself as a married man with children, and imagining that it was not him, but his son who rode to Venice (Hofmannsthal 1982a: 52).

Despite Andreas's aversion, Gotthelf's influence increases and the bond between the two grows stronger during the journey. He convinces Andreas to change his route and to go to Italy through Carinthia rather than the Tyrol. By riding too close to Andreas, he makes his horse stumble, after which the animal is injured, and Andreas is forced to ask for hospitality at the Finazzers' farm. Gradually, Gotthelf's violent temper is placed into relation with Andreas's thoughts. Although Andreas never even raises his voice against his servant, he feels on several occasions a desire to confront him physically. As they are riding together, he imagines pulling him down from his horse and hitting him 'savagely' (Hofmannsthal 1982a: 50). Later, as Gotthelf behaves inappropriately at the dinner table, he considers hitting him in the face until he falls unconscious (Hofmannsthal 1982a: 54). At the Finazzers' farm, Gotthelf's affair with the stable maid parallels Andreas's adventure with Romana; it begins at the same time, and follows the same stages. In a dream Andreas has on the night of the crime, Romana appears with torn clothes, as the maid does, and begs him not to tie her naked to the bed, as Gotthelf has done with his victim. Gotthelf's role is that of a disturber; as a doppelgänger, he stands between Andreas and Romana, in whom Andreas believes he has found a life companion. He substitutes homoeroticism for normative sexuality, and enacts Andreas repressed fantasies.[4]

Andreas's latent thoughts manifest through a series of anxious dreams, as well as through fantasies that take place in a state between wake and dream to which Hofmannsthal refers to as 'halb-geträumt' [dream-like state]. At night, he dreams of meeting Romana in Vienna, and as he pursues her in a dark alley, he is confronted with his first catechism teacher and his 'gefürchtete feste hand' [feared firm hand] (Hofmannsthal 1982a: 64), as well as with 'das Widerwertige Gesicht eines Knaben der ihm in dämmernder Abendstufe auf der Hinterstreppe erzählt hatte was er nicht hören wollte' [the repulsive face of a boy who as the night fell, at the back of the stairs, had told him what he did not want to hear] (Hofmannsthal 1982a: 64). These flashbacks associate sexuality with violence and sadism, and are followed by the memory of an act of cruelty he committed when, as a young boy, he broke a cat's back with an axle. In the dream, the cat returns to haunt Andreas with a 'dog-like face' and, taking a long time to die, stares at him with a gaze filled with 'lust and agony' (Hofmannsthal 1982a: 64). The following day, in a dream-like state, Andreas has a vision of the little dog he killed by stamping on its back as a twelve year old. The conflation between the animals hurt by Andreas and the dog poisoned by the servant unveils Gotthelf's sadistic urges as Andreas's very own.[5] In his notes from 1911–12, Hofmannsthal was planning for Andreas (who is in this version is called 'Leopold') an episode in which a countess was to treat him 'like a servant'. After the adventure, Andreas, in a state between wake and dreams, was to reflect that the adventure would have been wonderful if he had worn a mask (Hofmannsthal 1982a: 13). Besides confirming that Gotthelf and Andreas's actions are to a certain extent interchangeable, the note suggests that masking leads to a loosening of the *principium individuationis*, to the disruption of the boundaries that separate individuals from each other and from the external world, a phenomenon that Nietzsche associates with the Dionysian.

After Gotthelf is identified as a criminal in disguise, Andreas worries that his actions may cast a shadow on his own reputation, and reflects preoccupied on the saying 'Wie der Herr, so der Knecht' [like master, like servant] (Hofmannsthal 1982a: 67). In an act of introspection, he examines his family history — which, in many ways, parallels the family history of the author. Andreas, we learn, was named after his grandfather, Andreas von Ferschengelder, who arrived in Vienna from the outskirts of the Empire to serve the Emperor. Grateful for his loyalty, the Emperor granted him the noble title. Andreas, however, has little of his grandfather. He resembles his uncle Leopold, the black sheep of the family, who as a child was also dreamy, ill-tempered and cruel to animals and then became a violent man and discredited the family honour. As Andreas walks to the forest, the association with Gotthelf and Leopold loses the negative connotation. Andreas plays at hiding behind trees, experiences a temporary loss of the self, and finds a peculiar relief in imagining himself in other people's roles: 'endlich war sich selber entsprungen wie einem Gefängnis ... er wußte nichts von sich als den Augenblick, bald meinte er, er wäre Onkel Leopold, der wie <ein> Faun in Wald sprang einer Bauerndirn nach, bald er wäre ein Verbrecher und der Mörder wie der Gotthelf, dem die Häscher nachsetzten' [He had finally escaped himself, as from a prison... he knew nothing of himself, only the moment; now he thought he was Uncle Leopold pursuing a peasant girl like a faun in the forest, now he was a criminal and murderer like Gotthelf, with the sheriff's men after him] (Hofmannsthal 1982a: 71).

The state of inebriation is short-lasting, and juxtaposed with his reaction as he comes across a servant burying the Finazzers' dead dog. Devastated, Andreas drops to the ground and mourns the animal as if he were guilty of killing it himself:

> Hier! Sagte er vor sich hin: Hier! Das viele herumlaufen ist unnütz, man lauft sich selber nicht davon, bald zerrt einen dahin, mich haben sie diesen weiten Weg geschickt, endlich endet er auf irgendeinem Fleck, half auf diesem! Zwischen ihm und dem toten Hund war was, er wußte nur nicht was, so auch zwischen ihm und Gotthelf, der Schuld an dem Tod des Tieres war.
>
> ['Here!' he said to himself. 'Here! All this wandering about is futile, we cannot escape from ourselves. We are dragged hither and thither, they sent me all this long way — at last it comes to an end somewhere — here!' There was something between him and the dog, he did not know what, just as there was something between him and Gotthelf, who had brought about the dog's death.] (Hofmannsthal 1982a: 72)

Andreas is astonished by the warm, trusting relationship Romana enjoys with her parents. To the energy of Romana's father, and to the affection that he displays towards his daughter, he contrasts the cold and stiff manners of his own family. In the 1912–13 fragment, he reflects on how his parents have never enjoyed him, and compares his effort to make them happy to the struggle of warming up corpses.[6] The Finazzers' farm, and by extension the Carinthian countryside, is portrayed as a place of health and vigour, which stands in opposition to the capital, where people have nervous temperaments and are interested only in appearances (Hofmannsthal 1982a: 69). The Carinthian farm, however, has its dark side. Romana's father and mother, we learn from her account, are half-siblings who grew up together. Possibly as a consequence of inbreeding, five of Romana's siblings have died in infancy. As W. G. Sebald noted, the apparently radiant Finazzer family rests on 'decadence, dying and death' (1985: 71). The dream in which Andreas pursues Romana in Vienna, close to his parents' house, strangely dressed in 'half bäurischen halb städtische Kleider' [half peasant, half urban clothes] (Hofmannsthal 1982a: 64), underlines that the contrast between the capital and the countryside is only apparent. Moreover, the Carinthian atmosphere and characters find a double in their Venetian counterparts.

In Venice, the view of the *San Samuele* theatre, with its world-renowned performances, reminds Andreas of an amateur show that, as a child, he has seen in Vienna, where he had been filled by 'the most tender sensuality' and 'unspeakable longing' by the sight of a blue shoe glimpsed beneath the curtain (Hofmannsthal 1982a: 46). Through this flashback, Andreas's fascination with the stage is brought into connection with the half-seen and the fetish. The masked characters that he encounters in the city trigger similar emotions. Upon his arrival, Andreas feels vulnerable and exposed, a foreigner with bare features in a city of maskers. As the boatman leaves him on the dock with no guidance or direction, he compares the civility of the residents of his native city to the carelessness of the Venetians, and in doing so conflates Venice and Vienna: 'Als ließe man einen um 6h früh auf der Rossauerlände oder unter den Weißgärbern aus der Fahrpost aussteigen, der sich in Wien nicht auskennt. Ich kann die Sprache, was ist das weiter, deswegen machen sie aus mir, was sie wollen!' [You might as well turn a man out of the diligence on the Rossauerlände or under the Weissgärbern at six in the morning when he doesn't know his way about in Vienna. I can speak their language — what good is that? They'll do what they like with me all the same] (1982a: 40). In the 1911–12 versions, he first meets a company of actors (Hofmannsthal 1982a: 7); in the main fragment from 1912–13, he is greeted by a man in a 'domino', a term that Hofmannsthal uses to refer to a disguise consisting of a *bauta*, a mask with a prominent nose and a projecting chin that covers the whole face, and a red or black cape. This type of disguise, common in Venice in the eighteenth century, guaranteed anonymity by entirely covering the person and modifying the voice; it was traditionally worn by men, but could be occasionally worn by women, thereby effacing both class and gender. In *Andreas*, the masked man immediately offers his services, and, to gain Andreas's confidence, mentions his connection to the high Austrian aristocracy. Andreas does not notice that, in doing so, he repeats the actions of Gotthelf. If the criminal in disguise had broken the acceptable distance between him and his master by getting uncomfortably close to him, the masked man in Venice opens his cape and exposes his almost-naked body. Instead of pondering the reason for this eccentricity, Andreas responds by also opening his cape in the chilly morning air. The man, Andreas later finds out, has lost all his belongings by gambling, and works for Count Prampero, an impoverished aristocrat. Prampero's older daughter makes a living as a courtesan; the younger is organizing a lottery to sell her virginity and save the family from poverty. Throughout the novel, masking introduces the illegal, the illicit, the socially inacceptable.

Subsequent characters are introduced through a pattern in which each mimics the actions of the previous one or anticipates the next. Like Gotthelf, the Knight of Malta, Sacramozo (who in other notes is also called 'Sagrado') is both familiar and unfamiliar. He is twice a stranger, since he has lived in Venice for a long time and is originally from Malta. Yet he seems to know a great deal about Andreas and addresses him in flawless German. While Andreas is young and good looking but yet unsure of every step, travelling for the first time outside of his home city, the knight is ugly, long past youth, an experienced traveller and confident that nothing in his life has ever happened in vain. Numerous notes emphasize the importance that the character had in the book's conception, and shed light on Sacramozo's relationship to Andreas, his role as Andreas's double, and his key function for further developments for the novel, in which Hofmannsthal was planning to extend the action to Prague and to the Mediterranean, including North Africa. Through Sacramozo, Andreas is introduced to the Orient, a notion that for Hofmannsthal comprised the Arab world, China, Japan and Byzantium, as well parts of Eastern Europe (Stamm 2016: 107).

Hofmannsthal hesitated about the possible models for Sacramozo,[7] and in a note written sometime between 1917 and 1921 lent him the features of Stefan George, the Viennese poet who had fallen in love with him when he was a teenager. Although in the main fragment, the Knight writes unrequited love letters to Maria, Hofmannsthal envisioned an episode in which he shared with Andreas that he had 'never touched a woman'. Andreas would confess the same lack of experience, and the Maltese would congratulate him (Hofmannsthal 1982a: 23).[8] In the tradition of Wilde's *The Picture of Dorian Gray*, which had greatly impressed Hofmannsthal (Hammond 2012: 440), the motif of the double functions as a camouflage for same-sex desire.

Doubling, however, is not confined to male characters. The dissociated aspects of the male personality find a counterpart in female characters, which led Dieter Hornig to identify the main subject of the novel as the disintegration of women as triggered by the male gaze (1993: 91). Trapped in narcissism, Andreas projects upon the women who surround him aspects of his fragmented self. In the Carinthian dream, Romana is divided into an innocent, pure self and a lustful, aggressive personality: after begging him not to treat her like the maid, she kisses him passionately and then hits him with a rake (Hofmannsthal 1982a: 73). In Venice, Count Prampero's eldest daughter, Nina, whom Venetians hold in high esteem, is also split. Andreas longs to meet her, and when he is finally introduced to her, finds her lying on a couch in a pose reminiscent of Titian's and Giorgione's Venuses. This *tableau vivant*, which Andreas finds harmonious and charming, is contrasted to the unframed painting that lies on the floor, cut by a slash in the canvas: 'es waren Nina's Züge aber kalt, gemein. ... Es war eines von jenen peinlichen Porträts von denen man sagen kann daß sie das Inventarium eines Gesichtes enthalten, aber die Seele des Malers verraten' [Nina's features were there, but they looked cold and mean. ... It was one of those painful portraits of which it can be said that they contain the inventory of a face, but reveal the soul of the artist] (Hofmannsthal 1982a: 93).

Mesmerized by the portrait, Andreas asserts that it is very similar to its model, and yet very ugly. As, lost in a fantasy, he imagines himself as 'another self', a 'different Andreas', not a casual visitor but Nina's legitimate lover, the young woman undergoes a metamorphosis. She appears for a moment as Romana, and, as Andreas reaches out to hold her hand, she changes into the dark image of her portrait: 'ihr Blick verschleierte sich und das innere ihrer blauen Augen schien dunkler zu werden: die Ahnung eines Lächelns lag noch auf ihrer Oberlippe, aber ein vergehendes, beinahe angstvolles Lächeln schien einen Kuß dorthin zu rufen. Nicht konnte ihn tiefer erschrecken als diese Zeichen' [Her look became veiled, and the depths of her blue eyes seemed to darken; the hint of a smile still lay on her upper lip, but a fading, almost anxious smile that seemed to call for a kiss. Nothing could have startled him more deeply that such signs] (Hofmannsthal 1982a: 96).

In the notes from 1911–13, Nina finds her doppelgänger in Mariquita, the Spanish woman. In this version, Andreas meets Mariquita for the first time as she, masked, enters his room; she tries to drag him out to a gambling haunt and hints maliciously about his visit to Nina (Hofmannsthal 1982a: 31). In another note, as the masker talks about Nina, Andreas understands that they must somehow be the same person. In the main fragment, written in 1912–13, Nina and Maria become two different people, and each of them shares a separate double. Here Andreas meets Maria/Mariquita in church, on his way to Nina's, and Andreas refers to her as 'Die Maskierte' because of the suspicion that she might be a man in disguise. Both

Mariquita and Romana, with their child-like, boyish behaviour, embody what Hofmannsthal called '*das knaben-mädchenhafte*': an androgynous, still unfinished self (Ritter 2002: 70).

Maria and Mariquita, like Andreas and Gotthelf, were designed as opposites: Hofmannsthal describes Maria as somebody who is attracted to death, loves old people and has a horror of sex; Mariquita as frightened of death, close to children, restless and lustful, always busy with a 'puppet-like activity'. From Hofmannsthal's notes, we know he was planning an episode in which Maria would be able to observe her metamorphosis into Mariquita through a mirror. Maria and Andreas, at a masked ball, were to come together and undergo a reciprocal transformation and, in some versions, to overcome the dissociation of the self (Hofmannsthal 1982a: 191). The Knight of Malta was instead to facilitate Andreas's union with Maria, to commit suicide and to pass on his diplomatic tasks. The mask that was found in Sacramozo's room after his death symbolically represented these transformations.

The ongoing conflation between Romana/Nina, Nina/Maria, and their split into respective doubles, combined with the homoerotic allusions intertwined with the male doubles, underscore Andreas's difficulties in finding a stable love object. Throughout the narrative, Andreas is obsessed with the idea of having children, of giving his own parents the joy of becoming grandparents. He goes as far as wishing to be a woman, since, in his view, this would give him more control in generating offspring (Hofmannsthal 1982a: 63). As for nineteenth-century sexologists, for Andreas reproduction is the only acceptable outcome of sexuality. However, we learn through his dreams and fantasies that he is inclined to fetishism, same-sex desire, sadism and masochism. Andreas's apprenticeship, in this light, is also a journey from perversion to the location of a stable object of sexual desire (Romana) and to a sexuality geared towards reproduction (the children that he plans to have with her).

Andreas's adventures were initially planned as part of the 'Die Briefe des Zurückgekehreten' [The Letters of the Homecomer] (1907–08), a series of fictional letters in which an Austrian diplomat, who had been absent for eighteen years, relates the experience of coming back to Austria around 1900 and witnesses the profound changes in social and political structures (Hofmannsthal 1982b: 303–04). Besides recalling the adventures of an individual, Andreas's story was therefore intended from the outset as a commentary on modern Austria. When the novel grew into an autonomous project, Hofmannsthal decided to shift the setting to the eighteenth century. In a 1913 letter to his father, he explained this choice as a way to express his view on Austria-Hungary's political and ideological crisis while avoiding 'awkward references' to current events (Hofmannsthal 1982b: 367). For Hofmannsthal, the twentieth century was an age marked by decline.[9] The eighteenth century, in contrast, was the age of Haydn and Mozart, the time when Austria reached its cultural zenith. The novel's setting, then, served a dual purpose. On the one hand, it reflected the sphere of influence of the Hapsburg Empire, from Vienna to North-Eastern Italy, from Prague to the Mediterranean, and the Empire's rich cultural legacy.[10] On the other hand, the economic and political decline of the once powerful Republic of Venice symbolically represented the situation of Austria-Hungary at the beginning of the twentieth century.

In a letter written to Rudolf Pannwitz in 1917, Hofmannsthal addressed the novel's political implications and drew an outline of its sequel:

> Der Roman spielt, obwohl scheinbar rein privates Schicksal, im Todesjahr Maria Theresias. Der Held ist da 23 Jahre alt; im Nachspiel 1808–9 (Österreichs Erhebung) ist er ein hoher Beamter, sein Sohn dann Diplomat, sein Enkel in der Paulskirche 1848, damit deutet es in die Gegenwart herauf.

> [The novel, apparently simply the story of an individual, is set in the year of Maria Theresa's death. The hero is then 23 years old; in the sequel, 1808–9 (the period of Austria's rising), he is a senior civil servant, his son, then, a diplomat, and his grandson is in the Paulskirche in 1848; in this way the novel points to the present.] (1982b: 369)

By 1917, as Hofmannsthal was growing increasingly anxious about the disintegration of the aristocratic order, he planned to extend the plot to a span of time that included events such as Napoleon's conquest of Venice, Austria's subsequent acquisition of the city (1799), and the Congress of Vienna (1815), thereby mapping the history of Austria as a European power. In the first book, Hofmannsthal had reflected on Andreas's progenitors, his grandfather Andreas and his uncle Leopold, and on the impact of this heritage on his personality; in the notes for the sequel he mapped out Andreas's descendants, underlining how one's sense of self is shaped not only by personal experience but also by family history and cultural heritage that is passed on from generation to generation.

Hofmannsthal's work on the novel became increasingly fragmentary with the passing of time, and he often erased and rewrote versions of the same episodes. Several features, however, remain unchanged: the pivotal role of masks, Andreas's propensity for role play, his attraction for disguises, and his identification with the foreigners he encounters. For Hofmannsthal, the ability to mediate between cultures was a specifically 'Austrian' feature. The legacy of the cosmopolitan Hapsburg Empire gave Austria the capacity to act as a mediator between the Latin and the Slavonic world, between Western and Eastern Europe, Europe and Asia. Indeed, in the years in which he was working on *Andreas*, Hofmannsthal characterized Vienna, like Venice, as a *porta orientis* [gateway to the Orient] (1979: 195), and described Austria as a liminal and hybrid territory:

> ... zugleich Grenzmark, Grenzwall, Abschluß zu sein zwischen dem europäischen Imperium und einem, dessen Toren vorlagernden, stets chaotisch bewegten Völkergemenge Halb-Europa, Halb-Asien und zugleich fließende Grenze zu sein, Ausgangspunkt der Kolonisation, der Penetration, der sich nach Osten fortpflanzenden Kulturwellen, ja empfangend auch wieder und bereit zu empfangen die westwärts strebende Gegenwelle. (456)

> [... at once border marches, border wall, and settlement between the European Empire and an always chaotically moving mixture of peoples camped before its gates, half Europe and half Asia and at the same time a flowing border, a point of departure for colonization, for penetration, with cultural waves surging

toward the East, but also receiving and ready to receive the counter-wave beating its way westward.] (Hofmannsthal 1979: 456)

Precisely Austria's hybrid status, its configuration as 'half Europe, half Asia' in Hofmannsthal's eyes, made Austria essential in the new European order. As David Luft notes, for Hofmannsthal the role of Austria was 'to carry other cultures across to the rest of Europe, to mediate, to translate' (2011: 10). In *Andreas*, the Knight of Malta, who travels to Japan and Persia and acts as a mediator between Europe and the Orient, introduces the notion that Europe could reinforce its identity and rejuvenate itself through a dialogue with the East. In Hofmannsthal's plans, Andreas was to follow the Knight of Malta in his diplomatic mission. The young Austrian characterized by fluid borders of the self, who empathizes with the foreigners he encounters, increasingly dresses as a cultural mediator. His adventures, and those of his descendants, trace Austrian identity back to the high point of the Hapsburg Empire, and in doing so point to Austria's way out of the impasse and its new role in a changing European landscape. Andreas's fantasies and dreams, however, conjure a much darker scenario. In his subtext, rather than becoming a husband and a father, Andreas turns into the 'homosexual and narcissistic type' (Sebald 1985: 69).[11] Masks and doubling underline the fragility of the protagonist, and, in doing so, also address 'the crisis and anxieties of a destabilized male ego facing a world of disintegration of traditional values' (Berman 2002: 215).

'Outlived Culture and Healthy Barbarism': Bely's *Petersburg*

Designed by Tsar Peter the Great in 1703 to serve as a window to Europe for Russia's multi-ethnic empire, St Petersburg is nicknamed 'the Venice of the North' because of its many bridges and canals. Moreover, early twentieth-century St Petersburg shared with Venice a fascination with masks and masquerades. Costume balls were regularly held at the Winter Palace, but were also organized by aristocratic families and held in public theatres (Wiggins 2010: 181; McQuillen 2013: 9, 21). Alexandr Blok, Nikolai Evreinov and Igor Stravinsky all experimented with masks inspired by the *commedia dell'arte*. Vsevolod Meyerhold used to wear a Venetian *bauta* when he impersonated his alias, 'Dr Dappertutto', and named the journal he edited *The Love of Three Oranges* in celebration of the eighteenth-century Venetian playwright Carlo Gozzi. As Colleen McQuillen argues, the tribute to Venice involved a political connotation, since the comparison with early twentieth-century St Petersburg and the last years of the Venetian Republic emphasized the climate of instability that pervaded the Russian capital between the two revolutions (2004: 110). Bely engaged in this discourse by placing at the centre of *Petersburg*, the novel on which he was working from 1911 and that he published in *Sirin* in 1913–14, a Venetian costume and connecting it to the decline of the aristocracy and to revolutionary terror. Like Hofmannsthal, he used the term 'domino' for a disguise inspired by the Venetian *bauta*, consisting of a small black mask with a lace beard and a red, hooded mantle.

The action takes place in St Petersburg after Russia's defeat in the Russo-Japanese war, at a time when the country was overwhelmed by protests, strikes and terrorism. Nikolai Apollonovich, son of Senator Apollon Apollonovich Ableukhov, is a nervous young man who is unsuccessful with women and haunted by memories of a loveless childhood. In a moment of frustration after a romantic disappointment, he becomes involved with a terrorist party and says that, if the party required it, he would be ready to do away with his own father. He soon forgets about this promise and is seen around town wearing a red domino, a costume with which he intends to scare Sophia Petrovna, the woman who rejected him. One day, his friend Alexandr Ivanovich Dudkin, an agent of the revolutionary party, entrusts him with an object for safekeeping.

The story moves to its climax with a masked ball, which is attended by most of the characters in the novel. Here Sophia Petrovna hands to Nikolai, who is wearing his red domino, an anonymous letter which explains that the object that has been delivered to him is a sardine box containing a bomb. That same evening, the double agent Morkovin/Voronkov, who works for both the revolutionary party and the St Petersburg police, threatens to arrest Nikolai if he does not fulfil his promise. Mesmerized by the bomb, Nikolai activates the mechanism as if in a trance. When he comes to his senses, he is terrified and seeks help from Alexandr Ivanovich. The latter shows up in distress, declaring that he did not know the content of the parcel; he advises Nikolai to throw the bomb into the river and promises to mediate with the agent who has delivered the instructions. The party leader Lippanchenko (Morkovin in disguise) is not sympathetic and threatens to destroy both Nikolai and Alexandr if the crime is not committed. Nikolai returns to his home with the intention of getting rid of the bomb, but can no longer find it and is interrupted in his search by the return to St Petersburg of his mother. The bomb explodes at night in his father's studio, leaving the senator in a state of shock. Alexandr Ivanovich is haunted by hallucinations, goes mad, and murders Lippanchenko with a pair of scissors; Nikolai leaves for Egypt and does not return to Russia until the death of his parents.

The novel evokes an established model, the nineteenth-century realist novel, and disrupts the story line through a device that Olga Matich calls 'the spatialisation of time' (2010: 17), in which events seem to take place over a longer period of time than they actually do. The bomb that Nikolai keeps hidden in the residence he shares with his father is timed to go off after 24 hours, but the ticking of the clock does not rule over the dreams, memories and hallucinations that are interwoven in the narrative. Bely avoids the subjunctive, relating dreams and visions in the present tense, as if they were actual events. As a result, the reader is often unsure of whether events happen inside or outside the character's mind and the story line breaks into fragments.

The city landscape is also fragmented. The mainland is associated with reason, wealth, Apollo, the West; the Vasilevkii island with poverty, irrationality, Dionysus, the East. Senator Apollon Ableukhov and his son Nikolai, along with Nikolai's friend Sergei Sergeich Likhutin and his wife Sofia Petrovna, live on the mainland. The destitute agent Alexandr Ivanovich Dudkin, who throughout the narrative is addressed as 'the stranger', the powerful party leader Lippanchenko, who has

Mongol features, are residents of the island. However, divisions are not clear cut. As Maguire and Malmstad note, in the novel there are 'no private thoughts or private actions' and 'even something as concrete as a tic or gesture might be shared by a number of otherwise seemingly different personages' (1978: xiii). The islanders, 'neither men nor shadows' (Bely 1990b: 277), are at once independent characters and doppelgängers for the figures from the mainland. Alexandr Ivanovich, for instance, is both a messenger for the terrorist party and the double of Nikolai. He is initially introduced in contrast to Nikolai, since he is extremely poor, follows the preachings of Nietzsche, and is committed to revolution, while Nikolai is a neo-Kantian and belongs to a rich, aristocratic, conservative Russian family. The two are gradually brought closer as we learn that they share habits, memories, sexual perversions, and a state of obsession and confusion. Moreover, they are both haunted by masks, although these materialize in different ways: Nikolai develops a fixation with the domino; Alexandr is obsessed by the faces with the same imprint that he discerns on the damp, yellow wallpaper in his attic. Similarly, Senator Ableukhov and Lippanchenko, initially portrayed as opposites in their respective roles of representative of the Russian State and as leader of a terrorist organization, are brought together by their roles as father figures towards Nikolai and Alexandr, as well as by the 'Mongol' features that Nikolai and Alexandr perceive in them.

All characters are associated with masks: Nikolai's profile resembles a marble sculpture, Likhutin's face a wood carving, the senator's head recalls the head of the Gorgon and Alexandr Ivanovich's features, in his last appearance, are those of a clown. Each character is identified by a prominent trait: Nikolai and his father by huge ears; Likhutin by a shaven chin; Lippanchenko by narrow, 'Mongol', eyes. Communication, as if the characters were onstage, often takes place through gestures (Maguire and Malmstad 1978: xvi).

Masks hide the characters' inner divisions. The different components of Nikolai's personality are 'богоподобный лед' [godlike ice] and 'лягушечья слякоть' [froglike slime], a duality the narrator characterizes as 'feminine' and that parallels a division between a 'Western' and an 'Eastern' self (Bely 1990b: 76). Nikolai has two rooms in his father's house: he keeps one of them, decorated with a bust of Kant, for his library, while the other is furnished with an oriental couch, an Arab stool, and exotic objects such as African shields, Sudanese spears, incense burners and a multicoloured leopard skin. Moreover, he walks around the house in a Bukharan robe, Tartar skullcap and fur slippers, a masquerade that has effectively turned him into 'an oriental' (Bely 1990b: 57).

A traditional Venetian disguise, the domino finds a place in the oriental room. Nikolai wears it for the first time in a private ceremony in front of the mirror in which, 'like Narcissus', he becomes fascinated with his own image (Bely 1990b: 52). Staring at his reflection, he perceives his own face growing unfamiliar, has the feeling of losing his self, and becomes one with the pale demon in the mirror. By concealing his androgynous features, the costume reverses his sexuality, changing asexual temper into 'naked passion'. It also literally realizes a joke by Sopha Petrovna, who, in rejecting him, has called him a 'red clown' (Bely 1990b: 88).

Bold and confident in the domino, Nikolai experiences shame when his association with the costume is uncovered. When Alexandr Ivanovich catches a glimpse of the domino on the armchair, Nikolai's behaviour is compared to that of a thief caught red-handed: he blushes, covers the red silk with the Tartar gown and hurries to put it away. Sophia Petrovna, seeing the domino dancing on the bridge that connects the island to the mainland, discerns in it a satanic incarnation. She is, however, terrified only until a gust of wind blows the cloak open and exposes Nikolai's braces. Enraged, she tells the whole story to her husband, Sergei Likhutin, who connects the domino to 'satanic excess'. In a meeting with Lihkutin, Nikolai justifies his actions as the result of a nervous breakdown: 'врач сказал: рредкое такое — мозговое расстройство, такое-такое: домино и все подобное там... Мозговое расстройство...' [The doctor said: a very rare ... mental indisposition, all that business of the domino and suchlike... a mental indisposition ...] (Bely 1990b: 441). The domino is therefore associated with the illicit, characterized as socially inacceptable, and explained as a symptom of weak nerves and psychological exhaustion. It is also linked to a sexual pathology: stuck in a narcissistic phase, Nikolai is unable to relate to women and uses the domino to mediate with Sophia Petrovna.

At a fancy-dress ball, Nikolai receives a letter with the party's instructions. The event brings together the main characters, including Senator Apollon Apollonovich, Lippanchenko and Sophia Petrovna. As soon as Nikolai enters the ballroom, in his red domino, he is surrounded by dancing monks with skulls and cross bones embroidered on their chests, who sing a song announcing a time of terrorism (Bely 1990b: 229). Apollon Apollonovich sees in this performance a 'кровавые пляски' [sanguinary dance] (Bely 1990b: 217), while the 'кровавое домино' [blood red domino] fills him with revulsion (Bely 1990b: 217). He does not recognize his son, but thinks that somebody might be terrorizing him using red as a symbolic colour and later turns away in disgust, identifying in the costume an omen of terrorism: 'красный цвет, конечно, был эмблемой Россию губившего хаоса' [The red colour was, of course, an emblem of the chaos that was destroying Russia] (Bely 1990b: 184). Since Nikolai's father is also a high-ranking officer in the Russian Empire, the conflict between father and son symbolically stands for the conflict between the old establishment and the new generation (McQuillen 2013: 82). The domino, which Nikolai had initially worn for a personal reason, gradually acquires a meaning that goes beyond his intentions, and exposes him as a puppet of the revolutionary party.

Still masked, Nikolai returns home in the morning and comes face to face with his father in the drawing room walled with mirrors. Seeing his own image projected and multiplied by the mirrors, he experiences a division of the self and imagines himself projected into a murderer. The narrator recalls the vision in the past indicative, as if Nikolai were a third party witnessing the patricide:

> вдруг ему представился негодяй; лязгнули в пальцах у этого негодяя блиставшие ножницы, когда негодяй этот мешковато бросился простригать сонную артерию костлявого старикашки [...]

> Этот образ столь ярко предстал перед ним, будто он был уже только что.
>
> [He suddenly imagined the villain; a gleaming pair of scissors grasped in this villain's fingers, when he rushed clumsily to sever the scrawny old man's carotid artery; the villain slashed with the scissors across the scrawny old man's artery [...]
> This image appeared so vividly before him, as though it were something that had just happened.] (Bely 1990b: 272)

In a game of reflections, Nikolai and his father, from opposite sides of the room, see each other transformed respectively into a puppet, 'the fairground Petrushka ... bright red as blood' and into a dead man, 'a deadly skeleton in buttoned-up frock-coat' (Bely 1990b: 273). Douglas Clayton has noted that 'Petrushka' [little Peter], a puppet from the Russian folk tradition, was also a comic diminutive of Peter the Great, founder of St Petersburg and symbolic father of the Russian Empire (1994: 312). By turning Nikolai into Petrushka, the mirror reverses father and son's relationships; in charactering Petrushka as a 'bloody clown', it symbolically mirrors the conflicts that were pervading Russia (Clayton 1994: 14). The vision fulfils Nikolai's wish to see his father dead, and prefigures the murder which, with the same weapon, is later committed by Alexandr Ivanovich, whose features recall those of a clown.

While Nikolai becomes obsessed with the domino, Alexandr Ivanovich, messenger of the terrorist party, is haunted by a different type of mask, yellow faces with 'Tartars, Japanese or oriental' features, which seem to him 'пакостный отпечаток' [created from the same woodcut] (Bely 1900: 107). The eastern faces torment Alexandr mostly in his dreams, but even when he is awake, he continues to be taunted by a hallucination in which an oriental face with 'Mongoloid eyes' (Bely 1990b: 55) stares at him from a damp spot on his yellow wallpaper. When he meets the chief agent Lippanchenko to receive the package that he is to hand over to Nikolai, Alexandr recognizes in the man's yellow, fat, greasy features the faces that materialize in his attic. A few pages later, the narrator specifies that Lippanchenko, as if he were wearing a mask based on one of Alexandr Ivanovich's visions, looks like a mixture of Semite and Mongol. Alexandr cannot refrain from asking Lippanchenko whether he has Mongol origins, but Lippanchenko's answers remains vague, as he states that Mongol blood is a common feature in all the Russian population. The narrator notes that Lippanchenko has become Alexandr's personal fabrication: 'химера росла — по ночам: на куске темно-желтых обой усмехалась она настоящим монголом' [a chimera that grew with every night: on a patch of the dark-yellow wallpaper it grinned like a real Mongol] (Bely 1990b: 338).

Alexandr attributes the yellow masks to a mental ailment caused by the excessive consumption of alcohol: 'Ну, что такое монгол на стене? Бред. [...] Э, да болен он, болен... (349–50)' [What was the Mongol on the wall after all? Delirium. [...] Oh he was ill, ill!] (Bely 1990b: 349–50). The illness involves a deviation from the normative sexual drive. Portrayed as effeminate and squeamish, Alexandr confesses to Nikolai that he has never fallen in love with a woman, but that men have fallen in love with him. In addition, he develops an inclination towards fetishism: 'был влюблен, как бы это сказать: в отдельные части женского тела, в туалетные принадлежности, в чулки, например' [I was in love ... how shall I put it: with specific parts of woman's body, with articles of her toilet, stockings, for instance] (Bely 1990b: 111). Later, he correlates the sexual and the anthropological fetish, and brings both into connection with 'здоровое варварство' [healthy barbarism] (Bely 1990b: 360). In Freudian terms, he experiences a regression to an infantile stage of libidinal development that he associates with the type of thinking (fetishism and animism) that he sees as typical of primitive people, terrorists and 'Tartars, Japanese or oriental persons in general' (Bely 1990b: 107).

While the domino is interpreted as an emblem of revolutionary terror, the yellow faces are linked to the social revolts that take place in the Far East and that, in the fiction, spread first to the Vasilevkii Island and later to the mainland, as exemplified by the Manchurian hats worn by the St Petersburg demonstrators. Alexandr Ivanovich, Sophia Petrovna and Apollon Apollonovich all recognize in the protesting mob in St Petersburg 'желтые, монгольские рожи' [ugly, yellow Mongol faces] (Bely 1990b: 133).

Caught in the middle of the demonstration, Alexandr Ivanovich looks at the statue of Peter the Great and is enlightened by a prophetic glance into European history:

> ... желтые полчища азиатов, тронувшись с насиженных мест, обагрят поля европейские океанами крови; будет, будет — Цусима! Будет — новая Калка!...
>
> [...] под монгольской тяжелой пятой опустятся европейские берега, и над этими берегами закурчавится пена; земнородные существа вновь опустятся к дну океанов — в прародимые, в давно забытые хаосы... (121–22)
>
> ... yellow hordes of Asiatics, moving from the places they have settled, will turn the fields of Europe crimson with oceans of blood; there will be — Tsushima! There will be — a new Kalka! [...] the shores of Europe will sink under the Mongol heel, and above those shores foam will froth; the creatures of the earth will sink again to the bottom of the oceans — into primeval, long-forgotten chaos... (Bely 1990b: 121–22)

By evoking Tsushima, the battle in which the Japanese crushed the Russian navy during the Russo-Japanese war, the prophecy underscores anxieties about Russia's military and political crisis. References to Japan abound in the novel.[12] Alexandr also equates Russia's defeat by Japan with the thirteenth-century battle of Kalka, which opened the way for the Mongol conquest of Russia, and compares military weakness to a regression to an earlier state of evolution, the 'primeval, long-forgotten chaos' that he associates with the resurfacing of the primitive, or the so-called 'Mongol business' (Bely 1990b: 315). In the novel, anything yellow (like the faces in the wallpaper) or slimy (like the tin in which the bomb is hidden, like the lips of Lippanchenko) becomes an embodiment of this phenomenon.

Nikolai, whose twitching features' are compared to 'foglike slime' (Bely 1990b: 76), and who has promised to murder the senator, becomes part of this symbolic network. Indeed, his connection with the Mongols goes back to his family history.

The Ableukhovs, we learn, originated from 'the Kirgiz-Kaisak Horde' (Bely 1990b: 10), and the senator and his son are the last heirs of an ancient Mongol race. Before discovering that his son is behind the scandal of the red domino, Senator Ableukhov has a dream in which he recognizes Nikolai as a Mongol, more precisely as a Mongol that he had once met in Japan (Bely 1990b: 170). Similarly, after facing his father in the domino costume, Nikolai Apollonovich falls asleep and has a dream in which he sees an 'ancient Turanian' with the face of his father. When the Mongol enters the room in a colourful dressing gown, Nikolai identifies him as his ancestor Ab-Lai:

> [О]н — старый туранец — воплощался многое множество раз; воплотился и ныне: в кровь и плоть столбового дворянства Российской империи [...] на лице Николая Аполлоновича появилось теперь забытое, монгольское выражение; он кавался теперь мандарином Срединной империи, облеченным в сюртук при своем проезде на запад [...] Странное дело: как он вдруг напомнил отца!
>
> [[H]e — the old Turanian — had been embodied a multitude of times; he was embodied now: in the flesh and blood of the Russian imperial nobility of ancient lineage [...] on Nikolai Apollonovich's face a forgotten Mongol expression appeared; he seemed now to be a Mandarin of the Middle Empire, clad in a frock coat for his passage to the West. [...] How strange, he suddenly so resembled his father!] (Bely 1990b: 291)

In the dream, the old Turanian turns into Apollon Apollonovich, grabs Nikolai's exercise books and begins to instruct him in 'the Mongol business' and in the 'mission of the destroyer' (Bely 1990b: 291). Nikolai traces the roots of his neurosis to heredity, and fears that his aristocratic blood has been vitiated by 'yellow blood corpuscles' (Bely 1990b: 289). Since Nikolai's patricidal thoughts are interwoven with repressed memories of his childhood, the regression to Mongolism is also a leap into the depths of the psyche, the dimension that Freud classifies as the unconscious and that Rudolf Steiner, who influenced Bely, identified with the Dionysian (Wermuth-Atkinson 212: 76). Contemplating the bomb, Nikolai feels torn to pieces, as if his limbs were being pulled in different directions. Alexandr first interprets Nikolai's experience in Freudian terms, and tells him that his childhood has come back to haunt him. He then reverts to the Nietzschean (and theosophical) paradigm, and identifies Nikolai's experience as the suffering of Dionysus (Bely 1990b: 315).

Alexandr, who suffers from the same fragmentation as Nikolai, also experiences a division of the self. On his doorstep, he meets a Persian revolutionary and feels compelled to let him in into his apartment. The Persian's name, he learns, is Shishnarfne, an anagram of *Enfranshish*, the whisper that he has been hearing from the yellow faces.[13] Shishnarfne is both familiar and unfamiliar: he has oriental features, but no accent when he speaks Russian. Announcing that he has long been looking for Alexandr, he explains that he has come from Helsingfors, today's Helsinki, which at the time was part of the Russian Empire. Alexandr remembers how, in this city, he had spoken about the need to destroy European culture so as to bring about an age of 'healthy barbarism', inciting his audience to embrace Dionysian chaos:

> период историей изжитого гуманизма закончен и культурная история теперь стоит перед нами, как выветренный трухляк: наступает период здорового зверства, пробивающийся из темного народного низа (хулиганство, буйство апашей), из аристок-ратических верхов (бунт искусств против установленных форм, любовь к примитивной культуре, экзотика) и из самой буржуазии (восточные дамские моды, кэк-уок — негрский танец; и — далее); Александр Иванович в эту пору проповедовал сожжение библиотек, университетов, музеев; проповедовал он и призванье монголов (впоследствии он испугался монголов). Все явления современности разделялись им на две категории: на признаки уже изжитой культуры и на здоровое варварство, принужденное пока таиться под маскою утонченности (явление Ницше и Ибсена) и под этою маскою заражать сердца хаосом, уже тайно взывающим в душах.
> Александр Иванович приглашал посиять маски и открыто быть с хаосом.
>
> [The era of historically outlived humanism was at an end. All cultural history stood before us like an eroded ruin: a period of healthy barbarism was beginning, emerging from the depths of ordinary people (hooliganism, the riotous behaviour of the mob), from aristocratic high society (the uprising of the arts against established forms, love of primitive culture, the exotic), and from the bourgeoisie itself (oriental ladies' fashions, the cakewalk — a negro dance; and — so on); at the time Alexandr Ivanovich advocated the burning of libraries, universities and museums; he advocated the summoning of the Mongols (later he became afraid of the Mongols). All contemporary phenomena were divided by him into two categories: symptoms of outlived culture and healthy barbarism, which was compelled for the time being to conceal itself under a mask of refinement (the appearance of Ibsen and Nietzsche); and under that mask to infect the hearts of men with the chaos that was already secretly calling in their souls.
> Alexandr Ivanovich called on people to remove their masks and live openly with chaos.] (Bely 1990b: 360)

Through the flashback, degeneration, initially linked to the decay of the aristocracy, is explained as a phenomenon that encompasses the whole of Russian society, including the bourgeoisie and the lower classes, and that finds objective correlatives in the experience of the crowd, primitivism, orientalism and Japanophilia.

Alexandr soon notices that that the voice of Shishnarfne comes from his own throat. He considers escaping by jumping out of the window, but the narrator warns him that his attempt is useless: 'нужно было выскочить не из комнаты, а из тела' [he needed to spring out of his body, not his room] (Bely 1990b: 369). So far, Alexandr had perceived himself surrounded by threatening yellow masks. Now he recognizes that the threat comes from a estranged component in his own self: 'И пока это делалось с ним, он и думал, что они его ищут; а они были — в нем [all the while this was happening to him, he had thought that they were after him; but they — were inside him] (Bely 1990b: 101). Meanwhile Nikolai, lost in memories of his childhood, acknowledges that he has lived for years under a mask:

при нем кровью шутили, называли 'отродьем'; и над собственной кровью зашутил — 'шут'; 'шут' не был маскою, маской был 'Николай Аполлонович'...

Преждевременно разложилась в нем кровь.

[... they joked about his blood and called him 'sprog' and 'clown' — joked about his own blood; the 'clown' was not a mask, Nikolai Apollonovich was the mask...

His blood was prematurely decomposed.] (Bely 1990b: 408)

Both Alexandr and Nikolai suffer from a mental ailment, experience a deviation from normative sexuality, undergo a form of regression, and experience a fragmentation of the self. If, as Alexandr Ivanovich stresses, 'symptoms of outlived culture' and 'healthy barbarism' are the double face of the same reality, Nikolai's obsession with the domino, which symbolically exposes the decay of the aristocracy, and Alexandr's fixation with yellow masks, linked to Russia's past and present military defeats, are two sides of the same coin.

Bely encouraged an autobiographical interpretation of the novel by describing in his memoirs how, in the autumn of 1906, after his rejection by Blok's wife, Ljubov Mendeleeva, he spent many hours alone in his apartment, wearing a black mask and red cloak (Bely 1990a: 89–92). His political views continued to shift as he was working on the novel, and scholars generally agree that is pointless to attempt to identify a clear message (Langen 2010: 191). The novel, however, is filled with political references. In devising the plot, Bely drew on an incident involving the Minister of the Interior, Vycheslav von Plehve, assassinated by terrorists in 1905 (Peri and Evans 2010: 149–73). In his biography, he identified the murder as a turning point in history and a critical step in attacks on the Tsarist establishment. He also noted that the terrorist Boris Savinkov, who orchestrated the attack, served as a model for the party messenger Alexandr Ivanovich Dudkin (Bely 1990a: 65). Furthermore, he commented that the terrorist Evno Azef, who worked as a double agent for the Tsarist secret police and was known for his Mongolian appearance, served as a prototype for Lippanchenko. Vladimir Solovyov's philosophy, especially the poem 'Panmongolism' (1894), which predicts an invasion of Russia by Asians, was also an important source (Maguire and Malmstad 1978: 325). Bely and Blok referred to this idea as 'the yellow temptation', and believed that the revolutionary movement, which could count on collaborators in Finland, had been infiltrated by a destructive 'Eastern' element (Ljunggren 2005: 33).

When, after the ball, Apollon Apollonovich enters his son's room and removes the sardine tin, he casts a last glance at the forgotten costume and is astonished by its incongruity with its surrounding:

... во все стороны порезвились с табуретки кипящие красные складки пышно павшего домино, будто бьющиеся огни и льющиеся оленьи рога — прямо под голову пятнистому леопарду, распластанному на полу, с оскаленной головой ... шутовское и безголовое, раскидалось оно атласными полами и безрукими рукавами; на суданской ржавой стреле была повешена масочка.

> [...from the stool in all directions spread the seething scarlet folds of the flamboyantly discarded domino, like leaping flames and flowing antlers — right up to the head of the spotted leopard, spread-eagled on the floor with snarling jaws; ... it lay there, headless and preposterous, in satin folds and empty sleeves; on a rusty Sudanese arrow the little mask was hanging.] (Bely 1990b: 447)

In line with Freud's thoughts in *Totem and Taboo*, this image establishes a connection between the return of repressed childhood experiences, embodied by the mask, and primitivism, symbolized by the leopard skin and the Sudanese arrow. Since, in the novel, the fascination with primitive culture and the exotic (the African objects in Nikolai's room, Japanophilia) is conflated with the historically remote (the Mongol conquest of Russia), Nikolai's neurosis symbolically indicates Russia's decline. In linking the red domino, an emblem of terrorism, to the primitive weapon, the last manifestation of the costume also subscribes to the Lombrosian paradigm that saw in criminals and anarchists relics of the past, portraying threats to the Russian Empire as both internal and external, coming from the East as much as from the depth of the Western psyche.

Conclusions

Andreas and *Petersburg* evoke traditional models — the *Bildungsroman* and the nineteenth-century realist novel — but subvert them by dilating the time of narration through fantasies and dreams. Both challenge the boundaries between facts and imagination by addressing these experiences in the same narrative mode. By breaking the story line and adopting the fragment as a compositional principle and as a thematic motif, they participate in the *fin-de-siècle* preoccupation with the part–whole relationship. Both narratives project thoughts, ideas and memories that resemble one another onto a narrative segment — a mechanism that Freud, describing the language of dreams, identified as displacement — and in doing so rely on a metonymic logic. In drawing attention to facial features and identifying characters with a dominant trait, they make extensive use of synecdoche. Moreover, both foreground communication through gestures, and associate masks and disguises with the feeling of being constantly observed. The overarching metaphor is that of *theatrum mundi*, a stage on which fears and desires take a material shape, embodied by masks and doubles.

The main figures, Andreas and Nikolai, embody typical decadent heroes: they are the last offspring of a noble line, they are introverts with weak nerves and suffer from neurosis, and they have a difficult relationship to the opposite sex. Unloved during their childhood, they are unable to please their parents as adults, and see their craving for affection turn into negative emotions. Both experience a dissociation of the self, which results in the proliferation of masks and the production of doubles. They blame heredity for their mental ailments, but their dreams, fantasies and hallucinations trace their neurosis back to their childhood.

The inability to overcome childhood traumas and the conflict with their father results in a deviation from normative sexuality. For Freud, men were more likely to engage in perversions, whereas neuroses were typical of women, whom he saw as more passive and prone to repression (Schaffner 2012: 150). In this light, both Andreas and Nikolai suffer from a female affliction. Andreas is inclined to fetishism and sadism; Nikolai is androgynous and asexual. Both lack experience with women and are stuck in a narcissistic phase; in both texts, the hero's relationship with their double entails a homoerotic subtext. The deviation from a normative sexuality parallels a deviation from the law, as masking and doubling is on the one hand connected to narcissism and same-sex desire, and on the other to criminal, murderous impulses. Both Andreas and Nikolai are childless, a feature that symbolically addresses the extinction of their social class as well as the refusal to reproduce the established order.

In both novels, masking and doubling are found at the crossroad of Freudian psychoanalysis and Nietzsche's philosophy, related on the one hand to the resurfacing of the repressed and on the other to the loosening of the *principium individuationis*. Characters are initially presented as opposites (Andreas–Gotthelf/Maria–Mariquita; Nikolai–Alexandr/Senator Ableukhov–Lippanchenko) and then brought together by shared thoughts and experiences; the novels' imaginary geographies is initially fragmented into polarities, but eventually projected onto a single space. In *Andreas*, Venice, initially characterized in contrast to Vienna, becomes one with it in its role as a mediator between West and East, Europe and the Orient. Similarly, in *Petersburg*, the polarity between the island and the mainland, the capital of the Empire and its outskirts, disappears as they are both infected by social uprisings. In *Andreas*, the Orient functions at once as the counter-pole of Europe and its integral element; in *Petersburg* the 'East' is both a territory beyond the Empire and a constituent part of it. In both cases, the 'Orient' and the 'East' function as imaginary spaces connected to the Dionysian and to same-sex desire. Andreas and Nikolai run away from a threat that they connect to different social class and ethnicities, but that they find embodied in themselves.

By bringing masking and the compulsion to disguise into relation with the beginning of their family line and the experiences of childhood, both novels engage with the paradigm of regression. Masks and disguises foreground a process through which the mature man reverts to the mode of thinking of the child and criminal (*Andreas*), the pre-civilized and the primitive (*Petersburg*). This discourse is intertwined with the imperialist obsession with degeneration as a phenomenon taking place at the fringes of the Empire, and with the anxiety that it could spread to its core. The ongoing conflations of centre and margins (Vienna and Carinthia; St Petersburg and Manchuria) underscore this fear.

As emblems of neurosis, masking and doubling expose the process of degeneration that the authors saw as consuming the aristocracy from inside. In effacing the boundaries between characters, they facilitate the merging of social classes (aristocrats and the working classes) and of ethnicities (Austrians and Southern Europeans; Russian and Mongols), thereby challenging the hierarchies constitutive of the establishment. Finally, Venetian disguises such as the 'domino', which play a crucial role in both narratives, symbolically introduce a comparison with the climate of economical (and moral) decadence of eighteenth-century Venice. Andreas's and Nikolai's anxieties and their sexual crises reflect on the one hand the nervous disposition that Hofmannsthal and Bely believed characterized their contemporaries and the change of values experienced by the generation of 1905, and on the other hand the military and political crisis of Austria-Hungary and Tsarist Russia.

Notes to Chapter 6

1. Nina Berman describes Hofmannsthal's political vision as 'reactionary, problematic and paternalistic' (2002: 205).
2. 'Der Inhalt des neuen Idealismus ist Nerven, Nerven, Nerven und — Kostüm: Die Dekadence löst das Rokoko und die gotische Maskerade ab' [The content of new Idealism consists in nerves, nerves, nerves, and — costume: decadence replaces the rococo and the gothic masquerade] (Bahr 1891: 132).
3. Since Richard Alewyn published a critical study of the novel in 1958, *Andreas* has been interpreted through the categories that Hofmannsthal himself provided in the essay 'Ad me ipsum' — such as the concept of Pre-existence, which involves a unity between the self and world experienced in childhood, or the principle of reciprocal transformation that Hofmannsthal calls 'Das Allomatische' (Hofmannsthal 2015: 117–460). However, in this essay, Hofmannsthal was trying to formulate an interpretative key which would retroactively bring together all his writings. His interpretation, however, does not exhaust the meaning of the novel.
4. On Gotthelf's role as a double, see also Le Rider 1995: 145; Bergengruen 2010: 92.
5. For an analysis of Andrea's dreams in light of Freud's treatise, see Berger 1993.
6. 'als wären sie tot und er mußte sich auf sie legen, sie mit seinem Leib erwärmen' [as if they were dead and he had to lie down on them, to warm them with his body] (Hofmannsthal 1982a: 63, note 3).
7. Among models for the knight, Hofmannsthal mentions Harry Graf Kessler, Winckelmann, Rudolf Kassner and Rudolf Pannwitz (Hofmannsthal 1982a: 23).
8. On the role of the Knight of Malta in the novel, see also Sebald 1985: 68; Le Rider 1995: 159; Hornig 1993: 92).
9. In a letter to the German intellectual Eberhard von Bodenhausen, Hofmannsthal addressed his concerns about the political situation: 'Wir gehen einer dunklen Zeit entgegen, das fühlt jeder Mensch. Wir können von Schritt zu Schritt alles verlieren — und — das ist das schlimmste — auch wo wir siegen, nicht rechtes gewinnen als nur Verlegenheit' [We are approaching a dark time, we all feel it. We can lose everything from step to step — and — that's the worse — even if we win, we will not win anything positive, only embarrassment] (1953: 144).
10. The Hapsburg Monarchy, for Hofmannsthal, was the inheritor of the Holy Roman Empire; in line with this, he chose for his hero a bride called 'Romana'. Tyrol and Carinthia, the intermediate stops on Andreas's journey, exemplify the linguistic and cultural differences that characterized the Hapsburg Empire.
11. Mathias Mayer identifies the novel's modernity and strength precisely in Hofmannsthal's failure to follow the pattern of the *Bildungsroman* set out by Goethe's *Wilhelm Meister* (1992: 137).
12. Sophia decorates her apartment with Japanese prints and wears a pink kimono; with the intention of offending her, Nikolai calls her a 'Japanese doll' and she later receives an actual Japanese doll as a gift from the terrorist Lippanchenko. Senator Ableukhov has travelled to Japan; Alexandr's friend Styopka blames the Japanese for Russia's consumption of alcohol.
13. 'Shishnarfne' contains the sounds 'Shish' and 'Shishka', in Russian related to obscenity and provocation (Burkhart 1984: 148).

CONCLUSION

Throughout the 1890s, Lorenzo Tenchini assembled over seventy-seven death masks of inmates from the asylum and the prison in Parma for his small museum. Through this collection, he intended to establish a correlation between facial traits, brain features and criminal behaviour, and to display his innovative casting technique (Lorusso et al. 2007: 71). He created a plaster cast of the face of the deceased, filled it with wax, modelled the wax on plaster, and coloured the masks with particular attention to rendering the skin tone. As a last step, he incorporated the inmates' facial hair. Each effigy was mounted on a wooden plate with a silk cushion, a device that enabled the artefacts to be displayed on a flat surface or to be hung on a wall. On the back of the structure, Tenchini recorded the subject's brain's weight and size, as well as personal information such as age, origin, profession, family relations.

In 1906 — the same year in which Cesare Lombroso came into possession on Tenchini's masks, Rodin met Hanako at the Colonial Exhibition in Marseille and was fascinated by her acting of hara-kiri. Between 1907 and 1912, he modelled fifty-eight masks and heads of the actress. From Judith Cladel's biography, we know that he studied Hanako's features with the care and scrupulousness of an anatomist; he also experimented with different materials and was particularly pleased by the results in glass paste. At the Hôtel Biron, he placed Hanako's head on a pillow next to the masks of his partner and lover. In her description, Cladel underscored the mask's Asian features, and contrasted her own uneasiness towards the sculpture to Rodin's attachment to it (1918: 162).

Chapter 1 has looked at Tenchini's masks in the context of early anthropology and has examined their participation in a discourse shared by physiognomy, ethnography and anthropology. Chapter 2 has discussed Hanako's portraits in the context of symbolism. Unsettling parallels emerge, however, if one compares the two series. These consist, of course, of very different types of masks. Tenchini's waxworks are anatomical artefacts, Rodin's heads and busts works of art. Tenchini's works are the result of direct impression, Rodin's of sculpture. As medical and scientific tools, Tenchini's masks can be defined as anachronistic objects, dated in the age of photography. Moreover, his insistence on the authenticity of these effigies, his claim that they were impossible to duplicate, betrays Tenchini's opposition to technical reproducibility. Rodin's experiments with masks were instead considered too innovative, fragmentary and unfinished (Vitry 1903: 35).

From today's perspective, both series are unsettling. Firstly, we feel disturbed by the likeness to their models and, in Tenchini's case, by the organic material. Both wax, a material 'situated outside the limits of symbolisation' (Gombrich

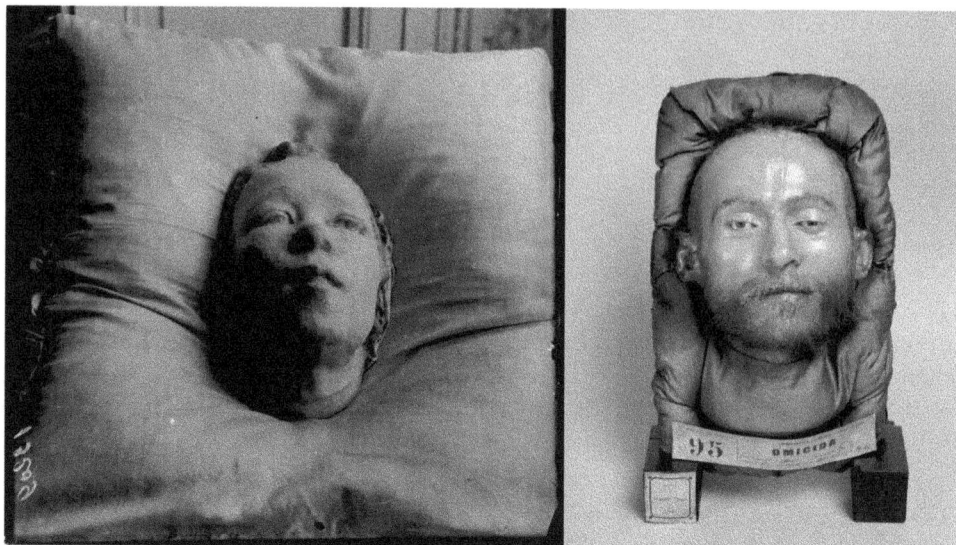

FIG. C.1. Left: Albert Harlingue, photograph of Hanako's mask lying on a pillow, 1912, 13 × 18 cm, Paris, Rodin Museum, Paris. Right: Lorenzo Tenchini, Wax masks mounted on wood, 'omicida'. Photograph by Paolo Giagheddu, by kind permission of the Museum of Criminal Anthropology 'Cesare Lombroso', University of Turin.

2000: 53), and glass paste reproduce the texture, density and translucency of the human skin. Excessive resemblance leads to a loss of symbolic meaning, and to sculptures becoming substitutes for the real, a process that Freud associates with the emergence of the uncanny (Freud 1955a: 244). Secondly, in portraying male inmates as effeminate, and Hanako as androgynous, Tenchini and Rodin reinforced sexual and racial stereotypes rooted in the paradigm of regression. Thirdly, both projects relied on the assumption of the observer's superiority and involved uneven power relations.[1] Finally, both series consist of fragments, portraits cut off at the neck, while the display on pillows and the author's attachment characterize them as fetishes. By having their eyes open, and, as Cladel puts it, 'looking into the unknown' (1918: 162), both Tenchini's criminals and Hanako stare back at the Western viewer, confronting them with the alterity of the 'criminal other' and of the 'Asian female', as well as with the 'otherness' of death.

The juxtaposition of the two series underscores the extent to which aesthetics, anthropology and anatomy overlapped at the turn of nineteenth century. In *fin-de-siècle* dramatic and literary texts, masks similarly reinforced the association between children, women, criminals and 'primitives' on the one hand, and the unconscious and the pre-historic on the other. Moreover, mask-imagery exemplifies how decadence, with its fascination with the peculiar, the perverse and the uncanny, provides another face of positivism, with its taxonomies, its classifications and its struggle to eliminate deviations from the norm. As objects of desire, as apotropaic artefacts and as commodities of exchange, masks assumed fetishistic connotations. In this guise, they participated in the elastic boundaries of the term 'sexual inversion'. In evoking the artificial and the subordination of the whole to the part, they also functioned as master tropes for decadent themes and style. Huysmans, Wilde, Beerbohm and Lorrain linked the mask to make-up and self-fashioning; Le Gallienne, Crommelynck, D'Annunzio, Hofmannsthal and Bely foregrounded the association between masks and fragments. Like Binet's and Freud's narrative of the fetish, these texts followed a metonymic logic and involved a focus on synecdoche.

Overall, the mask functioned as a changeable trope rooted in the material and in the linguistic order and exemplified the instability of the sign that critics identify as typical of decadent discourse (Sherry 2015: 22), and that is also found at the core of *fin-de-siècle* narratives of fetishism. By projecting the multiple meanings attributed to the term 'mask' from the axis of selection onto the axis of combination, these texts engage with the mask as an open, flexible signifier. The many manifestations of the mask, in turn, hark back to the themes of genius and madness and the period's preoccupation with degeneration, which, as Daniel Pick has demonstrated, was never reduced to a fixed theory but remained a protean notion, with terms such as madness, regression and atavism used interchangeably, often leading to one another or pointing to other signifiers (1989: 7). In the case studies examined in this book, the deferral of meaning from masks to busts, skulls and severed heads on the one hand, and the association with the unconscious and the primitive on the other, create a complex symbolic network. Since all these signifiers share the same elusive signified, the sign becomes unstable, and the gap between signifier and signified widens.

Vincent Sherry has drawn attention to how, in *The Origin of German Tragedy*, Walter Benjamin saw the slip of the signifier and the signified, in which critics identify a trademark of decadent style, as characterizing the allegorical mode (2015: 23). Curiously, the image that Benjamin chose to embody the allegorical is 'a face — or rather a death's head', which he associated with 'everything about history that, from the very beginning, has been untimely, sorrowful, unsuccessful' (Benjamin 1998: 166). He further defined mourning as 'the state of mind in which feeling revives the empty world in the form of a mask' (1998: 139). Benjamin's petrified face, with its emphasis on belatedness and untimeliness, suggests an outlook shared by many *fin-de-siècle* artists, who were convinced they were at the end of an era. Besides being portrayed as androgynous, the heroes in these tales embrace celibacy and share a proclivity for a female affliction (neurosis), while enacting their fantasies in dreams or through the adoptions of masks and doubling.

In an essay on post-revolutionary France, Neil Hertz demonstrated that, in the years following the French Revolution, political agitators used sexualized images of women faces to visualize revolutionary violence (Hertz 1985: 162). Elaborating on Freud's essay on Medusa, he interprets the fixation on women's faces as the objective correlative of a social and political transition. The case studies examined in this book traced a similar dynamic in texts produced between the end of the nineteenth and the early twentieth century, in which Medusa and her petrifying gaze continued to be evoked and her decapitation overlapped with the threat of Salomé. It is through the features of 'a hideous and fierce but not exactly sexless woman' (Hertz 1985:

161) that *fin-de-siècle* authors confronted new gender identities and the increasing presence of women in the public sphere at a time of intense political and social changes. In this light, the fixation with masks and faces represents both individual sexual disfunctions and anxieties about the virility of the nation.

Positioned between romanticism and positivism, between incarnations of the doppelgänger and manifestations of sexual perversions, masks embodied deviancy and regression, yet enabled the articulation of alternative forms of desire. In both cases, however, the use of the mask as tool of gender and sexual experimentation remained a male privilege. When masks were imposed on women, they either underlined their marginality or constrained their actions. When they were modelled on women, they betrayed little of those who inspired them and much more about the expectations and desire of the male artist.

The focus on male authors was conditioned by my aim to read *fin-de-siècle* masks in relation to the crisis of traditional masculinity that developed alongside the articulation of modern sexuality. While mask-making remains predominantly a male topos, there were female authors who engaged with masks and self-fashioning. In France, the most famous case is Lorrain's colleague and friend Rachilde, whose writings are replete with costumes, masked balls and animated puppets.[2] In the context of English literature, an example is Edith Cooper's fascination with death effigies and waxworks, which parallels her adoption of a literary persona.[3] Did these texts speak to one another in the same way as those examined in this monograph? Was there a female articulation of the mask, and did it develop an alternative point of view? These are, however, questions that deserve to be explored by further studies.

Notes to the Conclusion

1. The information provided by Tenchini indicates that the models came mostly from the lower classes, and had been driven to commit offences by poverty. Although Tenchini was in many ways a progressive researcher — he was a strenuous defender of patients' rights in mental hospitals (Lorusso et al. 2007: 358) — neither the inmates nor their families had a say in the production of these images. Unlike Tenchini's inmates, Hanako willingly posed for Rodin. However, Rodin was an international celebrity in a powerful colonial nation; Hanako a former geisha who had emigrated because of financial need, embracing a profession that was not deemed decent for women in her home culture.
2. On Rachilde's use of masking, see Felski 1995: 174–207.
3. On Edith Cooper's fascination with funerary effigies, see Maxwell 2018.

AFTERWORD

This book was written between two maternity leaves and the coronavirus pandemics. When the first lockdown began, I was working on a chapter on Rainier Maria Rilke's use of masks in *Die Aufzeichnungen des Malte Laurids Brigge* [*The Notebooks of Malte Laurids Brigge*] and on his use of masks as a trope that encapsulates the changes brought about by modernity. I would, however, have needed a library (not to mention the inter-library loan) to finish it, and I felt that, after so many delays, the project was long due and needed to come to a conclusion. Paradoxically (or perhaps fittingly), as I was revising the manuscript, masks became part of our daily life as well as an object of heated discussion. Moreover, they took on the role of a metaphor for our current age. The 2020 statement by the *British Comparative Literature Association* tellingly begins by quoting Descartes's dictum '*Larvatus prodeo*' [I advance wearing a mask], and suggests that Descartes's words have assumed a new meaning at a time when masks have become 'evocative of "viral modernity"'.[1] When I selected the image for the book cover, I could not help wondering how Ensor's painting would look if I modified it by adding on the artist's bare features a surgical mask.

The *fin-de-siècle* preoccupation with masks shares some similarities with current discourses about face coverings, since, in both cases, masks address changes in conventional understanding of the Self, a radical shift in the relationship between the Self and the World, and disruption to an established way of life. As I have argued throughout this monograph, *fin-de-siècle* masks both concealed and revealed, exemplifying a preoccupation with a divided consciousness, while at the same time challenging distinctions between Self and Other. Often, the mask functioned as a trope to question binary, essentialist 'either/or ontologies' that, between 1880 and 1914, were increasingly replaced by 'hybrid, both/and perspectives' (Saler 2015: 4). Today's face masks go a step further as they work entirely by effacement, creating a 'neutral' self that is then refracted across virtual reality, where it assumes new, diverse qualities. Contemporary masks, then, continue to be associated with multiplicity and becoming. Disguises and self-fashioning are just as prominent as they were in the late nineteenth century, although they are now projected into virtual space.

While the texts examined in this monograph are very much rooted in the cultural landscape of the *fin de siècle*, and engage with paradigms and beliefs that have today lost currency, they nevertheless underline the complexity of the mask as a metaphor and can inform research on the meaning that masks assume in the Covid-age. Developing this parallel further is, nevertheless, beyond the aim and scope of the present book.

Note to the Afterword

1. 'The Role of Literature in the Age of Confinement', BCLA 2020 Statement <https://bcla.org/covid-19-culture-and-quarantine/>.

BIBLIOGRAPHY

AALTONEN, SIRKKU. 2000. *Time-sharing on Stage: Drama Translation in Theatre and Society* (Clevedon: Multilingual Matters)
ADAMSON, WALTER. 2015. 'Italy', in *The Fin-de-siècle World*, ed. by Michael Saler (London: Routledge), pp. 167–84
ALEWYN, RICHARD. 1958. 'Andreas und die wunderbare Freundin', in *Über Hugo von Hofmannsthal*, by Richard Alewyn (Göttingen: Vandenhoeck & Ruprecht), pp. 105–41
ALSIP, BARBARA WITTMAN. 1971. 'Fernand Crommelynck, Spiritual Heir of Molière' (unpublished PhD thesis, Emory University, GA)
ANDREOLI, ANNAMARIA. 2001. *Il Vivere inimitabile: vita di Gabriele D'Annunzio* (Milan: Mondadori)
——2013. 'Il poeta, la folla e l'attrice divina', in *Tragedie, sogni e misteri*, by Gabriele D'Annunzio, ed. by Annamaria Andreoli (Milan: Mondadori), pp. 11–79
ANGIOLETTI, KATIA. 2010. *Il Poeta a teatro: Gabriele D'Annunzio e la riforma della scena drammatica* (Milan: Cuem)
ANTHONAY, THIBAUT D'. 2005. *Jean Lorrain: miroir de La Belle Époque* (Paris: Fayard)
APTER, EMILY. 1991. *Feminizing the Fetish: Psychoanalysis and Narrative Obsession in Turn-of-the Century France* (Ithaca, NY: Cornell University Press)
——AND WILLIAM PIETZ. 1993. *Fetishism as Cultural Discourse* (Ithaca, NY: Cornell University Press)
ASCHHEIM, STEVEN. 1993. 'Max Nordau, Friedrich Nietzsche and Degeneration', *Journal of Contemporary History*, 28.4: 643–59
AURNHAMMER, ACHIM. 1995. 'Andreas. Das Fragment als Erzählform zwischen Tradition und Moderne', *Hofmannsthal-Jahrbuch*, 3: 275–97
BABLET, DENIS. 1981. *The Theatre of Edward Gordon Craig* (London: Eyre Methuen)
BACHTIN, MICHAIL. 2009. *Rabelais and his World* (Bloomington: Indiana University Press)
BAHR, HERMANN. 1891. 'Die Überwindung des Naturalismus', in *Die Überwindung des Naturalismus*, by Hermann Bahr (Dresden and Leipzig: E. Pierson Verlag), pp. 152–58
BALL, HUGO. 1996. *Flight out of Time: A Dada Diary by Hugo Ball*, ed. by John Elderfield, trans. by Ann Raimes (Berkeley: University of California Press)
BAUDELAIRE, CHARLES. 1885. 'Éloge du maquillage', in *Le Peintre de la vie moderne, Œuvres complètes de Charles Baudelaire*, vol. III (Paris: Calmann-Lévy), pp. 99–104
——2012. 'In Praise of Cosmetics', in *Painter of Modern Life and Other Essays*, by Charles Baudelaire, ed. by Jonathan Mayne, trans. by Jonathan Mayne (London: Phaidon Press)
BECKSON, KARL. 1970. *Oscar Wilde: The Critical Heritage* (London: Routledge & Kegan Paul)
BEERBOHM, MAX. 1893. 'Oscar Wilde by an American', *Anglo-American Times*, 25 March
——1896. 'The Pervasion of Rouge', in *The Works of Max Beerbohm* (London: John Lane), pp. 97–124
——1914. *The Happy Hypocrite* (London: The Bodley Head)
——1953. 'The Spirit of Caricature', in *A Variety of Things* (London: Heinemann), pp. 139–49
——1964. *Max Beerbohm's Letters to Reggie Turner*, ed. by Rupert Hart-Davis (London: Soho Square)

—— 1972. 'A Peep into the Past', in *A Peep into the Past and other Prose Pieces*, by Max Beerbohm, ed. by R. Hart-Davis (Battleboro, VT: Stephen Green)

—— 1988. *Letters of Max Beerbohm, 1892–1956*, ed. by Rupert Hart-Davis (London: John Murray)

BEHRMAN, S. N. 1960. *Portrait of Max: An Intimate Memoir of Sir Max Beerbohm* (New York: Random House)

BELTING, HANS. 2017. *Face and Mask: A Double History*, trans. by Thomas S. Hansen and Anny J. Hansen (Princeton, NJ: Princeton University Press)

BELY, ANDREI. 1990A. *Mezhdu dvukh revoliutsii*, vol. III (Moscow: Khudozhestvennaia literatura)

—— 1990B. *Peterburg: roman v vos'mi glavakh s prologom i epilogom* (Kiev: Dnipro)

—— 2009. *Petersburg*, trans. by John Elsworth (London: Pushkin Press)

BENJAMIN, WALTER. 1998. *The Origin of German Tragic Drama*, ed. by George Steiner, trans. by John Osborne (London: Verso)

—— 1999. 'The Work of Art in the Age of Mechanical Reproduction', in *Illuminations*, ed. by Hannah Arendt, trans. by Harry Zorn (London: Pimlico), pp. 211–44

BENKARD, ERNST. 1929. *Undying Faces: A Collection of Death Masks*, trans. by Margaret M. Green (London: Hogarth)

BERGENGRUEN, MAXIMILIAN. 2010. *Mystik der Nerven: Hugo von Hofmannsthals literarische Epistemologie des 'nicht-mehr-Ich'* (Freiburg: Rombach)

BERGER, WILLY RICHARD. 1993. 'Die Träume in Hofmannsthals Romanfragment Andreas oder die Vereinigten', in *Das Wagnis der Moderne: Festschrift für Marianne Kesting* (Frankfurt am Main: Peter Lang), pp. 243–59

BERNHEIMER, CHARLES. 2002. *Decadent Subjects: The Idea of Decadence in Art, Literature, Philosophy, and Culture of the Fin de Siècle in Europe* (Baltimore, MD: Johns Hopkins University Press)

BERMAN, NINA. 2002. 'Hugo von Hofmannsthal's Political Vision', in *A Companion to the Works of Hugo von Hofmannsthal*, ed. by Thomas A. Kovach (Woodbridge and Rochester, NY: Camden House), pp. 205–25

BINET, ALFRED. 2011. *Le Fétichisme dans l'amour*, ed. by André Béjin (Paris: Payot)

BIRKETT, JENNIFER. 2000. 'Disinterested Narcissus: The Play of Politics in Decadent Form', in *Decadence and the fin de siècle: French and European Perspectives*, ed. by Patrick McGuinness (Exeter: University of Exeter Press), pp. 29–45

BISICCHIA, ANDREA. 1991. *D'Annunzio e il teatro: tra cronaca e letteratura drammatica* (Milan: Mursia)

BLANCHETIÈRE, FRANÇOIS. 2007. 'Un jeu de regards: Rodin et Hanako', in *Rodin: Le Rêve japonais*, ed. by Dominique Viéville (Paris: Musée Rodin, Flammarion), pp. 125–33

—— 2008. 'Hanako, la mort dans les yeux', in *Masques: de Carpeaux à Picasso*, ed. by Eduard Papet (Paris: Hazan), pp. 104–09

BOURGET, PAUL. 1883. *Essais de psychologie contemporaine* (Paris: Lemerre)

BRACK, O. M. 1987. *Twilight of Dawn: Studies in English Literature in Transition* (Tucson: University of Arizona Press)

BREDBECK, GREGORY. 1994. 'Narcissus in the Wilde: Textual Cathexis and the Historical Origins of Queer Camp', in *The Politics and Poetics of Camp*, ed. by Moe Meyer (New York: Routledge), pp. 51–74

BRICKMAN, CELIA. 2003. *Aboriginal Populations of the Mind: Race and Primitivity in Psychoanalysis* (New York: Columbia University Press)

BRISTOW, JOSEPH. 2010. 'Picturing his Exact Decadence: The British Reception of Oscar Wilde', *The Reception of Oscar Wilde in Europe*, ed. by Stefano Evangelista (London: Continuum), pp. 21–50

BROWN, BILL. 2001. 'Thing Theory', *Critical Inquiry*, 28.1: 1–22
BRUHM, STEVEN. 2001. *Reflecting Narcissus: A Queer Aesthetic* (Minneapolis: University of Minnesota Press)
BULEY-URIBE, CHRISTINA. 2007. 'Le Japon chez Rodin, entre symbolisme et décadence', in *Rodin: Le Rêve japonais*, ed. by Dominique Viéville (Paris: Musée Rodin, Flammarion), pp. 109–24
BURDETT, OSBERT. 1925. *The Beardsley Period* (New York: Cooper Square)
BURKHART, DAGMAR. 1984. *Schwarze Kuben-Roter Domino: eine Strukturbeschreibung von Andrej Belyjs Roman Peterburg* (Frankfurt am Main: Peter Lang)
CHARCOT, JEAN-MARTIN, and VALENTIN MAGNAN. 1882. 'Inversion du sens génital', *Archives de neurologie. Revue des maladies nerveuses et mentales*, 3.7: 53–60
CHOMEL, LUISETTA ELIA. 1997. *D'Annunzio: un teatro al femminile* (Ravenna: Longo)
CIMA, CHRISTOPHE. 2009. *Vie et œuvre de Jean Lorrain: ou chronique d'une 'guerre de sexes' à la Belle Époque* (Cannes: Alandis)
CIXOUS, HÉLÈNE. 1976. 'The Laugh of Medusa', *Signs*, 1.4: 875–93
CLADEL, JUDITH. 1918. *Rodin, the Man and his Art* (New York: The Century Co.)
CLAYTON, DOUGLAS. 1994. *Pierrot in Petrograd: The Commedia dell'arte/balagan in Twentieth-Century Russian Theatre and Drama* (Montreal: McGill-Queen's University Press)
CLIFFORD, JAMES. 1988. *The Predicament of Culture: Twentieth-century Ethnography, Literature and Art* (Cambridge, MA: Harvard University Press)
COHEN, ED. 1987. 'Writing Gone Wilde: Homoerotic Desire in the Closet of Representation', *PMLA*, 102: 801–13
COMPAGNON, ANTOINE. 1990. *Les Cinq Paradoxes de la modernité* (Paris: Seuil)
COQUIOT, GUSTAVE. 2006. 'Préface', in *Histoires de masques*, by Jean Lorrain, ed. by Sulpice Daviaux (Paris: Ombres), pp. 7–14
COWLING, MARY. 1989. *The Artist as Anthropologist: The Representation of Type and Character in Victorian Art* (Cambridge: Cambridge University Press)
CRACKANTHORPE, HUBERT. 1984. 'Roundabout Remarks', *The Yellow Book*: 266
CRAIG, GORDON. 1919. 'A Note on Masks', in *The Theatre Advancing*, by Gordon Craig (Boston, MA: Little Brown), pp. 113–27
CROMMELYNCK, FERNAND. 1967. 'Le Sculpteur des Masques', *Théâtre*, vol. 1 (Paris: Gallimard)
—— 1998. *The Theater of Fernand Crommelynck: Eight Plays*, ed. by Alain Piette and Bert Cardullo, trans. by Alain Piette and Bert Cardullo (Selingrove, PA: Susquehanna University Press)
D'ANNUNZIO, GABRIELE. 1902. *The Dead City*, trans. by Gaetano Ettore Raffaele Mantellini (Chicago, IL: Laird & Lee)
—— 1913. *Gioconda*, trans. by Arthur Symons (Chicago, IL: The Dramatic Publishing Company)
—— 1924A. 'Di Prometeo beccaio', in *Le faville del maglio: il venturiero senza ventura e altri studi del vivere inimitabile*, by Gabriele D'Annunzio (Milan: Treves), pp. 9–12
—— 1924B. 'La maschera aerea', in *Le faville del maglio: il venturiero senza ventura e altri studi del vivere inimitabile* (Milan: Treves), pp. 25–30
—— 1991. *The Flame*, trans. by Susan Bassnett (London: Quarter Books)
—— 1992A. 'Il futuro teatro d'Albano', in *La tragedia moderna e mediterranea: sul teatro di Gabriele D'Annunzio*, ed. by Valentina Valentini (Milan: Franco Angeli), pp. 80–83
—— 1992B. 'Lettera di Gabriele D'Annunzio a Ermete Zacconi, Corfù', in *La tragedia moderna e mediterranea: sul teatro di Gabriele D'Annunzio*, by Valentina Valentini (Milan: Franco Angeli), pp. 148–50
—— 2003A. 'Il caso Wagner I', in *Scritti giornalistici, 1889–1936*, ed. by Annamaria Andreoli (Milan: Mondadori), pp. 233–38

——2003B. 'La bestia elettiva', in *Scritti giornalistici, 1889–1936*, ed. by Annamaria Andreoli (Milan: Mondadori), pp. 86–94

——2003C. 'La gloria giudicata da un critico francese', in *Scritti giornalistici, 1889–1936*, ed. by Annamaria Andreoli, vol. II (Milan: Mondadori), pp. 374–77

——2003D. 'La rinascenza della tragedia', in *Scritti giornalistici, 1889–1936*, ed. by Annamaria Andreoli, vol. II (Milan: Mondadori), pp. 262–65

——2013A. 'La città morta', in *Tragedie, Sogni e Misteri*, ed. by Annamaria Andreoli and Giorgio Zanetti, vol. I (Milan: Mondadori), pp. 91–224

——2013B. 'La Gioconda', in *Tragedie, Sogni e Misteri*, ed. by Annamaria Andreoli and Giorgio Zanetti, vol. I (Milan: Mondadori), pp. 225–331

——2013C. 'La Gloria', in *Tragedie, Sogni e Misteri*, ed. by Annamaria Andreoli and Giorgio Zanetti, vol. I (Milan: Mondadori), pp. 334–448

——2016. *Il fuoco*, ed. by Pietro Gibellini and Filippo Caburlotto (Milan: Rizzoli)

DANSON, LAWRENCE. 2006. *Wilde's Intentions: The Artist in his Criticism* (Oxford: Clarendon Press)

DE GARIS, FREDERICK, and ATSUHARU SAKAI. 2002. *We Japanese: The Customs, Manners, Ceremonies, Festivals, Arts and Crafts of Japan* (London: Kegan Paul)

DE LAURETIS, TERESA. 1994. *The Practice of Love: Lesbian Sexuality and Perverse Desire* (Bloomington: Indiana University Press)

DELLAMORA, RICHARD. 1988. 'Representation and Homophobia in *The Picture of Dorian Gray*', *The Victorian Newsletter*: 28–31

DENISOFF, DENNIS. 2006. *Aestheticism and Sexual Parody, 1840–1940* (Cambridge: Cambridge University Press)

DICKSON, DONALD R. 1983. '"In a mirror that mirrors the soul": Masks and Mirrors in Dorian Gray', *English Literature in Transition, 1880–1920*, 26: 5–15

DOLLIMORE, JONATHAN. 1991. *Sexual Dissidence: Literatures, Histories, Theories* (Oxford: Oxford University Press)

DOWLING, LINDA. 1978. '"Rose Accurst": Yeats and Le Gallienne', *Victorian Poetry*, 16.3: 280–84

——1979. 'The Decadent and the New Woman in the 1890s', *Nineteenth Century Fiction*, 33: 434–53

DUNCAN, DEREK. 2006. *Reading and Writing Italian Homosexuality: A Case of Possible Difference* (Aldershot: Ashgate)

DU PLESSIS, MICHAEL. 2002. 'Unspeakable Writing: Jean Lorrain's *Monsieur de Phocas*', *French Forum*, 27.2: 65–98

DYER, TINA. 2005. 'Metaphysics and the Mask: Symbol of the Wildean Aesthetic', *The Wildean: Journal of the Oscar Wilde Society*, 27: 64–70

EDELMAN, LEE. 2004. *No Future: Queer Theory and the Death Drive* (Durham, NC: Duke University Press)

EINSTEIN, CARL. 1915. *Negerplastik* (Leipzig: Verlag der Weissen Bücher)

ELLIS, HAVELOCK, and JOHN A. SYMONDS. 1897. *Sexual Inversion* (London: Wilson and Macmillan)

ELLIS, HAVELOCK. 1897. *Studies in the Psychology of Sex* (London: The University Press)

——1932. 'A Note on Paul Bourget', in *Views and Reviews: A Selection of Uncollected Articles, 1884–1932* (Boston, MA: Houghton Mifflin)

ENSOR, JAMES. 1999A. *James Ensor: Lettres*, ed. by Xavier Tricot (Brussels: Labor)

——1999B. *Mes écrits, ou les suffisances matamoresques*, ed. by Hugo Martin (Brussels: Labor)

ESENBEL, SELÇUK. 2015. 'Japan', in *The Fin-de-siècle World*, ed. by Michael Saler (London: Routledge), pp. 254–65

EVANGELISTA, STEFANO. 2010. 'Introduction: Oscar Wilde: European by Sympathy', in *The

Reception of Oscar Wilde in Europe, ed. by Stefano Evangelista (London: Continuum), pp. 1–19
—— 2018. 'Aestheticism in Italy: a New Sense of Place', in *The Edinburgh Companion to Fin de Siècle Literature, Culture and the Arts*, ed. by Josephine M. Guy (Edinburgh: Edinburgh University Press), pp. 263–80
FABIAN, JOHANNES. 1983. *Time and the Other: How Anthropology Makes its Object* (New York: Columbia University Press)
FELSKI, RITA. 1995. *The Gender of Modernity* (Cambridge, MA: Harvard University Press)
FOLEY, KATHY. 1988. 'Hanako and the European Imagination', *Asian Theatre Journal*, 5.1: 76–85
FOUCAULT, MICHEL. 2003. *Abnormals: Lectures at the Collège de France, 1974–1975* (London and New York: Verso)
—— 1978. *The Will to Knowledge: The History of Sexuality*, vol. I, trans. by Robert Hurley (London: Penguin)
FREUD, SIGMUND. 1947. 'Das Unheimliche', in *Gesammelte Werke*, vol. XII (London: Imago), pp. 227–68
—— 1953. 'Three Essays on Sexuality', in *The Standard Edition of the Complete Psychological Works of Sigmund Freud*, ed. and trans. by James Strachey, vol. VII (London: Hogarth), pp. 125–248
—— 1955A. 'The Uncanny', in *The Standard Edition of the Complete Psychological Works of Sigmund Freud*, ed. and trans. by James Strachey, vol. XVII (London: Hogarth), pp. 222–55
—— 1955B. 'Totem and Taboo', in *Totem and Taboo and Other Works*, in *The Standard Edition of the Complete Psychological Works of Sigmund Freud*, ed. and trans. by James Strachey (London: Hogarth), pp. 1–100
—— 1978A. 'Fetishism', in *The Standard Edition of the Complete Psychological Works of Sigmund Freud*, ed. and trans. by James Strachey, vol. XXI (London: Hogarth), pp. 147–59
—— 1978B. 'On Narcissism: An Introduction', in *The Standard Edition of the Complete Psychological Works of Sigmund Freud*, ed. and trans. by James Strachey, vol. XIV (London: Hogarth), pp. 73–102
—— 2003. 'Medusa's Head and the Infantile Genital Organization', in *The Medusa Reader*, ed. by Marjorie Garber and Nancy J. Vickers (New York: Routledge), pp. 84–86
FRIEDERICI, ANGELIKA. 2009. *Castan's Panoptikum: Ein Medium wird besichtigt*, vol. VI (Berlin: Karl-Robert Schütze)
—— 2014. *Castan's Panoptikum: Ein Medium wird besichtigt*, vol. XX (Berlin: Karl-Robert Schütze)
FRYE, LAWRENCE. 1992. 'Masking, Doubling and Comedic Strategy in Hofmannsthal's Narrative Prose', in *Wir sind aus solchem Zeug wie das zu träumen ...: kritische Beiträge zu Hofmannsthals Werke*, ed. by Joseph P. Strelka (Bern, Berlin, and Frankfurt: Peter Lang), pp. 139–68
GAGNIER, REGENIA. 2010. *Individualism, Decadence and Globalization: On the Relation of Part to Whole, 1859–1920* (New York: Palgrave Macmillan)
GARBER, MARJORIE, and NANCY J. VICKERS. 2003. 'Introduction', in *The Medusa Reader*, ed. by Marjorie Garber and Nancy J. Vickers (New York: Routledge), pp. 1–9
GARNIER, BÉNÉDICTE. 2007. 'Une collection de rêve', in *Rodin: Le Rêve japonais*, ed. by Dominique Viéville (Paris: Musée Rodin, Flammarion), pp. 11–85
GAUTIER, THÉOPHILE. 1869. 'Introduction to C. Baudelaire', in *Les Fleurs du mal*, by Charles Baudelaire, ed. by Théophile Gautier (Paris: Lévy), pp. 1–75
GIBSON, MARY, and NICOLE HAHN RAFTER. 2006. 'Editors' Introduction', in *Criminal Man*, by Cesare Lombroso, ed. by Mary Gibson and Nicole Hahn Rafter, trans. by Mary Gibson and Nicole Hahn Rafter (Durham, NC, and London: Duke University Press), pp. 1–41

GILBART, OLYMPE. 2001. 'Mardi Littéraire', in *Monsieur de Phocas*, ed. by Hélène Zinck (Paris: Flammarion), pp. 333–34

GLICK, ELISA. 2001. 'The Dialectics of Dandyism', *Cultural Critique*, 46: 129–63

GOMBRICH, ERNST. 2000. *Art and Illusion: A Study in the Psychology of Pictorial Representation* (London: Folio Society)

GONSE, LOUIS. 1883. *L'Art japonais* (Paris: A Quantin)

GRAND, SARAH. 1894. 'The New Aspect of the Woman Question', *The North American Review*, vol. 158, no. 448: 270–76

GROSZ, ELISABETH. 1993. 'Lesbian Fetishism', in *Fetishism as Cultural Discourse*, ed. by Emily and William Pietz Apter (Ithaca, NY: Cornell University Press), pp. 101–15

GUERRERI, GERALDO. 1962. *Eleonora Duse e il teatro del suo tempo, 1858–1924*, in *Saggio critico di Gerardo Guerreri e catalogo della mostra* (Treviso: Canova)

HALL, JOHN. 2002. *Max Beerbohm: A Kind of Life* (New Haven, CT: Yale University Press)

HAMMOND, CHARLES H. 2012. 'Hugo von Hofmannsthal's *Das Märchen der 672. Nacht* and the Trials of Oscar Wilde', *Orbis Litterarum*, 67.6: 439–71

HÄRMÄNMAA, MARJA, and CHRISTOPHER NISSEN. 2014. 'Introduction', in *Decadence, Degeneration, and the End*, ed. by Marja Härmänmaa and Christopher Nissen (New York: Palgrave Macmillan), pp. 1–14

HARRIS SMITH, SUSAN. 1984. *Masks in Modern Drama* (Berkeley: University of California Press)

HEDERER, EDGAR. 1960. 'Andreas', in *Hugo von Hofmannsthal*, by Edgar Hederer (Frankfurt am Main: Fischer), pp. 268–87

HEIDEGGER, MARTIN. 1971. 'The Things', in *Poetry, Language, Thought*, ed. by Albert Hofstadter, trans. by Albert Hofstadter (New York: Harper & Row), pp. 174–82

—— 1997. *Kant and the Problem of Metaphysics*, vol. v, trans. by Richard Taft (Bloomington: Indiana University Press)

HEKMA, GERT. 1996. 'A Female Soul in a Male Body: Sexual Inversion as Gender Inversion in Nineteenth-century Sexology', in *Third Sex, Third Gender: Beyond Sexual Dimorphism in Culture and History*, ed. by Gilbert Herdt (New York: Zone Books), pp. 213–39

HERTZ, NEIL. 1985. 'Medusa's Head: Male Hysteria and Political Pressure', in *The End of the Line: Essays on Psychoanalysis and the Sublime*, by Neil Hertz (New York: Columbia University Press), pp. 161–93

HILLER, JONATHAN R. 2013. *The Cesare Lombroso Handbook*, ed. by Paul Knepper and P. J. Ystehede (London: Routledge)

HOFMANNSTHAL, HUGO VON. 1953. *Hugo von Hofmannsthal — Eberhard von Bodenhausen: Briefe des Freundschaft*, ed. by Dora von Bodenhausen (Düsseldorf: Diederichs)

—— 1979. 'Die Österreichische Idee', in *Reden und Aufsätze*, ed. by Bernd Schoeller and Rudolf Hirsch, vol. II (Frankfurt am Main: Fischer), pp. 453–58

—— 1980. 'Das Schriftum al Geistiger Raum der Nation', in *Reden und Aufsätze*, ed. by Bernd Schoeller, Ingeborg Beyer-Ahlert and Rudolf Hirsch, vol. III (Frankfurt am Main: Fischer), pp. 24–41

—— 1982A. *Andreas*, in *Sämtliche Werke. Kritische Ausgabe*, vol. XXX, ed. by Manfred Pape (Frankfurt am Main: Fischer), pp. 7–218

—— 1982B. *Sämtliche Werke*, by Hugo von Hofmannsthal, vol. XXX, ed. by Manfred Pape (Frankfurt am Main: Fischer)

—— 1988. *Andreas*, trans. by Marie D. Hottingen (London: Pushkin Press)

—— 1992. 'Die Briefe des Zurückgekehrten', in *Sämtliche Werke*, by Hugo von Hofmannsthal, ed. by Ellen Ritter, vol. XXXI (Frankfurt am Main: Fischer), pp. 151–416

—— 2011. 'The Austrian Idea', in *Hugo von Hofmannsthal and the Austrian Idea: Selected Essays and Addresses, 1906–1927* (West Lafayette, IN: Purdue University Press), pp. 99–102

———2015. 'Ad Me ipsum', in *Sämtliche Werke*, ed. by Ellen Ritter (Frankfurt am Main: Fischer), pp. 117–460
HORN, DAVID. 2003. *The Criminal Body: Lombroso and the Anatomy of Deviance* (New York and London: Routledge)
HORNIG, DIETER. 1993. 'Hofmannsthal romancier: Andréas', *Austriaca. Cahiers Universitaires d'Information sur l'Autriche*, 37: 85–100
HOSTYN, NORBERT, and PATRICK FLORIZOONE, EDS. 2000. *Art graphique d'Ensor en confrontation* (Ostend: Musée des beaux arts d'Ostende)
HUGHES-HALLET, LUCY. 2013. *The Pike. Gabriele D'Annunzio: Poet, Seducer and Preacher of War* (London: Fourth Estate)
HUTCHEON, LINDA. 2000. *A Theory of Parody: The Teachings of Twentieth-Century Art Forms* (Urbana: University of Illinois Press)
HUYSMANS, JORIS-KARL. 1884. *À Rebours* (Paris: G. Charpentier)
———1921. 'L'Émailleuse', in *Le Drageoir aux épices*, by Joris-Karl Huysmans (Paris: Les Éditions G. Crès et Cie), pp. 78–86
———1975. 'The Enameler', in *Down Stream and Other Works*, by Joris-Karl Huysmans, ed. by Samuel Putnam, trans. by Samuel Putnam (New York: Howard Fertig), pp. 255–61
———1998. *Against the Grain*, trans. by M. Mauldon (Oxford: Oxford University Press)
HYDE, H. MONTGOMERY. 1948. *The Trials of Oscar Wilde* (London: William Hodge)
HYMAN, TIMOTHY. 1997. 'James Ensor: A Carnival Sense of the World', in *James Ensor: Theatre of Masks*, ed. by Carol Brown (London: Lund Humphries Publishers), pp. 76–86
JONES, ERNEST. 1984. *Freud* (Barcelona: Salvat)
JONSSON, STEFAN. 2001. 'Society Degree Zero: Christ, Communism, and the Madness of Crowds in the Art of James Ensor', *Representations*, 75.1: 1–32
JUDRIN, CLAUDIE. 2002. 'Rodin dessine Hanako', in *Rodin et le Japon*, ed. by Claudie Judrin, Miyuki Minami and Hiroshi Kamiya (Tokyo: Contemporary Sculpture Center), pp. 20–21
JULLIAN, PHILIPPE. 1974. *Jean Lorrain ou le satiricon 1900* (Paris: Fayard)
KAPLAN, LOUISE J. 2006. *Cultures of Fetishism* (New York: Palgrave Macmillan)
KEENE, DONALD. 1972. 'Hanako', in *Landscapes and Portraits: Appreciations of Japanese Culture* (London: Martin Secker and Warburg), pp. 250–58
KINCAID, ZOË. 1928. 'Introduction', in *The Mask Maker*, by Kido Okamoto (London and New York: Samuel French), pp. 3–5
KINGCAID, RENÉE. 1992. *Neurosis and Narrative: The Decadent Short Fiction of Proust, Lorrain, and Rachilde* (Carbondale: Southern Illinois University Press)
KITZINGER, CHLOË. 2013. '"This ancient, fragile vessel": Degeneration in Bely's Petersburg', *The Slavic and East European Journal*, 57.3: 403–23
KNAPP, BETTINA. 1978. *Fernand Crommelynck* (Boston. MA: Twayne Publishers)
KOFMAN, SARAH. 1985. *The Enigma of Woman: Woman in Freud's Writings* (Ithaca, NY: Cornell University Press)
KOLBE, GEORGE. 1929. 'How Death Masks Are Taken', in *Undying Faces*, by Ernst Benkard, trans. by Margaret M. Green (London: Hogarth Press), pp. 43–46
KOOS, LEONARD K. 1999. 'Improper Names: Pseudonyms and Transvestites in Decadent Prose', in *Perennial Decay: On the Aesthetics and Politics of Decadence*, ed. by Liz Constable, Dennis Denisoff and Matthew Potolsky (Philadelphia: University of Pennsylvania Press), pp. 198–214
KOSOFSKY SEDGWICK, EVE. 2008. *Epistemology of the Closet* (Berkeley: University of California Press)
KRAFFT-EBING, RICHARD. 1965. *Psychopathia Sexualis with especial reference to antipathetic sexual instinct*, ed. by F. S. Klaf, trans. by F. S. Klaf (London: Staples Press)
KRISTEVA, JULIA. 1998. *Visions capitales* (Paris: Réunion des musées nationaux)

—— 2012. *The Severed Head: Capital Visions*, trans. by Jody Gladding (New York: Columbia University Press)

KYRIA, PIERRE. 1973. *Jean Lorrain* (Paris: Seghers)

LACAN, JACQUES, and WLADIMIR GRANOFF. 1956. 'Fetishism: The Symbolic, the Imaginary, and the Real', in *Perversions: Psychodynamics and Therapy*, ed. by Sándor Lorand and Michael Balint (New York: Random House), pp. 265–76

LACAN, JACQUES. 1977. *The Four Fundamental Concepts of Psycho-Analysis*, trans. by Alan Sheridan (London: Hogarth)

LANE, CHRISTOPHER. 1994. 'Framing Fears, Reading Designs: The Homosexual Art of Painting in James, Wilde, and Beerbohm', *ELH*, 61.4: 923–54

LANGEN, TIMOTHY. 2010. 'Andrei Bely's *Petersburg* and the Dynamics of Political Response', in *Just Assassins: The Culture of Terrorism in Russia*, ed. by Anthony Anemone (Evanston, IL: Northwestern University Press), pp. 191–208

LANKASTER, EDWIN R. 1880. *Degeneration: A Chapter in Darwinism* (London: Macmillan)

LAURENT, MONIQUE. 1979A. 'Rodin et les Japonaises Sada Yacco et Hanako', in *Rodin et l'Extrême Orient: exposition, Musée Rodin, 4 April–2 Juillet 1979* (Paris: Musée Rodin), pp. 23–25

—— 1979B. 'Sculptures', in *Rodin et l'Extrême Orient: exposition, Musée Rodin, 4 April–2 Juillet 1979* (Paris: Musée Rodin), pp. 26–39

LAVATER, JOHANN C. 1781. *Essai sur la physionomie, destiné à faire connaître l'homme et à le faire aimer*, vol. III (La Haye: Jaques Van Karnebeek)

LE BOEUF, PATRICK, ED. 2009. *Craig et la Marionette* (Paris: Actes Sud/Bibliothèque nationale de France)

LE GALLIENNE, RICHARD. 1895. *English Poems* (London: The Bodley Head)

—— 1896A. *Retrospective Reviews: A Literary Log*, vol. I (London: John Lane)

—— 1896B. 'The Boom in Yellow', in *Prose Fancies*, 2nd series (London: John Lane, The Bodley Head)

—— 1900. *The Worshipper of the Image* (London: John Lane, The Bodley Head)

LE RIDER, JACQUES. 1995. 'Andreas', in *Hugo von Hofmannsthal: Historismus und Moderne in der Literatur der Jahrhundertwende*, trans. by Leopold Federmair (Wien-Köln-Weimar: Böhlau Verlag), pp. 129–58

LEGRAND, FRANCINE-CLAIRE. 1971. *Ensor, cet inconnu* (Paris: La Renaissance du livre)

—— 1993. *Ensor, la mort et le charme* (Antwerp: Fonds Mercator)

LEMAÎTRE, JULES. 1898. 'Théâtre Japonais', in *Impressions de théâtre*, by Jules Lemaître, vol. III (Paris: Société française d'impression et de librairie)

LETKEMANN, PETER. 1973. 'Das Berliner Panoptikum: Namen, Häuser und Schicksale', *Mitteilungen des Vereins für die Geschichte Berlins*, 69: 319–27

LJUNGGREN, MAGNUS. 2005. 'The Missing Link in Andrei Bely's *Petersburg*', *Russian Literature*, 58: 115–26

LLOYD, JILL. 1991. *German Expressionism* (New Haven, CT: Yale University Press)

LOMBROSO, CESARE. 1864. *Genio e follia* (Milan: Giuseppe Chiusi)

—— 1876. *L'uomo delinquente* (Milan: Hoepli)

—— 1906. 'Du parallélisme entre l'homosexualité et la criminalité innée', in *Archivio di psichiatria, neuropatologia, antropologia criminale e medicina legale*, 27: 378–81

—— 2006. *Criminal Man*, ed. by Mary Gibson and Nicole Hahn Rafter, trans. by Mary Gibson, Mark Seymour and Nicole Hahn Rafter (Durham, NC, and London: Duke University Press)

LOMBROSO, CESARE, and GUGLIELMO FERRERO. 1893. *La donna delinquente, la prostituta e la donna normale* (Turin: Roux)

LOOS, ADOLF. 1964. 'Ornament and Crime', in *Programs and Manifestoes on 20th-Century*

Architecture, ed. by Ulrich Conrads, trans. by Michael Bullock (Cambridge, MA: MIT Press), pp. 19–24
—— 1998. 'Luxury Carriages', in *Ornament and Crime: Selected Essays*, by Adolf Loos, ed. by Adolf Opel, trans. by Michael Mitchell (Riverside, CA: Ariadne Press), pp. 75–82
LORRAIN, JEAN. 1895. 'Un démoniaque', in *Un démoniaque* (Paris: Dentu), pp. 3–54
—— 1929. 'L'homme aux têtes de cire', in *Buveurs d'âmes* (Paris: Fasquelle), pp. 123–34
—— 1994. *Monsieur de Phocas*, trans. by Francis Amery (Sawtry, Cambs: Dedalus)
—— 2001. *Monsieur de Phocas*, ed. by Hélène Zinck (Paris: Flammarion)
—— 2002. *Mes Expositions Universelles, 1889–1900*, ed. by Philippe Martin-Lau (Paris: H. Champion)
—— 2005A. 'Salomé et ses poètes', in *Jean Lorrain: miroir de La Belle Epoque*, ed. by Thibaut d'Anthonay (Paris: Fayard), pp. 444
—— 2005B. 'Une intoxiquée: Le Baron d'Adelswärd à Venise', in *Jean Lorrain: miroir de La Belle Epoque*, ed. by Thibaut d'Anthonay (Paris: Fayard), p. 819
—— 2006. *Histoires de masques*, ed. by Sulpice Daviaux (Paris: Ombres)
—— 2016. *The Soul-Drinker and Other Decadent Fantasies*, trans. by Brian M. Stableford (Snuggly Books, n.p.)
—— 2017. *Masks in the Tapestry*, trans. by Brian M. Stableford (Snuggly Books, n.p.)
LORUSSO, LORENZO, CARLO CRISTINI and ALESSANDRO PORRO. 2007. 'Lorenzo Tenchini (1852–1906): Neuroanatomy and Criminal Anthropology', in *Medicina nei secoli arte e scienza, Journal of History of Medicine*, 19.2: 353–60
LUFT, DAVID. 2011. 'Introduction', in *Hugo von Hofmannsthal and the Austrian Idea: Selected Essays and Addresses, 1906–1927*, ed. and trans. by David Luft (West Lafayette, IN: Purdue University Press), pp. 1–32
MACH, ERNST. 1886. *Beiträge zur Analyse der Empfindungen* (Jena: G. Fischer)
MACK, JOHN. 1994. 'Introduction', in *Masks: The Art of Expression*, ed. by John Mack (London: British Museum Press), pp. 8–31
MACKE, AUGUST. 1965. 'Die Masken', in *Der Blaue Reiter*, ed. by Wassily Kandinsky and Franz Marc (Munich: Piper), pp. 53–59
—— 2005. 'Masks', in *The blaue reiter almanac*, ed. by Wassily Kandinsky and Franz Marc (Boston, MA: Museum of Fine Arts), pp. 83–90
MACLEOD, KIRSTEN. 2006. *Fictions of British Decadence: High Art, Popular Writing, and the Fin de Siècle* (New York: Palgrave Macmillan)
MAGUIRE, ROBERT, and JOHN E. MALMSTAD. 1978. 'Introduction and Annotations', in *Petersburg* (Bloomington: Indiana University Press)
MANTEGAZZA, PAOLO. 1881. *Fisionomia e mimica* (Milan: Fratelli Colulard)
MARIANI, UMBERTO. 2008. *Living Masks: The Achievements of Pirandello* (Toronto: University of Toronto Press)
MARX, KARL. 1963. *Selected Writings in Sociology and Social Philosophy*, ed. by T. Bottomore and M. Rubel (London: Penguin)
MATICH, OLGA. 2010. 'Introduction', in *Petersburg/Petersburg: Novel and City, 1900–1921*, ed. by Olga Matich (Madison: University of Wisconsin Press), pp. 3–30
MAXWELL, CATHERINE. 2018. 'Michael Field, Death, and the Effigy', *Word and Image*, 34.1: 31–39
MAYBON, ALBERT. 1925. *Le Théâtre japonais* (Paris: Laurens)
MAYER, MATHIAS. 1992. 'Nachwort', in Hugo von Hofmannsthal, *Andreas*, ed. by Mathias Mayer (Stuttgart: Reclam), pp. 127–48
MAZZARELLO, PAOLO. 2011. 'Cesare Lombroso: An Anthropologist between Evolution and Degeneration', *Functional Neurology*, 26.2: 97–101
MCCLINTOCK, ANNE. 1995. *Imperial Leather: Race, Gender and Sexuality in the Colonial Contest* (New York: Routledge)

McIsaac, Peter. 2016. 'Castan's in Context: Introductory Remarks on a Bygone World in Wax', in *House of Wax: Anatomical, Pathological & Ethnographic Waxworks from Castan's Panopticum, Berlin, 1869–1922*, exhibition at the Morbid Anatomy Museum, 23 October 2015–June 2016 (Brooklyn, NY)

McQuillen, Colleen. 2004. 'The Dionysian Roots of Symbolist Masquerade Balls in "Petersburg" and "Poem without a Hero"', *Ulbandus*, 8: 106–18

—— 2013. *The Modernist Masquerade: Stylizing Life, Literature, and Costumes in Russia* (Madison: University of Wisconsin Press)

Miles, David. 1972. *Hofmannsthal's Novel 'Andreas': Memory and Self* (Princeton, NJ: Princeton University Press)

Minami, Miyuki. 2002. 'Rodin and Hanako', in *Rodin et le Japon*, ed. by Claudie Judrin, Miyuki Minami and Hiroshi Kamiya (Tokyo: Contemporary Sculpture Center), pp. 17–19

Mirabile, Andrea. 2014. *Multimedia Archaeologies: Gabriele D'Annunzio, Belle Époque Paris, and the Total Artwork* (Amsterdam: Rodopi)

Moers, Ellen. 1960. *The Dandy, Brummell to Beerbohm* (New York: Viking)

Monnier, Philippe. 1907. *Venise au dix-huitième siècle* (Paris: Perrin et cie)

Montaldo, Silvana. 2013. 'The Lombroso Museum from its Origins to the Present Day', in *The Cesare Lombroso Handbook*, ed. by Paul Knepper and P. J. Ystehede (London and New York: Routledge), pp. 98–112

Moran, Claire. 2007. 'The Aesthetics of Self-Skeletonization in James Ensor', in *Birth and Death in Nineteenth-Century French Culture*, ed. by Nigel Harkness and Lisa Downing (Amsterdam: Rodopi), pp. 239–51

Morel, Bénédict. 1857. *Traité des dégénérescence physiques, intellectuelles et morales de l'espèce humaine* (Paris: J. B. Baillière)

Moulin, Jeanne. 1978a. *Fernand Crommelynck ou le théâtre du paroxysme* (Brussels: Palais des académie)

—— 1978b. *Fernand Crommelynck* (Brussels: Palais des académies)

Mulvey, Laura. 1996. *Fetishism and Curiosity* (Bloomington: Indiana University Press)

—— 1999. 'Visual Pleasure and Narrative Cinema', in *Film Theory and Criticism: Introductory Readings*, ed. by Leo Braudy and Marshall Cohen (New York: Oxford University Press), pp. 833–44

Murray, Alex, and Jason David Hall, eds. 2013. *Decadent Poetics: Literature and Form at the British Fin de Siècle* (London: Palgrave Macmillan)

Musumeci, Emilia. 2009. 'Le maschere della collezione Lorenzo Tenchini', in *Il museo di antropologia criminale 'Cesare Lombroso'*, ed. by Silvano Montaldo and Paolo Tappero (Turin: UTET), pp. 69–76

Nancy, Jean-Luc. 2005. 'Masked Imagination', in *The Ground of the Image*, trans. by Jeff Fort (New York: Fordham University Press), pp. 80–100

—— 2008. 'Masqué, démasqué', *Masques: de Carpeaux à Picasso*, ed. by Edouard Papet (Paris: Hazan), pp. 14–15

Nelson, James. 1971. *The Early Nineties: A View from the Bodley Head* (Cambridge, MA: Harvard University Press)

Nietzsche, Friedrich. 1967. *The Birth of Tragedy*, trans. by Walter Kaufman (New York: Vintage Books)

—— 1972. *Beyond Good and Evil*, trans. by R. J. Hollingdale (Harmondsworth: Penguin)

—— 1995. *Unfashionable Observations*, trans. by Richard T. Gray (Stanford, CA: Stanford University Press)

—— 2009. 'On Truth and Lie in an Extra-Moral Sense', in *Writings from the Early Notebooks*, by Friedrich Nietzsche, ed. by Raymond Geuss and Alexander Nehamas, trans. by Ladislaus Löb (Cambridge: Cambridge University Press), pp. 253–64

NIKOPOULOS, JAMES. 2010. 'The Spirit of the Chorus in D'Annunzio's *La città morta*', *Comparative Drama*, 44: 155–78

NOCHLIN, LINDA. 1994. *The Body in Pieces: The Fragment as a Metaphor of Modernity* (London: Thames and Hudson)

NOIR, PASCALE. 2004. 'Radiographie d'une fin de siècle: Jean Lorrain et l'art du portrait', in *Portraits de femmes*, by Jean Lorrain, ed. by Pascale Noir (Paris: L'Harmattan), pp. 65–192

NORDAU, MAX. 1993. *Degeneration*, ed. by George L. Mosse (Lincoln and London: University of Nebraska Press)

OHI, KEVIN. 2011. *Henry James and the Queerness of Style* (Minneapolis: University of Minnesota Press)

OKAMOTO, KIDO. 1928. *The Mask-Maker*, trans. by Hanso Tarao (London and New York: Samuel French)

—— 1974. *Shuzenji Monogatari: hitomaku sanba*, ed. by Koichi Toshikura (Tokyo: Kokuritsu Gekijo)

OKAMOTO, KYOICHI, ED. 2006. *Kido Nendaiki* (Tokyo: Seia Bo)

OOSTERHUIS, HARRY. 2012. 'Sexual Modernity in the Works of Richard von Krafft-Ebing and Albert Moll', *Medical History*, 65.2: 133–55

OVID. 2000. 'The Metamorphoses', in *Poetry in Translation*, trans. by A. S. Kline <https://www.poetryintranslation.com/PITBR/Latin/Ovhome.php>.

PATER, WALTER. 1976. *The Renaissance: Studies in Art and Poetry*, the Limited Editions Club at the Stamperia Valdonega (Verona: Collins & Co.)

PERI, ALEXIS, and CHRISTINE EVANS. 2010. 'How Terrorists Learned to Map: Plotting in Petersburg and Boris Savinkov's Recollections of a Terrorist and the Pale Horse', in *Petersburg/Petersburg: Novel and City, 1900–1921*, ed. by Olga Matich (Madison: The University of Wisconsin Press), pp. 149–73

PERRIA, PIERA. 1992. *Tra applausi e fischi: La gioconda di Gabriele D'Annunzio* (Florence: Atheneum)

PHILLIPS, DAVID. 1982. 'In Search of an Unknown Woman: L'Inconnue de la Seine', *Neophilologus*, 66.3: 321–27

PICK, DANIEL. 1989. *Faces of Degeneration: A European Disorder, 1848–1918* (Cambridge: Cambridge University Press)

PIETTE, ALAIN, and BERT CARDULLO. 1997. *The Crommelynck Mystery: The Life and Work of a Belgian Playwright* (Selingrove, PA: Susquehanna University Press)

PINET, HÉLÈNE. 2002. 'L'Eau, la femme, la mort: le mythe de l'Inconnue de la Seine', in *Le Dernier Portrait* (Paris: Réunion des Musées Nationaux), pp. 175–90

POGGIOLI, RENATO. 1968. *The Theory of the Avant-Garde*, trans. by Gerald Fitzgerald (Cambridge, MA: Harvard University Press)

PONNAU, GWENHAËL. 1991. 'L'Écriture dans les marges', *Europe*, 27.2: 84–91

POTOLSKY, MATTHEW. 2013. *The Decadent Republic of Letters: Taste, Politics, and Cosmopolitan Community from Baudelaire to Beardsley* (Philadelphia: University of Pennsylvania Press)

POTTIER, EDMOND. 1890. 'Grèce et Japon', *Gazette des Beaux-Arts*, 4: 105–32

POWELL, BRIAN. 1990. *Kabuki in Modern Japan: Mayama Seika and his Plays* (London: Macmillan)

—— 2016. *Japan's Modern Theatre: A Century of Change and Continuity* (London: Routledge)

PRAZ, MARIO. 1970. *The Romantic Agony* (Oxford: Oxford University Press)

PRINCE, MORTON. 1906. *The Dissociation of a Personality* (London and New York: Longmans, Green)

RANK, OTTO. 1971. *The Double: A Psychoanalytic Study*, trans. by Harry Tucker (Chapel Hill: University of North Carolina Press)

RAPETTI, THALIE. 2009. 'Le Portrait de Lorrain en Dorian Gray', in *Jean Lorrain, Produit d'extrême civilisation*, ed. by Jean de Palacio and Éric Walbecq (Mont-Saint-Aignan: Universités de Rouen et du Havre), pp. 121–48

RE, LUCIA. 2004. 'D'Annunzio, Duse, Wilde, Bernhardt: Author and Actress between Decadence and Modernity", in *Italian Modernism: Italian Culture between Decadentism and Avant-Garde*, ed. by Mario Moroni and Luca Somigli (Toronto: University of Toronto Press), pp. 86–129

RICHTER, VIRGINIA. 2011. *Literature after Darwin: Human Beasts in Western Fiction* (London: Palgrave Macmillan)

RILKE, RAINIER MARIA. 1910. *Die Aufzeichnungen des Malte Laurids Brigge* (Leipzig: Insel)

—— 1979. *Rodin*, trans. by Robert Firmage (Salt Lake City, UT: Peregrine Smith)

RIMER, J. THOMAS. 2016. *Toward a Modern Japanese Theatre: Kishida Kunio* (Princeton, NJ: Princeton University Press)

RITTER, ELLEN. 2002. 'Hofmannsthal's Narrative Prose: The Problem of Individuation', in *A Companion to the Works of Hugo von Hofmannsthal*, ed. by Thomas A. Kovach (Woodbridge and Rochester, NY: Camden House)

ROYLE, NICHOLAS. 2003. *The Uncanny* (Manchester: Manchester University Press)

SAID, EDWARD. 1979. *Orientalism* (New York: Vintage Books)

SALER, MICHAEL. 2015. 'Introduction', in *The Fin-de-siècle World* (London: Routledge), pp. 1–8

SALIOT, ANNE-GAËLLE. 2015. *The Drowned Muse: Casting the Unknown Woman of the Seine across the Tides of Modernity* (Oxford: Oxford University Press)

SANTOS, JOSÉ. 1995. *L'Art du récit court chez Jean Lorrain* (Paris: Nizet)

SAVARESE, NICOLA. 1988. 'A Portrait of Hanako', *Asian Theatre Journal*, 5.1: 63–75

SAWADA, SUKATARO. 1984. *Little Hanako* (Nagoya: Chunici Pub)

SCHAFFNER, ANNA K. 2012. *Modernism and Perversion: Sexual Deviance in Sexology and Literature, 1850–1930* (Basingstoke and New York: Palgrave)

SCHNAPP, JEFFREY. 1988. 'Nietzsche's Italian Style', in *Nietzsche in Italy*, ed. by Thomas Harrison (Stanford, CA: ANMA Libri), pp. 247–77

SCHNITZLER, GÜNTER. 2011. 'Quellendichte und Unabschließbarkeit; Zu Hofmannsthals Andreas-Roman', *Realität als Herausforderung: Literatur in ihren konkreten historischen Kontexten*, ed. by Ralf Bogner (Berlin and New York: Walter de Gruyter & Co), pp. 447–62

SCHOONBAERT, LYDIA. 1989. 'James Ensor', in *James Ensor: Belgien um 1900* (Munich: Hirmer), pp. 11–34

SCHOPENHAUER, ARTHUR. 1891. *Die Welt als Wille und Vorstellung* (Leipzig: Brockhaus)

SCHWOB, MARCEL. 1991. 'Le Roi au masque d'or', in *Le Roi au masque d'or* (Toulouse: Éditions Ombres), pp. 13–28

SEBALD, W. G. 1985. 'Venezianisches Kryptogramm: Hofmannsthals Andreas', in *Die Beschreibung des Unglücks: zur österreichischen Literatur von Stifter bis Handke* (Wien: Residenz Verlag), pp. 61–77

SHAW, GEORGE BERNARD. 1911. *The Sanity of Art: An Exposure of the Current Nonsense about Artists* (London: Constable)

SHEEHY, HELEN. 2003. *Eleonora Duse: A Biography* (New York: Alfred Knopf)

SHEPPARD, ANTHONY. 2001. *Revealing Masks: Exotic Influences and Ritualized Performance in Modernist Music Theatre* (Berkeley, CA: Berkeley University Press)

SHERRY, VINCENT. 2015. *Modernism and the Reinvention of Decadence* (Cambridge: Cambridge University Press)

SHIONOYA, KEI. 1986. *Cyrano et les samuraï: le théâtre japonais en France et l'effet de retour* (Paris: Publications orientalistes de France)

SIEBERS, TOBIN. 2003. 'Medusa as Double', in *The Medusa Reader*, ed. by Marjorie Garber and Nancy J. Vickers (London: Routledge), pp. 196–97

SIGHELE, SCIPIO. 1906. 'L'opera di Gabriele D'Annunzio davanti alla psichiatria', in *Letteratura tragica*, by Scipio Sighele (Milan: Treves), pp. 3–94
SINFIELD, ADAM. 1994. *The Wilde Century: Effeminacy, Oscar Wilde, and the Queer Movement* (London: Cassell)
SPACKMAN, BARBARA. 1989. *Decadent Genealogies: The Rhetoric of Sickness from Baudelaire to D'Annunzio* (Ithaca, NY: Cornell University Press)
—— 1996. *Fascist Virilities: Rhetoric, Ideology, and Social Fantasy in Italy* (Minneapolis: University of Minnesota Press)
STAMM, ULRIKE. 2016. 'Orient', in *Hofmannsthal-Handbuch. Leben-Werk-Wirkung*, ed. by Mathias Mayer and Julian Werlitz (Stuttgart: Metzler), pp. 107–08
STANFORD, DEREK. 1970. *Critics of the Nineties* (London: John Baker)
STEWART, SUSAN. 1984. *On Longing: Narratives of the Miniature, the Gigantic, the Souvenir, the Collection* (Durham, NC: Duke University Press)
SYMONS, ARTHUR. 1899. *The Symbolist Movement in Literature* (London: Archibald Constable)
SYRIMIS, MICHAEL. 2017. 'The Light that Blinds: On Art in D'Annunzio's La Gioconda' *Forum Italicum*, 51.2: 378–95
THORNTON, R. K. R. 1989. 'The Mask in Wilde and Yeats', in *Die Modernisierung des Ich: Studies zur Subjektkonstitution in der Vor- und Frühmoderne*, ed. by Manfred Pfister (Passau: Rother), pp. 269–74
—— AND MARION THAIN. 1997. *Poetry of the 1890s*, 2nd edn (Harmondsworth: Penguin)
TREBBI, FERNANDO. 1996. 'Figurazioni del femminile sulla scena della Gioconda', in *Gesto e parola: aspetti del teatro europeo tra ottocento e novecento*, ed. by Umberto Artioli and Fernando Trebbi (Padua: Esendra), pp. 115–25
TRICOT, HAVIER. 1997. 'James Ensor and English Art', in *James Ensor: Catalogue* (London: The Barbican Art Gallery), pp. 105–10
TRICOT, XAVIER. 2008. 'James Ensor, Prince des Masques', in *Masques: de Carpeaux à Picasso*, ed. by Édouard Papet (Paris: Hazan), pp. 162–67
TRICOT, HAVIER (n.d.), 'Who is hiding behind the mask in The Astonishment of the Mask Wouse', in *James Ensor online museum*, web publication (Gent: Museum von Schoene Kunsten), <http://jamesensor.vlaamsekunstcollectie.be/en/sources/online-publications/who-is-hiding-behind-the-mask-in-the-astonishment-of-the-mask-wouse>
VALENTINI, VALENTINA. 1992. *La tragedia moderna e mediterranea: sul teatro di Gabriele D'Annunzio* (Milan: Franco Angeli)
VATTIMO, GIANNI. 1974. *Il soggetto e la maschera: Nietzsche e il problema della liberazione* (Milan: Bompiani)
VIEGNES, MICHEL, and SABRINA GRANGER. 2009. 'Marcel Schwob ou la dissonante symphonie des signes', in *Contes Symbolistes*, 1 (Grenoble: Ellog), pp. 269–83
VITRY, PAUL. 1903. 'Masques', *Art et Décoration*, 14: 345–54
WEBER, SAMUEL. 1973. 'The Sideshow, or: Remarks on a Canny Moment', *Comparative Literature*, 88.6: 1102–33
WEIHE, RICHARD. 2009. 'Person und Maske: "Sua cuique Persona" als Schema der Maskierung', in *Wir sind Maske*, ed. by Sylvia Ferino Pagden (Milan: Silvana Editore), pp. 21–28
WEIR, DAVID. 1996. *Decadence and the Making of Modernism* (Amherst: University of Massachusetts Press)
WERMUTH-ATKINSON, JUDITH. 2012. *The Red Jester: Andrei Bely's Petersburg as a Novel of the European Modern* (Zurich: LIT-Verlag)
WETMORE, KEVIN J. 2006. 'Modern Japanese Drama in English', *Asian Theatre Journal*, 23.1: 179–205
WHITELEY, GILES. 2017. *Oscar Wilde and the Simulacrum: The Truth of Masks* (London: Legenda)

WHITTINGTON-EGAN, RICHARD, and GEOFFREY SMERDON. 1960. *The Quest of the Golden Boy: The Life and Letters of Richard Le Gallienne* (London: Unicorn)

WIGGINS, CAMERON. 2010. 'The Enchanted Masquerade: Alexander Blok's *The Puppet Show* from the Stage to the Streets', in *Petersburg/Petersburg: Novel and City, 1900–1921*, ed. by Olga Matich (Madison: University of Wisconsin Press), pp. 174–93

WILDE, OSCAR. 2005. 'The Picture of Dorian Gray', in *The Complete Works of Oscar Wilde*, ed. by Josephine M. Guy, vol. III (Oxford: Oxford University Press), pp. 165–357

——2007A. 'Pen, Pencil and Poison', in *The Complete Works of Oscar Wilde*, ed. by Josephine M. Guy, vol. IV (Oxford: Oxford University Press), pp. 104–22

——2007B. 'The Critic as an Artist', in *The Complete Works of Oscar Wilde*, ed. by Josephine M. Guy, vol. IV (Oxford: Oxford University Press), pp. 162–206

——2007C. 'The Decay of Lying', in *The Complete Works of Oscar Wilde*, ed. by Josephine M. Guy, vol. IV, Oxford University Press, pp. 72–103

WINN, PHILLIP. 1997. *Sexualités décadents chez Jean Lorrain: le héros fin de sexe* (Amsterdam: Rodopi)

WITT, MARY ANNE FRESE. 2001. *The Search for Modern Tragedy: Aesthetic Fascism in Italy and France* (Ithaca, NY: Cornell University Press)

——2007. *Nietzsche and the Rebirth of the Tragic* (Madison and Teaneck, NJ: Fairleigh Dickinson University Press)

WOODHOUSE, JOHN R. 2008. *Gabriele D'Annunzio: Defiant Archangel* (Oxford: Oxford University Press)

YEATS, WILLIAM BUTLER. 1921. *Four Plays for Dancers, 1865–1939* (London: Macmillan)

ZIEGLER, ROBERT. 1994. 'The Narrative of Masks in Jean Lorrain', *Selecta: Journal of the Pacific Northwest*, 15: 31–35

——2008. 'The Mask of the Blinded Toad: Jean Lorrain 1900', *Dalhousie French Studies*, 84: 29–40

ZINCK, HÉLÈNE. 2001A. '"Ai-je lu quelque part?" ou la question de l'intertextualité', in *Monsieur de Phocas*, ed. by Hélène Zinck (Paris: Flammarion), pp. 303–14

——2001B. 'Le Roman à clefs: Robert de Montesquiou...et les autres', in *Monsieur de Phocas*, ed. by Hélène Zinck (Paris: Flammarion), pp. 315–26

INDEX

❖

Adamson, Walter 6, 109
aesthetes, aestheticism 3, 37–38, 76–77, 79, 81, 84, 86, 96–97, 100, 109, 121, 134
aesthetic costume 36–37
African art 27–28, 163
  masks 27–28 fig. 1.8, 52
Agamemnon Mask 104, 106 fig. 4.3
Alewyn, Richard 146, 165 n. 3
Angioletti, Kata Laura 105, 112
anthropology, anthropologists 1–2, 8, 16–19, 21, 23, 33, 37–39 n. 2, 70, 95, 118, 144, 167–68
  criminal anthropology 21, 23–25 figs. 1.5 & 1.6
Apollo, Apollonian 32, 110, 119 n. 3
aristocracy 35, 96–97, 105, 124, 128–29, 136, 139, 143–44, 150, 153–54, 160–62,
  fears of decay of 153–54, 160–62, 164
Art et Décoration 25–26 fig. 1.7
atavism 2, 23, 33, 38, 169
Aurnhammer, Achim 145

Bahr, Hermann 144
Bakhtin, Mikhail 52, 72 n. 6
Ball, Hugo 34
barbarism 2, 6, 39,
  'healthy barbarism' 38–39 n. 5, 154, 159, 161–62
Baudelaire, Charles:
  'Éloge du maquillage' ['In Praise of Cosmetics'] 37–38, 39–40 n. 6, 79, 130
  Les Fleurs du mal 12
bauta (mask) 150, 154
Beardsley, Aubrey 78, 82
Beau Brummell 27, 80, 124
Beerbohm, Max 73–74, 79–80, 82–85, 93
  'A Defence of Cosmetics' (or 'The Pervasion of Rouge') 79–80, 82–85
  The Happy Hypocrite: A Fairy Tale for Old Men 73–74, 80–85
  on masks 74, 80, 84–85, 93, 169
  on 'New Women' 80, 84–85
Belanger, Enrico 117
Belting, Hans:
  Face and Mask: A Double History 13, 18, 21
Bely, Andrei (neé Boris Nikolaevich Bugaev) 143–44, 154, 162, 165, 169
  Petersburg 15, 143, 154–65
Benjamin, Walter 6, 169
  The Origin of German Tragedy 169
  'The Work of Art in the Age of Mechanical Reproduction' 6
Benkard, Ernst:
  Das Ewige Antlitz [The Eternal Face] 21
Berman, Nina 154, 165 n. 1
Bernhardt, Sarah 33, 63, 105
Bernheimer, Charles 95
Binet, Alfred 8, 100, 104
  'Le Fétichisme dans l'amour' 95–96
Bisicchia, Andrea 120 n. 16
Blanchetière, François 63, 65, 68, 72 n. 13
Blok, Alexandr 154, 162
Bodley Head, The 78, 85
Bredbeck, Gregory 78
Brown, Bill 17
Bourdelle, Antoine 25, 36–37
Bourget, Paul 12, 77
  on decadence 12, 16 n. 12, 37, 86, 144
Brack, O. M. 5, 73, 86
Bréal, Michel 125
Bredbeck, Gregory 78, 87
Brickman, Celia, 5
Bruhm, Steven 78

caricature 42, 53, 55, 57, 70, 79, 127, 130
Carriès, Jean 25, 30
  Horror Mask 39 fig. 1.9
carnival 5, 41–42, 51–53, 57, 72 n. 6, 127, 146
  Bakhtin 52
  carnival masks 30, 41–42, 51
Castan's Panopticon 19, 39 n. 1
castration 112, 139
  anxiety 8–9, 16 n. 10, 95, 116, 118, 122, 141 n. 10
Cellini, Benvenuto:
  Perseus with the Head of Medusa 11 fig. I.5, 12, 100, 101 fig. 4.1, 104, 119 n. 4 & 7
Cézanne, Paul 27
Charcot, Jean-Martin 3, 122, 124, 129
  on 'sexual inversion' 3, 5
Cixous, Hélène 10
Cladel, Judith 65, 67–69, 167–68
class 81, 105, 113, 123–24, 127, 129–30, 136, 139, 143, 150, 161, 164, 170 n. 1
Clayton, Douglas 158
Clifford, James 27–28
Cohen, Ed 73, 84
Colonial Exhibition of Marseilles (1906) 64, 167

colonialism 7, 28, 139, 170 n. 1
commedia dell'arte 33, 133, 146, 154
Compagnon, Antoine 14, 17
Coquiot, Gustave 126–27
cosmopolitanism 13, 38, 57, 143, 153
Copeau, Jacques 33
Cowling, Mary 18
Craig, Edward Gordon 34
criminal anthropology 21, 23, 24–25 figs 1.5 & 1.6
Crommelynck, Fernand 53–54, 56–57, 70–71, 169
 Le Sculpteur de masques 53–57
cross-dressing 5, 62, 72 n. 10, 76, 90, 122, 124, 140
crowd 52, 54, 113–14, 115–16, 120 n. 19, 125, 127, 136, 161
cubists 27, 52
 'cubist gaze' 28
cultural appropriation 14, 17, 37, 41, 52

dadaism 33–34
dandyism 36–38, 74–77, 79–80, 84, 93, 96, 119 n. 2, 121, 124–25, 128, 131
D'Annunzio, Gabriele 13, 15, 95–99, 105, 109, 113–19, 119 n. 1
 works:
  Il Fuoco [*The Flame*] 12, 96–102, 104–05, 107–08, 118
  'La bestia elettiva' [The Elective Beast] 96–97
  La città morta [*The Dead City*] 33, 96, 104–09, 119 n. 9
  La Gioconda 96, 109–14, 116, 119 n. 9
  La Gloria 96, 109, 113–19, 120 n. 16
 and Eleonora Duse 97–98, 107, 109, 112, 119 n. 2, 120 n. 19
 and fetishism 96, 109, 118
 and fragments 111–12, 169
 influence of Lombroso on 109, 120 n. 19
 influence of Nietzsche on 96–97, 118, 119 n. 3
 and masks 10, 33, 95–96, 98–99, 104–05, 107, 118, 119 n. 9, 169
 on Italian culture and politics 96–97, 105, 109, 117, 120 n. 16
Danson, Lawrence 76
Darwin, Charles 2, 18, 39 n. 4, 130
 Influence on Lombroso 2
death masks 3 fig. I.1, 6, 10, 18–23 figs 1.1, 1.2, 1.3, 1.4, 60–61, 68, 87, fig. 4.3, 135, 167–68 fig. C.1
 in D'Annunzio's *La città morta* 104–07
decadence, decadents, decadent style 2–3, 7, 12–14, 27, 33–35, 37–39, 71, 73–74, 77–80, 85–87, 93, 96, 104, 115, 123, 144, 169,
 Le Gallienne's criticism of 86, 92
 Havelock Ellis on 12–13
 Max Nordau's criticism of 38, 77
 as theorised by Paul Bourget 12, 144
 as defined by Renato Poggioli 39
 as defined by Théophile Gautier 12
decapitation 7, 10, 12, 16 n. 10, 69, 99, 109, 113, 119, 120 n. 16, 121, 125, 134–36, 139, 141, 169

De Garis, Frederic and Atsuharu Sakai 62
degeneracy, degeneration 1–3, 12–13, 16 n. 1, 26, 38, 40 n. 7, 77–78, 91, 106, 122–23, 128, 136, 143, 161, 164, 169
 Lombroso on 2, 106, 118
 Jean Lorrain on 122–23, 125, 136, 139
 and masks 128, 143, 164
 Nordau on 1–3, 38, 77, 91–92, 106, 118, 139
Dellamora, Richard 76
Denisoff, Dennis 79
De Quincey, Thomas 76
Dionysian, Dionysus 31–33, 109–10
 and Bely 160–61, 164
 and D'Annunzio 98, 109–10, 115, 120 n. 15
 Dionysian artist 57, 61
 Vattimo on 32–33
 Nietzsche on 31–32, 119 n. 3, 148
Dollimore, Johnathan 75, 79
domino (mask) 141 n. 3, 150, 154–57,
 in Bely's *Petersburg* 157–60, 162–65
doubles, doubling 10, 15, 37, 84, 89–90, 125, 137–39, 144, 163–64, 169
 in Hofmannsthal's *Andreas* 144, 150–52, 154, 163–64
 in Bely's *Petersburg* 163–65
Dowling, Linda 85, 87
Duse, Eleonora 33, 97–98, 105, 107, 109, 112–13, 116–17, 119 n. 2 & 7

'East, the' 15, 120 n. 16, 162, 164
 in Bely's *Petersburg* 155–56, 158–59, 162–64
 in Hofmannsthal's *Andreas* 153–54, 164
East Asian masks 6, 30, 41–42, 46–47, 51–53
Ego-mania 74, 77, 91, 118
 Nordau on 77, 91, 93, 118
Einstein, Carl:
 Negerplastik 27–28 fig. 1.8
Ellis, Havelock 12, 73, 78, 86–87, 126
 Sexual Inversion 73, 87, 126
 Studies in the Psychology of Sex 78
Ensor, James 6, 15, 30, 32, 41–54, 70–71, 126–27, 129, 134, 171
 The Astonishment of the Mask Wouse 47 fig. 2.5
 on carnival 42, 52–53
 The Entry of Christ into Brussels 42, 47, 53
 The Intrigue 50 fig. 2.9, 72 n. 5
 Influence on Jean Lorrain 126–27
 Man of Sorrows 49 fig. 2.7, 51
 'Masque divers' (lecture) 51
 Masks fig. 1.10
 on masks 6, 15, 30, 41, 44, 46, 51–54, 57, 70–71, 121, 126–27
 The Scandalized Masks 42–43 fig. 2.1
 Self-Portrait with Masks 47–48 fig. 2.6
 The Skeleton Painter 50 fig. 2.8
 Skeletons in the Studio 47
 Skeleton Looking at Chinoiserie 45 fig. 2.3, 47

Skulls and Masks 46 fig. 2.4
Still Life with Chinoiseries 44 fig. 2.2
ethnic impersonation 36–37
ethnography 14, 17–19, 167,
  ethnographic masks and busts 18, 23, 167
  'ethnographic surrealism' 28
Euripides 32
Evans, Christine 162
Evreinov, Nikolai 33, 154
Expressionism, expressionists 15, 33, 46, 56, 65, 67–69, 84
  German Expressionism 27, 30, 34, 52

Fabian, Johannes 7
Felski, Rita 36, 75, 93
femininity 36–37, 52, 54, 57, 71, 85, 93, 100, 116, 118, 131, 139, 156,
feminist criticism/theory 10, 16 n. 6, 36, 41, 57, 118, 131
fetish, fetishism 8–9, 13, 15, 16 n. 6, 37, 57, 78, 88, 92–93, 95–96, 100, 104, 109, 118, 122, 169
  and Bely 159
  Binet on 95–96, 104
  and D'Annunzio 96, 100, 104, 109, 112, 118, 120 n. 16
  Freud on 8–9, 95–96, 122
  Lacan on 8
  and Lorrain 124, 133
  the mask as a fetish 27, 37, 68, 71, 73–74, 87, 122, 124, 168
Flemish carnival 41–42, 51, 53
Foley, Kathy 64
Foucault, Michel 73, 123
fragment, fragmentation 7, 13–15, 39, 57, 92–93, 112
  and Bely 155, 162–64, 169
  and D'Annunzio 96, 106, 109, 111–13, 118
  Freud on 7
  and Hofmannsthal 145, 151, 163–64, 169
  and Lorrain 124, 132
  as characteristic of modernity and decadence 7, 13–14, 17, 26, 38–39, 144
  masks as fragments 7, 13, 15, 17, 39, 71, 96, 135, 169
  and Rodin 67, 69–70, 167–68
French, Samuel 59 fig. 2.10, 62,
Freud, Sigmund 5, 7–10, 15, 84, 95, 122
  works:
    Beyond the Pleasure Principle 131
    The Interpretation of Dreams 144
    Three Essays on Sexuality 5, 78, 144
    Totem and Taboo 163
    'The uncanny' 7, 8, 122, 126, 131, 168
    'Fetishism' 8
    'On Narcissism: A Introduction' 78
    'Medusa's Head and the Infantile Genital Organization' 9, 96
  on fetishism 8–9, 16 n. 6–8 & 10, 37, 57, 95–96, 122
  on homosexuality and narcissism 5, 16 n. 7, 78, 122, 140 n. 2, 144
  on Medusa and the castration complex 8–10, 16 n. 10, 95–96, 116, 118
  on the uncanny 7–8, 13, 53, 71, 122, 126, 131, 140, 168
Frye, Lawrence 146
Fuller, Loïe 58, 63–64, 71

Gagnier, Regenia 13–14, 16 n. 12
Garnier, Bénédicte 63, 67
Gauguin, Paul 27, 29, 51, 63
Gautier, Théophile 12
gaze 10, 28, 41, 57, 110
  and D'Annunzio 110, 114
  Lacanian gaze 10, 15, 41, 51, 53, 71
  and Lorrain 128–29, 132–35
  male gaze 151
  of Medusa 68, 91, 109–10, 169
Gémier, Firmin 62
gender 1–2, 15–16, 37, 61, 71, 72 n. 10, 74, 124–26, 140, 170
  as performative 1, 122
gender blurring/ambiguity 2–3, 5, 36, 85, 90, 93, 116, 119, 125, 127, 136, 139–40, 142 n. 11
genius 1–2, 23, 169
  Lombroso on 2, 21, 23, 77, 109
  Genio e follia [Genius and Madness] 2
  Nietzsche on 30
Gioconda, La (da Vinci's) 90–91, 113–14, 119 n. 11, 120 n. 15
Glick, Elisa 78, 90
Gombrich, Ernst 167
Gonse, Louis 28, 36, 63
Gorgon, *see* Medusa
gothic fiction 41, 74, 87, 139, 165 n. 2
Gothic art 25–27, 39
Goya, Francisco 134
Grand, Sarah:
  'The New Aspect of the Woman Question' 79
Granoff, Wladimir 8
green 86–87, 126

Hanako (Hisa Ōta) 6, 14, 30, 63–65, 66 figs 2.11–13, 67–69, 70 fig. 2.16, 71, 72 n. 13, 167, 168 fig. C.1, 170
  Judith Cladel on 65, 67–69, 167
Hammond, Charles H. 151
Härmänmaa, Marja 12
Hederer, Edgar 146
Heidegger, Martin 10, 14, 17
Hertz, Neil 169
Hoffmann, Ernst Theodor Amadeus 15, 52, 121–24, 127, 129, 134
  'The Sandman' 122, 124, 129, 138
Hofmannsthal, Hugo von 15, 47, 143–46, 150–54, 165, 165 n. 1, 9 & 10, 169
  Andreas 15, 47, 143–54, 165 n. 3 & 11
Hogarth, William 134
Hokusai 42

homosexuality 2, 5, 14, 73, 77–78, 120 n. 19, 122–23,
        126, 141 n. 4,
    and Beerbohm's circle 82–84, 92
    Freud on 5, 8–9, 16 n. 7, 78, 96, 122, 133, 140 n. 2
    Havelock Ellis on 73
    as an identity 73
    Lombroso on 2, 120 n. 19
    And Lorrain 121–23, 136–38, 140
    medico-legal debates about 14–15, 73, 77–78
    and Wilde and *The Picture of Dorian Gray* 15, 73,
        76–78, 82, 84, 92
Hornig, Dieter 151, 165 n. 8
Hostyn, Norbert, and Patrick Florizoone 42
Huysmans, Joris-Karl 35, 37, 74, 169
    À *Rebours* [Against Nature] 35, 74–76, 94 n. 4, 128
    L'Émailleuse [The Enameller] 35–37

Ichitawa, Sadanji 58, 62
Imaginary, the (Lacan) 8
Inconnue de la Seine 6, 7 fig. 1.3, 21, 87, 92 fig. 3.1, 134
individualism 13, 77, 109, 148

Japanese art 25, 42, 57, 62–64
Japanese masks 25–28, 30, 36, 38, 42, 47, 56, 133
Japanese theatre and carnival (see also kabuki and Nō)
    25, 26, 33–34, 41, 53, 56–58, 60–64, 71, 72 n. 10
Japanophilia, *Japonisme* 28, 42, 63–64, 161
Jarry, Alfred 33
Jonsson, Stefan 127
Jullian, Philippe 122, 126, 128

kabuki 57–58, 61–65, 71
    'new' (shin-)kabuki 58, 61–65, 71
    see also Shuzenji Monogatari
Kandinsky, Wassily, 27
Kaplan, Louise 16 n. 6, 88
Kawakami, Otojirō 58, 63, 71, 72 n. 8
Kincaid, Zoë 62
Kingcaid, Renée 126
Kirchner, Ernst Ludwig 27
Knapp, Bettina 53–54
Kolbe, George 21, 23
Krafft-Ebing, Richard von 1, 139
    on fetishism 8
    on gender-crossing 5, 124
    on sexuality 3, 5
    Psychopathia Sexualis 73, 122

Lacan, Jacques:
    on fetishism 8
    Lacanian gaze 10, 15, 41, 51, 53, 71
Langen, Timothy 144, 162
Lane, Christopher 82
Laurent, Monique:
    on Rodin and Hanako: 65, 68–69
Lavater, Johann Caspar:
    Essays on Physiognomy 18

Le Gallienne, Richard 6, 73, 85–87, 90–93, 169
    works:
        'The Boom in Yellow' 86
        The Worshipper of the Image 6, 14, 73–74, 87–93
    subjects:
        on decadence 86, 92–93
        on Wilde 87
Legrand, Francine-Claire:
    on Ensor 42, 51
Lemaître, Jules 64
Ljunggren, Magnus 144, 162
Lloyd, Jill:
    on masks in the work of Ensor and Nolde 30
Lombroso, Cesare 2, 16 n. 3, 21, 23
    works:
        L'uomo delinquente [Criminal man] 2, 16 n. 3,
            21
        Genio e follia [Genius and Madness] 2, 16. n. 2
    subjects:
        atavism 2, 23, 38, 129, 144
        criminality, genius, madness and homosexuality
            2, 21, 23, 109, 120 n. 19, 122
        and D'Annunzio 120 n. 19
        death masks 3 fig. I.1, 22 figs 1.3, 1.4, 23
        methodology 21
    also see Museum of Criminal Anthropology
        'Cesare Lombroso' (University of Turin)
Loos, Adolf 38, 40 n. 7
Lorrain, Jean (née Paul Duval) 15, 36, 72 n. 12, 121–40
    works:
        'Chez l'une d'elles' 125
        Histoires de masques 121–26, 141 n. 3 & 7
        'La Dame aux portraits' [The Lady with the
            Portraits] 124
        'Lanterne magique' [The Magic Lantern]
        'Le Coup de grâce' [The Mortal Blow] 124
        'Le Masque' [the mask] 126
        'Les Trous du masque' [The Holes in the Mask]
            126
        'L'Homme au bracelet' [The Man with the
            Bracelet] 124
        'L'Homme au complet mauve' [The Man in the
            Mauve Suit] 124
        'L'Un de d'Eux' [One of Them] 123, 126
        Monsieur de Phocas 15, 4, 121–22, 127–39,
            141 n. 9, 141–42 n. 10–13 & 15
        'Trio de masques' [Three Masks] 123–24
    subjects:
        on degeneration 15, 122, 125, 128–30, 136, 138
        dress/cross-dressing 121–22, 124
        and masks 6, 10, 57, 122–27, 129–40, 169
        on narcissism 133, 139
        on sexuality, 'sexual inversion' 123, 131, 133, 136,
            140, 142 n. 11

Mach, Ernst 144
Mack, John 18

Macke, August 27
   'Die Masken' 38–39
Magnan, Valentin 3, 124, 129, 139
   and 'sexual inversion' 5
Malmstad, John 156, 162
Mantegazza, Paolo 18
   Fisionomia e mimica [*Physiognomy and Expression*] 18
Marc, Franz 27
masked balls 75, 122, 125–26, 132, 141 n. 3, 145–46, 152, 155, 170
mask-making 1, 10, 23, 26, 28, 30, 41, 54, 62–63, 70–71, 80–81, 126 170 n. 1
   in Crommelynck's *Le Sculpteur de masques* 54–56
   as a gendered practice 14, 41, 170
   as a form of cultural appropriation 41, 52
   in Okamoto's *Shuzen-ji Monogatari* 60–63
   and Rodin 65, 67–69, 70 fig. 2.16
   as ritual 71
mask-phobia 51, 121–24, 132–33, 135, 158–59, 163
masks
   African 27–28 fig. 1.8, 52
   as allegorical 127, 169
   as anachronistic 6–7, 167
   blurring class, gender, ethnicity 1, 3, 5, 37, 57, 85, 90, 93, 122, 125–27, 140, 150, 164
   as caricatures 55, 57, 70, 130, 141 n. 8
   as a commodity 6, 37, 168
   carnival masks 30, 41–42, 51
   contemporary use/meaning 171
   associated with death 8, 10, 30, 52–54, 68, 71, 84, 87–88, 90, 127, 134, 140, 168
   associated with 'the primitive' 6, 8, 15, 27, 39, 40 n. 7, 53, 159, 163–64, 168–69
   associated with 'savagery' 8, 15, 51, 69, 125, 144
   associated with terrorism 15, 157, 159, 162–63
   as cultural appropriations 14, 17, 37, 41, 52
   also see death masks
   as emblems/symbols of decadence/degeneration 26–27, 38, 57, 122–23, 143, 161–62
   in connection with decapitation 7, 10, 69, 99, 113, 119, 121, 134–36
   as disguise 1, 7, 14–15, 32–33, 38, 73–76, 81, 87, 89, 93, 115, 122, 143, 146, 150, 153–54, 156, 163–64, 171
   as embodiments of repressed desires 8, 57, 122
   as ethnographic busts 18, 23, 167
   as fetish objects 27, 37, 68, 71, 73–74, 87, 122, 124, 168
   as figurations of alterity 1, 7, 13, 41, 70–71, 168
   as flexible, open, empty signifiers 12, 15, 39, 125–26, 140, 141 n. 6, 169
   as fragments 7, 13, 15, 17, 39, 71, 96, 135, 169
   as iconic of modernity 6, 13–14, 17, 39, 41
   Japanese 25–28, 30, 36, 38, 42, 47, 56, 133
   liminal character 17, 30
   and mirrors 10, 15, 37, 74, 82, 90, 125–26, 133, 156–57
   as portraiture 1, 6, 17–19, 23, 27–28, 30, 39, 41, 53–57, 60, 63, 71, 87–88, 93, 123–24, 135, 141 n. 6, 167–68
   as a female portrait 10, 54, 62, 135
   and the 'return of the repressed' 2, 6, 8, 13, 15, 71, 122, 139, 163–64
   and refractions of the self 6, 12, 30–32, 33–34, 53, 71, 74, 80, 93. 100, 115, 118, 137–40, 144–46, 151–52, 156–57, 161–63, 170–71
   self-objectification 28
   as severed heads 13, 15, 68–69, 71, 96, 99, 109, 118–19, 123–25, 134–36, 139, 169
   shifts of function 12, 14, 17, 21, 39, 41–42
   and skulls 10, 23, 42, 46 fig. 2.4, 47 fig. 2.5, 51, 53–54, 56, 71, 127, 169
   as a substitute 8, 16 n. 7, 32, 37, 71, 92, 168
   and the rebirth of Western civilisation 6–7, 27, 34, 38–39, 71
   as synecdoches 8, 13, 169
   as theatrical props 1, 25, 30–31, 38–39, 41, 53, 63, 70, 105, 122, 133, 139
   tragic masks 31, 33, 96, 98–99
   as tropes in decadent art and literature 1, 13–14, 16–17, 35, 38–39, 41, 169
   and the uncanny 1, 8, 13, 53, 68, 71, 122, 126, 132, 139, 168, 171
masquerades 5, 15, 36–37, 41–42, 124, 144, 154
Maguire, Robert 156, 162
Matich, Olga 155
McClintock, Anne 6
McQuillen, Colleen 13, 30, 154, 157
Medusa 9 fig. I.4, 10, 11 I.5, 12, 16 n. 10, 91, 92 fig. 3.1, 95–96, 99–102, (101 fig. 4.1), 108–10, 112–13, 115–17, 117 fig. 4.5, 118, 119 n. 11, 120 n. 16, 135, 169
   Medusa Ludovisi 111 fig. 4.4
metonymy 8, 13, 33, 69, 95–96, 102, 109, 146, 163, 169
Meyer, Mathias 165 n. 11
Meyerhold, Vsevolod 33, 154
Miles, David 145
Mirbeau, Octave 28, 63
mirrors 10, 12, 15, 35, 37, 74–76, 81–82, 90, 104, 125–26, 133, 152, 156–58
misogyny 1–2, 10, 62, 85, 93, 115, 130, 132, 168, 170
modernity 6, 13–14, 17, 39, 41, 63, 83, 98, 144, 165 n. 11, 171
modernism 6, 13, 27, 39, 143
Monet, Claude 28
Mongols 21, 68–69, 156, 158–64
Monnier, Philippe 146
Morasso, Mario 109
Moreau de Tours, Paul 3, 122
Moreau, Gustave 104, 119 n. 5, 129, 138
   Orpheus 103 fig. 4.2
Mulvey, Laura 41, 57
museums 19, 21, 25–26, 39 n. 2, 132, 134

Anatomical Museum of the University of Edinburgh 19, 20 figs 1.1, 1.2
Bavarian State Museum of Ethnology 27
Berlin Ethnological Museum 30
Castan's Panopticon 19, 39 n. 1
'Cesare Lombroso' Museum of Criminal Anthropology, University of Turin 3 fig. I.1, 4 fig. I.2, 23, 24 fig. 1.5, 25 fig. 1.6
Gustave Moreau Museum 135, 138
Louvre 25–26, 132
National Archaeological Museum Athens 105, 106 fig. 4.3
Rodin Museum 66 figs 2.11–2.13, 67 fig. 2.15, 168 fig. C.1
Schiller National Museum 21, 22 figs 1.3, 1.4
Tenchini Anatomical collection, Parma 167
Trocadero 27
Vienna Museum 21
Musumeci, Emilia 23
mutilation 13, 39, 109–10, 112–13, 115, 118, 120 n. 16

Nancy, Jean-Luc 10
narcissism 5, 73–74, 77–78, 91, 93, 94 n. 5, 95–96, 100, 104, 108–09, 119, 123, 132–33, 139, 151, 154, 156–57, 164
  Binet on 95, 104, 118
  Freud on 5, 78, 95, 133, 140 n. 2, 144
  Max Nordau on 77, 93
  Otto Rank on 78
Neurosis 8, 12, 15, 98, 122, 128–29, 144, 160, 163–64, 169
'New Women' 79–80, 84–85
Nietzsche, Friedrich 13, 30–34, 38, 39 n. 5, 96–97, 109, 148, 164
  Jenseits von Gut und Böse [Beyond Good and Evil] 32
  Die Geburt der Tragödie aus dem Geiste der Musik [The Birth of Tragedy from the Spirit of Music] 30–32, 60, 97, 119 n. 3
  on masks as emblematic of the death of tragedy and civilisational decay 31–32, 38
  'Über Wahrheit und Lüge im aussermoralischen Sinne' [On Truth and Lies in a Nonmoral Sense] 32
  Unzeitgemässe Betrachtungen [Unfashionable Observations] 30, 32–33 Nō 14, 26, 33–34, 36, 41–42, 51, 53, 56–58, 60, 62–63, 67
Nissen, Christopher 12
Nochlin, Linda 13, 39
Nolde, Emil 6, 30
  'Masks' 31 fig. 1.10
Nordau, Max 1–3, 6, 38, 77, 91, 106, 118, 130, 139, 144
  Degeneration 2–3, 38, 77
  on decadence 3, 38, 77, 86, 144
  on ego-mania 77, 91, 93, 118
  on gender 3, 139
  on genius 1–2
  on Wilde 77, 91, 93

Okamoto, Kido 14, 41, 57–62, 70–71, 72 n. 9 & 10
  Shuzen-ji Monogatari [The Tale of *Shuzen-ji*] 41, 58, 59 fig. 2.10, 60–62
onnagata 58, 61, 72 n. 10
'Orient', the, oriental 6, 27, 34, 37, 41–42, 51, 125, 131, 135, 137–38, 142 n. 14, 150, 153–54, 156, 158–59, 161. 164
Orientalism 37, 41, 161

part-whole relationship 8, 12–13, 37, 74, 86, 95–96, 163, 169, 13, 96
Pater, Walter 90, 94 n. 9, 109–10, 113–14, 119 n. 12 & 15, 134
Peri, Alexis 162
Perseus 9–11 fig. I.5, 12, 96, 99–100, 101 fig. 4.1, 102, 104, 109, 111, 120 n. 16, 135
Petrushka 158
phrenology 18–19, 21, 23, 70
physiognomy 14, 17–18, 21, 146, 167
  moral physiognomy 54, 75, 84, 88, 146
Picasso, Pablo 6, 27
Pick, Daniel 1, 169
Pisarro, Camille, 28, 63
Poggioli, Renato 39
portraiture 1, 6, 10, 15, 17–19, 23, 27–28, 30, 39, 41, 51, 55–57, 60, 63, 65, 67, 70–71, 74–76, 87–88, 90–91, 93, 94 n. 4 & 5, 123–24, 135, 141 n. 6, 151, 167–68
Potolsky, Matthew 14, 37, 73,
Pottier, Edmond 63–64, 71
Praz, Mario 119 n. 11, 121
primitive 3, 5–6, 8, 15, 21, 26, 39, 40 n. 7, 53, 63, 72 n. 12, 93–94 n. 3, 95, 122, 140 n. 2, 144, 159, 161, 163–64, 168–69
primitivism 15, 27, 39, 161, 163
psychoanalysis 1, 5, 15, 77–78, 121, 139, 144, 164

queerness 12–13, 122, 140
  Lee Edelman on 140

Rachilde (neé Marguerite Vallette-Eymery) 122, 170
Rank, Otto 77–78
  'Beitrag zu Narzissismus' [Essay on Narcissism] 78
  on *The Picture of Dorian Gray* 77–78, 84
Real, the (Lacan) 8, 10
regression 1–3, 5, 21–22, 39 n. 5, 71, 93–94 n. 3, 127–28, 144, 159–60, 162, 164, 168–70
Renoir, Pierre-Auguste 51
repressed, the 2, 8, 13, 15, 57, 71, 122, 139, 147, 163–64
Rilke, Rainier Maria 16, 32, 112–13, 116, 119 n. 14
  Die Aufzeichnungen des Malte Laurids Brigge [The Notebooks of Malte Laurids Brigge] 171
Ristori, Adelaide 98
Ritter, Ellen 152
Rodin, Auguste 8, 14, 30, 41, 63–65, 67–71, 72 n. 11, 112–13, 167–68

and Hanako 8, 14, 30, 41, 64–65, 67–71, 167, 170 n. 1
and Japanese art 63, 72 n. 11
Masks of Hanako 66 figs 2.11, 2.12., 2.13, 70 fig. 2.16
Royle, Nicholas 13, 71
Rops, Félicien 134
Rousseau, Henri 27
Rowlandson, Thomas 134

Said, Edward 41
Saler, Michael 14, 171
Salomé 69, 79, 119 n. 5, 135–36, 140 n. 1, 169
Saussure, Ferdinand de 125
'savage', the 8, 15, 37–38, 39–40 n. 6, 51, 69, 93–94 n. 3, 125, 139, 144
Savarese, Nicola 65, 72
Sawada, Sukataro 64–65, 68–69, 72
Schaffner, Anna 1, 5, 184,
Schellong, Otto 19, 21, 39 n. 3
Schniztler, Günter 145
Schoonbaert, Lydia 42, 51, 72
Schopenhauer, Arthur 30–31, 39 n. 4, 144
  The World as Will and Idea 30
Schwob, Marcel 15, 121, 123, 125, 127, 141 n. 5,
  'Le Roi au masque d'or' 125, 145 n. 6
Sebald, W.G. 149, 154, 165 n. 8
Sedgwick, Eve Kosofsky 78
self, the 6, 12, 15, 30–34, 53, 71, 74, 80–81, 93, 95, 100, 104, 118, 137–40, 144–48, 151–54, 156–57, 160, 162–63, 165 n. 3, 171
self-fashioning 32, 36, 38, 73, 93, 96, 128, 169–71
self-referentiality 14, 17, 37, 39, 118
Seurat, Georges 51
severed heads 13, 15, 68–69, 71, 96, 99, 102, 104, 109, 118–19, 123–25. 134–36, 139, 169
Sheehy, Helen 112
Sherry, Vincent 13, 169
Shionoya, Kei 61, 71
Siebers, Tobin 100
Signac, Paul 51
signified, signifiers 12, 15, 39, 69, 125–26, 140, 141 n. 6, 169
Smerdon, Geoffrey 86–87, 92, 94 n. 10
Spackman, Barbara 10, 96, 100, 111–12, 120 n. 19
Stamm, Ulrike 150
statues 12, 100, 109–14, 120 n. 15, 128, 132, 136, 139, 142 n. 13
stewart, Susan 23
Stravinsky, Igor 154
Symbolic, the (Lacan) 126, 140
symbolism, symbolists 3, 13, 15, 30, 33, 38, 57, 123, 141 n. 6, 167
Symonds, John Addington 73, 87, 100
  Sexual Inversion 73
Symons, Arthur 13, 35, 86,
synecdoche 8, 13, 95, 163, 169

Tairov, Alexandr 33
Tardieu, Ambroise 122
Tenchini, Lorenzo 23, 167–68, 170 n. 1
  wax masks 24–25 figs 1.5, 1.6, 168 fig. C.1
theatre 31–34, 41, 57–58, 61–65, 72 n. 8, 97, 100, 104–05, 107, 109, 119 n. 4
  see also Japanese theatre
tragedy 31–33, 60, 63, 79, 96–97, 99–106, 113, 119 n. 4
  and D'Annunzio 96–106, 116
Tricot, Xavier 42, 72
Turner, Reginald 79–80, 82–83, 94 n. 7

uncanny, the 1, 7–8, 10, 13, 53, 71, 122, 126, 131–32, 139–40
  Freud's essay, 'The Uncanny' 7–8, 122, 126, 131, 140, 168

Valéry, Paul 133
Van Gogh, Vincent 28, 51, 63
Vattimo, Gianni 32–33
Venice, Venetian 97, 133–34, 145–47, 149–50, 153–54, 156, 164–65
Vienna 38, 143, 145, 148–50, 152–53, 164
Vitry, Paul 25–27, 38,
  'Masks' (essay) 25

Weihe, Richard 10
'West, the', Western 6–8, 14, 17–18, 27–28, 38, 39 n. 5, 41, 53, 56–57, 62–64, 70, 73, 120 n. 16, 153–56, 164, 168,
Whistler, James Abbott McNeill 28, 63, 86, 129, 141 n. 9
Whittington-Egan, Richard 86–87, 92, 94 n. 10
Wiggins, Cameron 154
Wilde, Oscar 14–15, 35, 73–93, 128, 141 n. 5, 169
  'The Decaying of Lying' 74
  'The Disciple' 78
  'Pen, Pencil and Poison' 78, 87
  The Picture of Dorian Gray 14–15, 35, 73–78, 80–83, 87–93, 93 n. 3, 94 n. 5, 128, 138–39, 151
  Salomé 78–79, 140 n. 1
Winn, Phillip 122, 138, 142 n. 15
Witt, Mary Ann Frese 96, 100, 106, 108, 116, 119 n. 3, 120 n. 16,

Yacco, Sada (Sadayakko Kawakami) 56, 58, 63–64, 67
Yeats, William Butler 15, 33–34, 72 n. 7, 85–86
  The Hour Glass 34
'yellow book' (in general) 75–76
  The Yellow Book 78–80, 85–86

Zacconi, Ermete 109, 113, 116, 119 n. 9
Zinck, Hélène 129, 141 n. 9

www.ingramcontent.com/pod-product-compliance
Lightning Source LLC
LaVergne TN
LVHW061251060426
835507LV00017B/2014